Daan Apeldoorn

Comprehensible Knowledge Base Extraction for Learning Agents
– Practical Challenges and Applications in Games

Daan Apeldoorn

Comprehensible Knowledge Base Extraction for Learning Agents
—
Practical Challenges and Applications in Games

Verlagshaus Mainz GmbH, Aachen

Daan Apeldoorn
Comprehensible Knowledge Base Extraction for Learning Agents –
Practical Challenges and Applications in Games

ISBN: 978-3-95886-490-0
1. Auflage 2023

Bibliografische Information der Deutschen Bibliothek
Die Deutsche Bibliothek verzeichnet diese Publikation in der Deutschen Nationalbibliografie; detaillierte bibliografische Daten sind im Internet über www.dnb.ddb.de abrufbar.

Das Werk einschließlich seiner Teile ist urheberrechtlich geschützt. Jede Verwendung ist ohne die Zustimmung des Herausgebers außerhalb der engen Grenzen des Urhebergesetzes unzulässig und strafbar. Das gilt insbesondere für Vervielfältigungen, Übersetzungen, Mikroverfilmungen und die Einspeicherung und Verarbeitung in elektronischen Systemen.

Vertrieb:	Herstellung:
© Wissenschaftsverlag Mainz - Aachen	Druckerei Mainz GmbH Aachen
Süsterfeldstr. 83, 52072 Aachen	Süsterfeldstraße 83
Tel. 0241 / 87 34 34 00	52072 Aachen
www.Verlag-Mainz.de	www.DruckereiMainz.de

This work represents the dissertation of Daan Apeldoorn and has been accepted at the Department of Computer Science of TU Dortmund University, Germany.

Some contents have been published (in similar form) in preliminary works by the author (and further co-authors). To comply to the copyright requirements of the respective publishers (IEEE, Springer), copyright remarks are provided in Algorithm 3.3, Figure 4.5 and Figure 5.9 (in addition to referencing the original works).

For IEEE, according to:
https://journals.ieeeauthorcenter.ieee.org/choose-a-publishing-agreement/avoid-infringement-upon-ieee-copyright/
For Springer, according to:
https://www.springer.com/gp/rights-permissions/obtaining-permissions/882

Figure 3.2 shows an excerpt from an educational exhibit software created by the author for Z Quadrat GmbH Mainz.

The sprites of the games shown in Figure 4.1 and Figure 5.7 are the property of the GVGAI competition and Oryx Design Lab and are allowed to be used in corresponding academic papers, according to their license files.

Quotations are provided (in addition to referencing the original works) with the author names, publication years and publisher names (for the initial quotation and for page 127: Rowohlt Taschenbuch, for page 62: Springer Vieweg).

Cover image and Figure 3.3 are stemming from a teaching software by the author used in artificial intelligence courses held for Z Quadrat GmbH Mainz.

The work has been created (besides common tools bundled with operating systems) with the help of free and open source software, mainly: Computer Modern Unicode fonts, Gummi, Inkscape, LaTeX, LibreOffice, Lyric Hyphenator, TexMaths.

In case any copyright requirements are not handled accordingly, please contact the publisher or the author.

printed in Germany

To my parents and to Viola

„[...] Spielen war immer eine wichtige Methode zur Vorbereitung auf den Ernstfall. Man sollte es in gezielter Weise verwenden. [...] Wer Spiel nur als Spiel betrachtet und Ernst nur als Ernst, hat beides nicht verstanden!"

> taken from: Dietrich Dörner, Die Logik des Mißlingens [27], p. 309
> (1992, Rowohlt Taschenbuch)

"[...] Playing has always been an important method for preparing serious tasks. One should deploy it specifically on purpose. [...] Those, who are looking at games only as games and on serious tasks only as serious tasks, do not understand both of them!"

> taken from: Dietrich Dörner, The Logic of Failing [27], p. 309
> (1992, Rowohlt Taschenbuch, translated from German)

Preface

The first time I remember getting in touch with the idea of intelligent machines, was at the age of about twelve, when one of my parents gave me a book by Fritz R. Glunk et al. with the title "Computer und Roboter" [33]. While being a book for children on the general topic of computers and robots, it still contains some fascinating stories, e. g., about the famous chess playing Mechanical Turk which was constructed by Baron von Kempelen in 1769 (and which was in fact controlled by a small human hidden inside), or the well-known "artificial psychotherapist" ELIZA by Joseph Weizenbaum. These stories certainly inspired me already in my childhood to become interested in computers—especially in the field of artificial intelligence.

During my last years at secondary school, my computer science teacher Josef Glöckler was the first introducing me to the basic ideas behind neural networks and fuzzy logic.

At the beginning of my computer science studies, I became also very interested in the field of software engineering and later, at the Johannes Gutenberg University of Mainz, I was lucky to attend the great artificial intelligence lectures by Prof. Dr. Thomas Uthmann, where I started focusing my artificial intelligence interests on subsymbolic learning aspects and, especially, on agent-based approaches. During that time, also my first publications in the field of software engineering appeared and first ideas for a multi-agent simulation platform with applications in logistics crossed my mind (which later became the multi-agent simulation system ABSTRACTSWARM [3]).

At University of Hagen, where I finished my master's degree, I could further focus my studies on artificial intelligence and I was able to study a course called "Methoden der Wissensrepräsentation und -verarbeitung" ("Methods of Knowledge Representation and Processing") by Prof. Dr. Christoph Beierle and Prof. Dr. Gabriele Kern-Isberner (and a following seminar), which introduced me to the broad field of knowledge representation and the "symbolic world" of artificial intelligence.

After a short time at University of Koblenz-Landau, I started my PhD studies in 2015 at TU Dortmund University supervised by Prof. Dr. Gabriele Kern-Isberner. I learned a lot from her, both deepening and widening my knowledge representation skills and I am very thankful for that.

Getting more and more in touch with symbolic knowledge representation inspired me to bring closer together both worlds of artificial intelligence (with traditionally rather disjoint communities) and I started focusing on the explanation of learned agent behavior by extracting knowledge from learning agents as well as the exploitation of such extracted knowledge during an agent's learning process.

After the publications [7, 8] on these topics together with my PhD supervisor, a cooperation with Dr. Vanessa Volz (formerly at Algorithm Engineering Chair of TU Dortmund University, at time of writing at Queen Mary University of London and modl.ai, Copenhagen) emerged, where we used one of the knowledge base extraction approaches to create a measure for the subjective strategic depth experienced by humans when playing video games. The work resulted in a paper [11] with promising results that were presented in New York in 2017 at the conference on *Computational Intelligence in Games* (CIG 2017), which connected me to the *Artificial Intelligence in Games* community.

I met Jun.-Prof. Dr.-Ing. Alexander Dockhorn (from Leibniz University Hannover) at CIG 2017 and it turned out that the knowledge base extraction approaches also fit very well to his research in the field of *General Video Game Playing Artificial Intelligence* (GVGAI)—a field aiming at the creation of agents that are able to play different (a priori unknown) video games. Being practically dependent on real-time capabilities in this field, I was more influenced toward practical applicability of the developed knowledge extraction approaches. The following fruitful cooperation with Jun.-Prof. Dr.-Ing. Alexander Dockhorn resulted in two further publications (a conference paper [26] and a journal article [5]), where the extraction of knowledge bases was used to learn *forward models* (i.e., "how a game works") from a priori unknown video games. We could show that our approach outperformed other general video game playing agents.

My current work in the artificial intelligence group of the Medical Informatics department at the Institute of Medical Biostatistics, Epidemiology and Informatics (IMBEI) at the University Medical Center of the Johannes Gutenberg University in Mainz incorporates multi-agent simulations of hospital processes (e.g., for the optimization of a priori unknown scenarios). Moreover, the work also raised interest in learning knowledge bases from data sets (see [10]). Especially the possibility of automatically checking the certainty of a knowledge base against a provided data set was further stimulated in this context.

The efficient knowledge base extraction approach and related approaches that are yielded by this work resulted in the implementation of the open-source software INTEKRATOR [38], which allows for applying them not only in the context of games, but also in other domains (e.g., in medical informatics).

The present work summarizes my experiences from the last years, combining the topics of agents and knowledge base extraction/exploitation with a general focus on practical applications and a special focus on applications in games.

Mainz, December 2022

Daan Apeldoorn

Acknowledgments

Writing a PhD thesis is usually a huge process over a long period of time with a lot of people being directly or indirectly involved. This is the place where I would like to thank all of them, starting with some very personal thanks to those people in my life, with whom I share so many profound experiences and memories:

I would like to thank my family, especially my parents Felicitas Apeldoorn and Johannes Apeldoorn, who inspired me already as a child (which was certainly one of the very first elements of the causal chain leading to this work, see Preface) and who supported me in my early youth when I really needed their help to find back to the right way. Without their help, this thesis certainly would not have become reality. My warmest thanks go to my wife Viola, who really suffered from me spending a huge amount of the spare time remaining from my regular jobs for my PhD work over the past years. While this was a very hard time for her (especially during the COVID-19 pandemic, where social contacts were extensively restricted), she never gave up supporting me with all her love and her energy that she could raise besides her own working obligations.

My very special thanks go to my supervisor Prof. Dr. Gabriele Kern-Isberner. I learned a lot from her and she contributed over a long period of time with many discussions and advises to this work. I would like to thank her for all the time she took for me, for fruitful discussions, her valuable advises and for the freedom she gave to me.

In the following, if not explicitly intended or stated otherwise, all persons appearing in enumerations will be mentioned in alphabetical order of their surnames, without any further implications:

My special thanks go to Prof. Dr. Heinrich Müller for accompanying me over the past years in the context of the TU Dortmund PhD mentoring program with advice and many motivating words.

My special thanks also go to the further members of the examination board, which (besides my supervisor) are: My (external) second reviewer Prof. Dr. Simon Lucas, the examination board's chair Prof. Dr. Günter Rudolph, and Prof. Dr. Johannes Fischer. I want to thank them for their work and for supporting me on the last steps toward my PhD with their stimulating questions and valuable feedback.

Acknowledgments

I would like to thank my additional co-authors, with whom I was able to work and publish together during my PhD time, which lead to further results and thereby also contributed to this work (see bibliographic remarks of Section 3.7, Section 4.4 and Section 5.4): Jun.-Prof. Dr.-Ing. Alexander Dockhorn, Lars Hadidi, Corinna Krüger, Dr. Torsten Panholzer, and Dr. Vanessa Volz.

Moreover, I want to thank my proofreaders Dr. Peter Dauscher, Jun.-Prof. Dr.-Ing. Alexander Dockhorn, Jennifer Hahn, Dr. Dativa Tibyampansha, and Dr. Nils Vortmeier for their ambitious proofreading, their valuable feedback and for fruitful discussions that helped improving the quality of this work.

I am thankful for the working environment at my former working place, the Chair 1 of the Department of Computer Science at the TU Dortmund University, which I was able to benefit from during my time as a PhD student there. Besides my supervisor, I also want to thank my former colleagues at Chair 1, especially the leader of the chair, Prof. Dr. Thomas Schwentick, as well as the scientific staff members of my former working group: Tanja Bock, Dr. Christian Eichhorn, Diana Howey, Dr. Patrick Krümpelmann, Dr.-Ing. Steffen Schieweck, Andre Thevapalan, and Marco Wilhelm. Moreover, I also want to thank my former colleagues Anja Flehmig, Dr. Lars Hildebrand, Jan Eric Lenssen, Wolfgang Hunscher, Prof. Dr.-Ing. Dr. h. c. Claudio Moraga, Prof. Dr. Peter Padawitz, Dr. Nils Vortmeier, and Prof. Dr. Thomas Zeume, as well as my other former colleagues there.

I also want to thank my (current and former) colleagues of my current primary working place, the Medical Informatics department of the Institute of Medical Biostatistics, Epidemiology and Informatics (IMBEI) at the University Medical Center of the Johannes Gutenberg University Mainz, for creating a stimulating environment both for my former and my current research, as well as a perspective for applications and future works. Especially, I would like to thank the director of the institute, Prof. Dr. Konstantin Strauch, as well as the leader of the Medical Informatics department, Dr. Torsten Panholzer together with Lars Hadidi and Dr. Dativa Tibyampansha from our AI working group. Moreover, I also want to thank Dr. Emilio Gianicolo, Chung Shing Rex Ha, Franziska Härtner, Dr. Jochem König, Barbara Linkerhägner, Fabian Linkerhägner, Dr. Federico Marini, Dr. Gerrit Toenges, as well as my other colleagues there.

Furthermore, I would like to thank my current second affiliation, the Z Quadrat GmbH Mainz, especially Stella Zerbe and Kai Zerbe, as well as Petra Eckert, who gave me the opportunity to contribute to the realization of several creative educational works, such as AI-related exhibits (one of which traveled around German and Austrian cities on board of the exhibition ship *MS Wissenschaft* in 2019 and finally made it to the *Deutsches Museum Bonn* in 2021) and AI-related courses (e. g, at the Otto-Schott-Gymnasium in Mainz-Gonsenheim and at institutions of the Human Help Network Foundation Thailand in Pattaya). I am thankful for being a part of the company and for all our joint successes during the past years.

Additional thanks go to (ordered chronologically here): Jan Hangen for profound and stimulating mathematical foundations, Joseph Glöckler, who was the first introducing me to some basic ideas of AI approaches, Henrik Heimbürger, with whom I published my very first paper in 2004, Prof. Dr. Thomas Uthmann, who gave the first AI lectures I attended during my bachelor's studies and who passed away already in 2005, Prof. Dr. Christoph Beierle for further supporting my AI interests during my master's studies, Prof. Dr. Lars Mönch for offering me my very first student position in academia, Prof. Dr. Steffen Staab for giving me the opportunity of collecting my first experiences as a scientific staff member of his former institute at University of Koblenz-Landau, Prof. Dr. Matthias Thimm for his ambitious support during my time in Koblenz, and Prof. Dr. Leszek Wojnowsky for his motivating words.

Last but not least, I would like to thank the numerous further people I worked with and who crossed or partly joined my academic paths during the past years. These are especially (among many others): Boian Balouchev, Cedric Perez Donfack, Manuel Feilen, Dr. Marc Finthammer, Prof. Dr. Joachim Hertzberg, Dr. Dominik Jain, Amelie Koch, Iona Kuhn, Steven Kutsch, Dr. Kai Lingemann, Kevin Majchrzak, Prof. Dr. Abhaya Nayak, Richard Niland, Dr. Nico Potyka, Bianca Ruland, Kai Sauerwald, Prof. Dr. Jacob Schrum, Dr. Christoph Schwering, Dr. Christiane Spisla, Prof. Dr. Frieder Stolzenburg, and Prof. Dr. Geoff Sutcliffe.

My very warm final thanks go to my friends at the *Protestant Church Community of Mainz-Gonsenheim* and the *Protestant Deanery of Mainz* as well as to all my other friends for patiently and understandingly staying on my side and giving me strength, although I certainly was neglecting them oftentimes when being "unavailable" and into my work. I am especially remembering Claudius Euteneuer, who passed away during the time of writing the thesis.

I am very thankful for being allowed to share experiences with all these people— also for those that are not explicitly mentioned here—and I am very sorry, if I forgot to mention someone, whose name should have been included.

About This Work

How can learned agent behavior be *explained*? *Compactly* and in a *human-readable* way, such that it is also *accessible to people not familiar with logic or knowledge representation* approaches?

This work tries to find answers to these questions from a practical point of view in the context of games.

Games provide an application domain with excellent properties for testing and evaluating artificial intelligence (AI) approaches—especially regarding learning agents:

- Many games are highly dynamic environments.
- Games are diverse and scalable problems (both in size and complexity).
- Players can be intuitively modeled as agents.
- Games are easily accessible to many people with different backgrounds, which is a clear advantage when working at the intersection of the traditionally rather disjoint fields of machine learning and knowledge representation.

Moreover, concepts and approaches that have once successfully been applied in the context of games, may have the potential to be transferred to other domains as well.

This work focuses on the *intuitive* and *comprehensible* extraction of rule-based knowledge bases from agent behavior, that is learned, e. g., by sub-symbolic (or other) machine learning approaches—or even human agents. One of the main goals is to be able to render such extracted knowledge accessible to people with different backgrounds and who are not necessarily familiar with logic or knowledge representation.

Furthermore, it will be demonstrated that the presented approaches may also serve as an interface for combining knowledge representation with machine learning and other techniques in the context of games, e. g., to accelerate learning processes of agents or to create hybrid symbolic/sub-symbolic learning agents.

More detailed, after providing an introduction in Chapter 1, the foundations as needed in the following will be introduced in Chapter 2 and related work will be considered there.

After that, in Chapter 3, a knowledge representation scheme will be described, that originates from the idea of representing behavior learned by an (artificial or human) agent in a compact and human-readable way. The described approach is able to represent more extensive amounts of knowledge clearly arranged and intuitively comprehensible, such that it is also accessible to people without deeper knowledge in logic or knowledge representation. A reasoning algorithm will be described that allows for efficient reasoning based on the described approach. To underpin the comprehensibility and the reasoning efficiency, a study by Krüger, Apeldoorn and Kern-Isberner [41] will be presented, in which the comprehensibility is evaluated and compared to a state-of-the-art approach. At the end of Chapter 3, algorithms will be provided that are able to create such comprehensible representations from data (e. g., from learned multi-dimensional weight matrices or from play traces resulting from the behavior of learning agents).

Chapters 4 and 5 consider applications of the presented approaches: In the recent years, the presented approaches have been used in numerous different applications, mostly in the context of learning agent models. Applications comprise:

- estimating the subjective strategic depth of games from human play traces [11],
- detecting and exploiting heuristics from observations in unknown environments [7, 9],
- learning and revising forward models in a priori unknown video games [5, 26].

In a paper by Kuhn [42], some of the approaches have also been used to extract and exploit human intuitions for solving job-shop problems.

By outlining the variety of applications (especially in the context of games), besides Chapter 3, both Chapter 4 and Chapter 5 represent the most important chapters of this work. In accordance with my earlier experiences in the field of software engineering, the agent models considered for the applications here will be designed in a modular way, such that both the underlying learning approaches and the knowledge extraction methods can be easily substituted.

Finally, Chapter 6 provides conclusions and an outlook on future work.

The appendix completes the work by referring to the implementation of the most essential results in the INTEKRATOR toolbox [10, 38] as well as to further online (video) material accompanying this work.

Most of the contents throughout the chapters are underpinned by comprehensible (running) examples, also further stressing the practical potential of this work. The chapters have a transitive linear dependency and can be best followed in their sequential order.

Contents

Preface 1
Acknowledgments 5
About This Work 9
Table of Notations 15
1. Introduction 19
   1.1 Motivation 19
   1.2 Aims and Scope 21
   1.3 Contributions 21
   1.4 Remarks on Joint Works 24
2. Foundations of Learning Agents 27
   2.1 Basic Agent Model 28
       2.1.1 Sensors, Percepts and States 30
       2.1.2 Actions 31
       2.1.3 State Transitions and Partial Observable Markov Decision Processes 32
       2.1.4 Definition of an Agent 35
       2.1.5 Agent Behavior 37
       2.1.6 Knowledge-Based Agents 41
       2.1.7 Learning Agents and the Black Box Problem 42
   2.2 Another "Black Box": Comprehensible Representation of Agent Behavior 47
   2.3 Related Approaches 48
       2.3.1 Learning Approaches for Structural Insights 50
       2.3.2 Comprehensible Representations for Knowledge Learned by Agents 52
       2.3.3 Learning and Hybrid Agent Models for Games 54
   2.4 Summary 56
3. Knowledge Base Extraction 57
   3.1 Definition of HKBs 58
       3.1.1 From Non-Deterministic to Deterministic State-Action Sequences 58
       3.1.2 Rules and HKBs 59
   3.2 Reasoning for HKBs 62
   3.3 HKBs for Knowledge Engineering 64
   3.4 Basic Knowledge Base Extraction Approaches 66
       3.4.1 Basic Ideas 67
       3.4.2 A Preliminary Algorithm 68
       3.4.3 Incorporating the Apriori Algorithm 75

- 3.5 Advanced Knowledge Base Extraction..80
  - 3.5.1 Advanced HKB Extraction Algorithm...............................80
  - 3.5.2 Completeness of the Approach....................................87
  - 3.5.3 Learning HKBs from Numeric Data................................91
  - 3.5.4 Handling Higher-Dimensional Data..............................97
- 3.6 Summary..99
- 3.7 Bibliographic Remarks...100
4. Explaining and Analyzing Agent Behavior...103
  - 4.1 Knowledge Base Extraction in Games.......................................104
    - 4.1.1 Selected Games...104
    - 4.1.2 Modeling the State-Action Spaces..................................106
    - 4.1.3 Resulting HKBs..108
  - 4.2 Subjective Strategic Depth...113
    - 4.2.1 Subjective Strategic Depth Measure................................113
    - 4.2.2 Evaluation..117
    - 4.2.3 Results...119
  - 4.3 Summary...121
  - 4.4 Bibliographic Remarks..122
5. Enhancing Learning Agents..125
  - 5.1 Accelerating an Agent's Learning Process by Knowledge Base Extraction....125
    - 5.1.1 Extracting and Exploiting HKBs during Learning...................126
    - 5.1.2 A Combined HKB/Reinforcement Learning Agent Model................134
    - 5.1.3 Integrating A Priori Knowledge through HKBs......................144
  - 5.2 Forward Model Learning...148
    - 5.2.1 Learning Forward Models of Games..................................149
    - 5.2.2 Revising Forward Models of Games..................................156
    - 5.2.3 An Agent Model Combining Learning and Revision....................161
  - 5.3 Summary...164
  - 5.4 Bibliographic Remarks..164
6. Conclusion and Future Work...167
  - 6.1 Summary of the Results and Conclusions..................................167
  - 6.2 An Outlook on Future Work..171
Appendix...173
A. Introduction to the InteKRator Toolbox..175
  - A.1 Basic Interface...175
  - A.2 Learning..176
  - A.3 Reasoning...178
  - A.4 Revision..178
  - A.5 Checking..179

B. Online Appendix..181
List of Algorithms...183
List of Figures..184
List of Tables...185
References...187
Index..193

Table of Notations

Notation	Description
$:=$	"is defined as"; in algorithms: assignment
$\{...\}$	Ordered set
a	Action symbol; i.e., a symbol representing an agent's action.
$a_{\mathbf{p}}, a_\rho$	Action symbol belonging to a state-action pair $\mathbf{p}$ or a rule ρ, respectively (in the latter case, a_ρ is the conclusion of ρ).
$\mathbb{A}$	Action symbol set; i.e., a set of all action symbols representing an agent's possible actions.
$\mathfrak{D}(st)$	An agent's decision component that returns an action as decision for a perceived state st.
$\mathcal{KB}$	Knowledge base
$\mathbf{p} := (st_{\mathbf{p}}, a_{\mathbf{p}})$	A state-action pair consisting of an agent's state (according to its perceived sensor values) and an action that was performed in that state.
$P(a)$	Probability/relative frequency of an action (according to a state-action sequence).
$P(\bigwedge_{s \in S} s \wedge a)$	Probability/relative frequency of a (partial) state and an action (according to a state-action sequence).
$P(a \mid \bigwedge_{s \in S} s)$	Conditional probability/relative frequency of an action given a (partial) state.
$Q := (q_{s_1,...,s_n,a})$	A (multi-dimensional) weight matrix, which contains weights for state-action pair combinations (where one of an agent's sensors represents one dimension, with an additional action dimension).
$\mathfrak{R}(\mathcal{KB}, st)$	Short hand for the reasoning algorithm for exception-tolerant hierarchical knowledge bases (Algorithm 3.1), which returns one (or more) action(s) inferred from the provided knowledge base $\mathcal{KB}$ given the perceived state st.

Table of Notations

Notation	Description
R_j	The j-th level of an exception-tolerant hierarchical knowledge base (starting with R_1 as topmost level); i.e., a set of rules.
$R_{j<j'}$	Short hand for R_j, $j < j'$; i.e., $R_{j<j'}$ is the j-th level of an exception-tolerant hierarchical knowledge base with j being lower than j' (see also $R_{j'<j<j''}$).
$R_{j'<j<j''}$	Short hand for R_j, $j' < j < j''$; i.e., $R_{j'<j<j''}$ is the j-th level of an exception-tolerant hierarchical knowledge base with j being higher than j' and lower than j'' (see also $R_{j<j'}$).
$\mathcal{SA}$	State-action sequence; i.e., an ordered set of state-action pairs. In cases where the order is not of importance, it may also refer to an unordered set of state-action pairs.
$\mathcal{SA}^*$	Deterministic state-action sequence; i.e., a state-action sequence, where pairs with the same state also always have the same action (but not necessarily vice-versa).
s_i	A sensor symbol representing a value of an agent's i-th sensor. (It is assumed that every s_i can be uniquely associated with its corresponding sensor symbol set $\mathbb{S}_i$—in practice, e.g., by a prefix naming convention for the symbol names.)
$\mathbb{S}_i$	Sensor symbol set; i.e., a set of all symbols representing the sensor values of an agent's i-th sensor.
$st := s_1 \wedge ... \wedge s_n$	An agent's (complete) state; i.e., a conjunction of all state symbols s_i representing the values perceived by all n sensors of the agent. (In other words, st represents the state an agent is assumed to be in, iff all s_i are known according to the agent's sensors.) A state $\tilde{st} := \bigwedge_{s \in \tilde{S}} s$ with $\tilde{S} \subset S := \{s_1, ..., s_n\}$ denotes a partial state with not all sensors being involved.
$st_\mathbf{p}, st_\rho$	An agent's state belonging to a state-action pair $\mathbf{p}$ or a rule ρ, respectively (in the latter case, st_ρ is the premise of ρ and may refer to a partial state).
st^a	A state-action conjunction, i.e., $st^a := s_1 \wedge ... \wedge s_n \wedge a$, used in the context of forward models to represent an action a performed in a state st.

Table of Notations

Notation	Description
st'	Subsequent state information; in the context of forward models, the information may be partial or may only represent specific aspects of a subsequent state (e. g., a score change).
S	State symbol set; i. e., a set containing the symbols of the sensor values that describe an agent's state (set representation of a state st).
$S_{\mathbf{p}}, S_\rho$	State symbol set belonging to a state-action pair $\mathbf{p}$ or a rule ρ, respectively (the latter is also called *premise set*, which must not necessarily contain a symbol for each of the agent's sensors).
$\top$	Tautology symbol, used for empty premises/states.
$\square$	Halmos-style finality symbol, used for indicating the end of a contextual unit (e. g., a definition, an example or a proof).

1. Introduction

1.1 Motivation

In these days, artificial intelligence (AI) experiences a new prominence. With the ideas of deep and convolutional neural networks in conjunction with the development of corresponding frameworks, especially the machine learning area has gained a lot of attraction (again) during the last years. Promoted by impressive applications for learning agents, like DEEPMIND's ATARI-playing AI [49] (which learned to play several ATARI video games without any a priori knowledge) or the renowned ALPHAGO [60] (which was the first computer program known to beat Lee Sedol, one of the best go players in the world), sub-symbolic learning approaches seem to be the ultimate solution in the context of learning agents.

Nevertheless, also the symbolic world of AI did not stand still during the last years and one can observe some movements toward a fusion of symbolic and sub-symbolic approaches as the possible next step in AI. Moreover, knowledge representation approaches have a huge potential to solve several (partly well-known and sometimes ignored) problems of sub-symbolic approaches and are even known to be stronger in some aspects:

- First of all, using sub-symbolic machine learning approaches like (deep) neural networks, the learned knowledge is implicitly encoded in millions of weights and is therefore usually not comprehensible to humans after the learning process. This is currently maybe one of the most debated drawbacks of these kinds of approaches.

- The learning process of common sub-symbolic machine learning approaches for agents does not appear to be learning in a "human-like" manner: Oftentimes hundreds or thousands of iterations are needed until adequate learning results can be observed.

- Using pure sub-symbolic machine learning approaches, usually everything is learned from scratch, including those parts of the knowledge that are a priori available. E. g., in the context of an agent that learns to play a game, there is

1. Introduction

no obvious possibility to distinguish between learning the rules of the game (which are usually known in advance) and a good strategy how to play it.

- Machine learning can be accelerated incorporating symbolic knowledge in several ways: Not only by supporting the learning process with a priori knowledge (as already mentioned before), but also by reincorporating symbolic knowledge that was extracted or mapped (or otherwise learned) from a sub-symbolic learning approach during the learning process (e. g., [9, 31]).

- Finally, belief revision (i. e., incorporating new knowledge into an existing knowledge base), as the "symbolic approach to machine learning", does not only seem to be a more natural way of learning in some situations, but can potentially also be much more efficient than sub-symbolic machine learning approaches: New knowledge can be incorporated properly into what is already known without the need for thousands of iterations to adapt to the dynamics of observations. (An efficient belief revision approach geared to practical eligibility will be presented in Chapter 5.)

Besides this great potential, on the other hand, many symbolic AI approaches suffer from being inefficient when it comes to practical applications, where fast reasoning and/or belief revision capabilities are needed.

In the following, these considerations will be examined by investigating methods that provide possibilities of combining symbolic and sub-symbolic aspects in the context of learning agents with a focus on practical applicability. For this purpose, a knowledge representation approach will be described that allows for the extraction of compact knowledge bases from learned agent behavior as well as for efficient reasoning and belief revision on the extracted representations: On the one hand, such an approach must be lightweight and easily comprehensible—especially when addressing applications from a different community (e. g., real-time applications such as games). On the other hand, the approach should be designed in a way that renders it independent from a specific underlying machine learning paradigm and thereby allows for combining it with different machine learning approaches.

The techniques presented here will be underpinned by numerous examples and their practical applicability will be demonstrated in the context of different applications in games, starting from the extraction of knowledge up to a modular agent model incorporating learning with knowledge base extraction, belief revision and further techniques.

1.2 Aims and Scope

This work aims at bringing closer together ideas from machine learning and knowledge representation approaches in the context of agents. This will be addressed with practical applications in mind: A knowledge base extraction approach will be fleshed out that is able to learn a knowledge base from data representing the behavior of an agent. Following common modularization principles, this approach will not rely on a single sub-symbolic machine learning paradigm (e. g., reinforcement learning with one specific kind of neural network as function approximator), such that the underlying learning approach can be exchanged in a modular way.

The provided methods allow for easily combining knowledge representation techniques with machine learning approaches in the context of learning agents, such that

- knowledge learned by agents with common machine learning techniques can be explicitly represented (e. g., to render it comprehensible to humans),
- agents based on machine learning approaches can benefit from advantages of knowledge representation, symbolic reasoning and belief revision (e. g., by exploiting reasoning and belief revision techniques for symbolic knowledge that becomes explicit during a machine learning process) and,
- an agent model can be elegantly combined by incorporating the former two aspects.

The major concepts of this work will be implemented in a ready-to-use toolbox [38] aiming at practical applications in a general way, even beyond the scope of agents.

1.3 Contributions

This work contributes in several ways to the incorporation and practical usage of knowledge representation in the context of AI and agents in games (cf. [29]). Furthermore, being geared toward practical applicability, the results have also the potential of being used in other contexts outside the scope of games (which will be outlined at the end of this work).

The work is mainly based on the nine peer-reviewed papers [5–11, 26, 41], which have been published over the past years in the context of this dissertation. On seven of which [5–11], the author appears as first author and on the remaining two [26, 41], the author appears as second author. The papers have been published on a variety of international conferences and journals/series, such as the *Global Conference on Artifi-*

1. Introduction

cial Intelligence (GCAI 2016) in Berlin, the yearly conference of the *Florida Artificial Intelligence Research Society* (FLAIRS 2017) on Marco Island, the *IEEE Conference on Computational Intelligence and Games* (CIG 2017 and 2018) in New York and in Maastricht (which became the *IEEE Conference on Games*, COG, in 2019), the *International Symposium on Commonsense Reasoning* (COMMONSENSE 2017) in London, as well as the *Multi-disciplinary International Conference on Artificial Intelligence* (MIWAI 2021; held as a virtual/online conference due to the COVID-19 pandemic), among others. Furthermore, publications have also been placed in the IEEE journal *Transactions on Games*, as well as in *Studies in Health, Technology and Informatics*, the latter is covering medical informatics research. Moreover, a bachelor's thesis [40] and a master's thesis [12] at TU Dortmund University emerged in the context of this work.

The main contributions that will be described here are the following:

- A comprehensible multi-abstraction-level knowledge representation approach, which is geared toward learning human-readable knowledge in the context of agents and which has advanced comprehensibility and reasoning efficiency properties (Chapter 3):
The described approach is accessible to people without profound knowledge in the fields of knowledge representation or logic and it can therefore serve for didactical purposes or for building a bridge between different communities. Moreover, due to its reasoning efficiency, it is eligible for practical applications and has been shown to be useful in the context of agents, e. g., in [5–7]. To some extend, the described approach can be considered similar to the state-of-the-art approach of answer set programming (ASP) [19], in the sense that it makes use of similar ideas from default reasoning (e. g., [55]). In a joint study [41] together with Corinna Krüger, it was compared to ASP and the ASP solver CLINGO [22].

- A novel measure for the subjective strategic depth experienced by humans when playing (video) games (Chapter 4):
Several measures for strategic depth of games already existed before. However, according to [11], these measures are different in what they actually measure and how the measurement is realized. The approach that will be described here was developed in a joint work with Dr. Vanessa Volz in [11] and is novel in the sense that it measures the strategic depth that is subjectively experienced by players (instead of other properties, such as the computational resources needed, as described in [11]). To achieve this, the measure that will be described here relies on the knowledge needed by a human player to successfully play a game. This knowledge is collected by one of the knowledge base extraction approaches that were developed in the context of this thesis. Mainly being a side product at

first, the measure was later also incorporated in artificial agents to allow them to estimate the difficulty of their surrounding environment.

- Two agent models integrating (reinforcement) learning and knowledge representation (and other state-of-the-art approaches for games) for advanced learning performance, resulting in a progress in general video game artificial intelligence (GVGAI) [53] (Chapter 5):
  Besides investigating the incorporation of knowledge representation and learning techniques in the context of agents, the main contribution here is an agent model that allows for combining learning, knowledge representation and other techniques such as monte carlo tree search (MCTS) [21]. In joint works with Jun.-Prof. Dr.-Ing. Alexander Dockhorn, the resulting agent model was evaluated in the context of the GVGAI competition [65] and could outperform other GVGAI agents. Furthermore, this agent model also allows for exploiting techniques such as MCTS, which are well-established for non-learning GVGAI agents: Such agents for the so-called "planning track" of the GVGAI competition usually rely on a known forward model of a game (i.e., the a priori knowledge how the game works). With this contribution, it is possible to benefit from established techniques from the GVGAI planning track also in the context of learning agents (for the "learning track" of the competition), where no forward model is provided to an agent.

- An educational exhibit consisting of a multi-level game which estimates the difficulty subjectively experienced by a player and which can teach basic ideas of knowledge representation in the form of rules and exceptions:
  The exhibit makes use of approaches that emerged in the context of this PhD research [8, 11] and was originally created for the *Z Quadrat GmbH*.[1] It was accepted for the educational exhibition ship *MS Wissenschaft* [50] and traveled around different German and Austrian cities in 2019. It was subsequently selected for the *ScienceStation* travelling exhibition (a further project of the German scientific communication organization *Wissenschaft im Dialog*, WiD) [59] and, in this context, it was available at several train stations in Germany in 2019. Finally, it became a selected exhibit of the *Deutsches Museum Bonn* (German Museum in Bonn) [24] for its new exhibition on AI [48]. Although only the underlying approaches (and not the exhibit itself) will be considered directly in this work, it contributes to education. Moreover, parts of it will be used as an example in the context of different approaches in this work (see Figure 3.2).

---

[1] Z Quadrat is an educational company mainly focusing on mathematics and computer science didactics. It is the author's second affiliation at time of writing.

- The INTEKRATOR toolbox for creating knowledge bases from data by incorporating machine learning and knowledge representation techniques (Appendix A): In contrast to other software concerning knowledge representation (such as the TWEETYPROJECT [66] and CLINGO [22]), the INTEKRATOR toolbox is much more lightweight and focuses on learning knowledge bases from data. In the study [41], its reasoning algorithm turned out to be much more efficient than that of CLINGO. Moreover, it can also be used outside the scope of agents: In a joint paper with Dr. Torsten Panholzer, it was recently proposed to be used for the automated creation of expert systems [10].

For distinguishing the author's parts of the contributions from those of further co-authors, remarks on joint works are provided in the next section (Section 1.4).

1.4 Remarks on Joint Works

Besides the joint publications together with the author's PhD supervisor Prof. Dr. Gabriele Kern-Isberner, this thesis also comprises results that emerged from joint works with other co-authors. For this purpose, this section briefly summarizes the joint works with the aim of distinguishing the own contributions from those of others.

From the nine peer-reviewed papers [5–11, 26, 41] that are related to this thesis, six of them [5, 6, 10, 11, 26, 41] have co-authors besides or in addition to the author's PhD supervisor. These will be briefly considered in the following (mainly according to the order of their appearance):

- The paper [11] emerged from a cooperation with Dr. Vanessa Volz (formerly at TU Dortmund University, at time of writing at Queen Mary University of London and modl.ai, Copenhagen). In this paper, a measure for subjectively experienced strategic depth in the context of games has been developed, based on some of the approaches that will be presented here. The measure has been evaluated in the context of a study involving a survey software which was especially developed for that purpose. The author contributed mainly to the development of the strategic depth measure, as well as by developing the survey software and evaluating the data retrieved from the study. The results have been incorporated into Section 4.2 as well as Section 5.1.2 (the latter being a follow-up application by the author). Another follow-up emerging from this work was the educational exhibit that makes use of the strategic depth measure (see the second to last bullet point in Section 1.3), which was also developed by the author. (See also bibliographic remarks in Section 4.4.)

- The first author of the paper [41] is Corinna Krüger. The paper resulted from her bachelor's thesis, which was co-supervised by Prof. Dr. Gabriele Kern-Isberner and the author. In this work, a comparison has been done between some of the approaches that will be presented here and the state-of-the-art approach of *answer set programming* (ASP) [19]. Both a survey as well as experiments have been performed. The author contributed directly to the survey as well as indirectly to the whole work in the context of co-supervising the bachelor's thesis. The original work [41] is referenced at several places here. (See also bibliographic remarks in Section 3.7.)

- The paper [26] and later the journal article [5] both emerged from a joint work together with Jun.-Prof. Dr.-Ing. Alexander Dockhorn (from Leibniz University Hannover). The first author of the former work is Jun.-Prof. Dr.-Ing. Alexander Dockhorn, the first author of the latter is the author. In these two publications, some of the approaches presented here are used for learning and exploiting forward models in the context of *general video game artificial intelligence* (GVGAI) [53] and the GVGAI competition [65]. The author's contributions mainly comprise the development of the agent model that involves the approaches presented here as well as the development, integration and evaluation of a revision algorithm for learned forward models. Parts of these results have been incorporated in Section 5.2. Moreover, Section 5.2 also refers to and analyzes some of the results that were mainly provided by Jun.-Prof. Dr.-Ing. Alexander Dockhorn. (See also bibliographic remarks in Section 5.4.)

- The paper [6] emerged in the context of the author's work at the Medical Informatics department of the Institute of Medical Biostatistics, Epidemiology and Informatics (IMBEI) at the University Medical Center of the Johannes Gutenberg University Mainz. Co-authors are Lars Hadidi and Dr. Torsten Panholzer. In [6], parts of the work that will be presented here are applied for learning guidelines in the form of rules with exceptions for optimizing hospital processes by means of agent-based simulations. The author contributed the learning algorithm (cf. Algorithm 3.3) as well as the first ideas for the proof of the algorithm's completeness, which were later incorporated and further elaborated in this work (see Section 3.5.2). (Moreover, the experiments for the agent-based simulations and their evaluation were also contributed by the author, but are not part of this thesis.)

- Finally, also the publication [10] with Dr. Torsten Panholzer as co-author emerged in the context of the author's work at IMBEI. In this work, the INTEKRATOR toolbox [38] (an implementation of parts of the thesis work) is proposed for automatically creating expert systems from data. The author con-

1. Introduction

tributed the implementation of the INTEKRATOR toolbox (see Appendix A) as well as the description of the toolbox's application in the context of expert systems. (The latter aspect is only considered roughly in the outlook on future work here, see Section 6.2.)

Further information on joint works can also be found in the respective bibliographic remarks sections at the end of the chapters 3–5 (i.e., Section 3.7, Section 4.4 and Section 5.4).

2. Foundations of Learning Agents

The first conceptual ideas of agents already came up in the early beginning of AI history. However, original research fields on agent-specific topics developed later, like the field of *agent architectures*, which emerged first in the mid-1980s (according to [69], pp. 394–396). Over the decades, the agent paradigm became further established and nowadays, agents are a central concept which is widely used in different fields of AI research. The development of intelligent agents, which are able to act, adapt, learn and communicate autonomously in an environment, can be considered one of the central joint objectives of AI research (cf. [14], p. 338).

Agents serve as a comprehensible generic model for autonomous systems with sensory inputs ("percepts") and the ability of performing actions within an environment. Due to the generality of the model, many different physical and virtual systems (e. g., robots, software/web services, smartphone devices, etc.) can be considered agents. The principle of the basic agent model is a useful conceptual framework which can be used for many AI-related technologies and applications. Some selected examples (among many others) are:

- *Autonomous mobile robots* [36]:
  Equipped with sensors (like cameras or laser scanners) and motors (for performing actions), robots can be able to navigate and perform tasks in a (limited) environment.

- *Games*:
  A player (partially) perceives the state of a game (e. g., the board, cards or—in case of a video game—objects or pixels on the screen) and performs moves as actions. Here, the game represents the environment. In the research field of *general (video) game playing*, as an additional challenge, the game to be played can be a priori unknown to the game playing agent (see GVGAI competition [52]).

- *Agent-based simulations*:
  In agent-based simulations, agents are simulated as autonomous entities that can interact cooperatively (or competitively) with each other and with the simulated environment. Examples are the simulation league of the *RoboCup* soccer competition [56] or systems for simulating public transport networks [34], trading simulations [44] or for multi-agent modeling of logistics processes [3].

Apart from technical systems, the agent model can also be applied to animals and even humans (cf. the second example in the above list with a human player in mind), which can help to analyze and understand their behavior. (Later, in Chapter 4, an extended example of analyzing human behavior in the context of games will be presented.)

Due to its comprehensibility, the basic agent model can also be seen as a didactic tool to explain different AI approaches (e. g., also Russel and Norvig refer to the idea of an agent as a unifying concept in their classic book [57], p. viii). Even though many of the concepts that will be introduced here can in general also be used apart from agents, the agent model will play a central role in this work for introducing and explaining the concepts.

At first, the basic agent model (as used throughout this work) will be introduced and both symbolic and sub-symbolic approaches and their respective challenges will be discussed in the context of agents (Section 2.1). After that, the problem of representing complex agent behavior in a compact and human-readable way will be outlined (Section 2.2). Finally, related approaches will be presented and discussed (Section 2.3).

2.1 Basic Agent Model

This section provides the main ideas and relevant details of the basic agent model which is used throughout this work to introduce further concepts. The presentation is mostly limited to the *relevant* aspects that are needed here as preliminaries for the following chapters (especially Chapter 3). The main goal of this section is to be able to represent deterministic (and non-deterministic) agent behavior in a simple and adequate way that can be easily used later for the extraction of knowledge bases, as in Section 3.5 (see Algorithm 3.3).

Due to the generality of the agent model and the diversity of different agent types and applications, it is hard to provide a sound and complete definition of what exactly an agent is (see, e. g., [14], p. 338 or [70] pp. 4–5). A rather general definition, which can be found likewise in the literature, is that of *a system that is able to act autonomously in an environment to fulfill its (designated) tasks* (cf. [14], p. 339). Following this idea, as a first approach, an agent and its environment can be modeled as in Figure 2.1a. The figure shows the basic interaction of an agent with its environment; similar figures can be found in literature on agents (e. g., [14, 70]) or robotics [36].

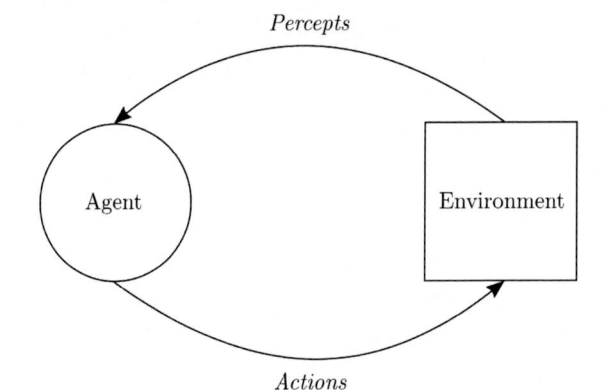

Figure 2.1a (Basic Agent Model) (Source: adapted from [14])
The inputs of an agent are information about its environment in form of *percepts* (which are perceived through the agent's sensors). The outputs are *actions*, which are performed by the agent and which can change the state of the environment. After performing an action, information about the changed environment can be perceived anew by the agent.

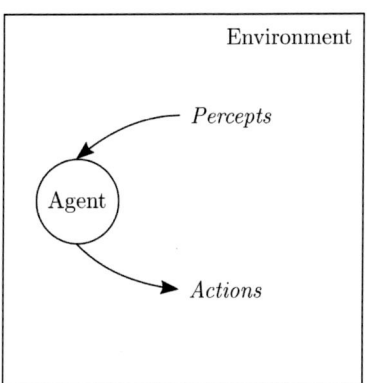

Figure 2.1b (Basic Agent Model: Alternative Representation)
Inputs and outputs of the agent are the same as in Figure 2.1a. However, this representation of the basic agent model emphasizes that an agent itself can be considered a part of its environment. This can be of interest, e. g., if an agent changes its position in the environment by performing a movement action.

2. Foundations of Learning Agents

Although Figure 2.1a is a common and comprehensible visualization of an agent model's basic ideas, it lacks outlining explicitly that an agent itself can often be considered a part of its environment. Since this will be important for most examples and applications of this work, Figure 2.1b shows an alternative representation, which emphasizes this idea more explicitly.

Based on the ideas of an agent interacting with its environment, a closer look on the agent itself will be provided in the following.

2.1.1 Sensors, Percepts and States

In the context of this work, an agent is supposed to have a fixed number of n sensors. The sensor values, that can be perceived by the agent, are represented by the elements of the *sensor symbol sets* $\mathbb{S}_1, ..., \mathbb{S}_n$: Every $\mathbb{S}_i$ is a finite set, whose elements represent the distinct values that can be perceived by the agent through its i-th sensor.[2] Furthermore, it is assumed that every element $s \in \mathbb{S}_i$ can be uniquely associated with its corresponding sensor symbol set $\mathbb{S}_i$, such that $\bigcap_{i=0}^{n} \mathbb{S}_i = \emptyset$. In practice, this can be achieved by providing a unique *symbol name* for every $s \in \mathbb{S}_i$ (e.g., by a prefix naming convention where the prefix reflects the respective sensor symbol set).

Note that, depending on the application, an agent may or may not know all possible sensor values in advance. If an agent does not know all possible sensor values in advance and a previously unknown sensor value is perceived for the first time, the corresponding sensor symbol set can be extended by adding a symbol for this newly perceived value. By this, an agent is able to successively collect representations for all occurring sensor values, e.g., when exploring a (partially) unknown environment.

A perceived *state* of an agent can now be represented as a set $S := \{s_1, ..., s_n\}$, with every $s_i \in S$ being a symbol of the corresponding sensor symbol set $\mathbb{S}_i$. This set-theoretic representation is similar to those used in classical planning (see [32], Section 2.2), except that the symbols here are more tightly coupled to their corresponding sensors (e.g., by the aforementioned naming convention). Equivalently to the set-theoretic representation, a state st of an agent can also be denoted as $st := \bigwedge_{s \in S} s$, i.e., a conjunction of all state symbols representing the values perceived by the respective sensors of the agent.

---

[2] This may sound limiting, since it implies that only discrete information can be perceived by the agent. However, in practical applications, the sensory inputs are often inherently discrete or can be discretized easily; e.g., a simple light sensor of a robot with 1024 shades of gray or a board game with a board consisting of discrete cells. (More advanced techniques related to discretization are considered later in Section 3.5.3.)

In many real-world applications, an agent's state is *incomplete* in the sense that it is oftentimes not possible to cover all of the environment's (potentially relevant) aspects with sensors. However, apart from that, the following definition (adapted from the original definition in [8]) will help to distinguish states that are completely known according to the sensors of an agent (i. e., where all of the agent's sensors are involved) from those that are only partially known (i. e., where only a subset of the agent's sensors are involved).

Definition 2.1 (Complete State/Partial State) A *complete state* is a conjunction $st := \bigwedge_{s \in S} s$ over a state set $S := \{s_1, ..., s_n\}$ of sensor symbols $s_i \in \mathbb{S}_i$, that represent the sensor values currently perceived by an agent through all its sensors (with n being the number of sensors). A *partial state* is a conjunction $\tilde{st} := \bigwedge_{s \in \tilde{S}} s$ over a subset $\tilde{S} \subset S$ of a complete state's state set. □

The provided definition will also be relevant later for the concepts and algorithms that will be considered throughout this work.

2.1.2 Actions

The possible actions that can be performed by an agent are modeled by the finite *action symbol set* $\mathbb{A}$, where every $a \in \mathbb{A}$ represents a distinct action. The agent model considered here only allows for performing one action at a time.

In many cases, the action symbol set of an agent is fixed and a priori known. However, there are also applications imaginable where not all actions are known in advance (e. g., if the the agent's possible actions depend on its current state). In such cases, the action symbol set can be extended by a new, previously unknown action whenever it becomes available for the first time.

As it is the case for the sensor symbol sets described in Section 2.1.1, in this way, an agent can successively extend its action symbol set when exploring a (partially) unknown environment, where not all possible actions are known in advance.

Figure 2.2 provides an abstract visualization of the agent model described so far including its sensors and possible actions.

2. Foundations of Learning Agents

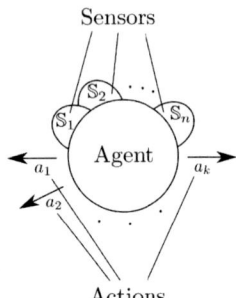

Figure 2.2 (Agent, Sensors, Actions) (Source: a. f. FLAIRS'17 poster by Apeldoorn & Kern-Isberner)
The sensors through which the agent can perceive its environment are represented by the semicircular areas here, annotated with their corresponding sensor symbol sets. The possible actions through which the agent can change the state of the environment are represented by the arrows, annotated with the elements $a_1, ..., a_k$ from the agent's action symbol set $\mathbb{A}$.

2.1.3 State Transitions and Partial Observable Markov Decision Processes

After having considered states and actions in the previous sections, this section now considers some basic concepts of transitions from one state to another resulting from an agent performing actions in its environment. The principal aim here is to create a simple yet sufficient conceptual base for easily describing the data resulting from an agent's behavior (as needed later, e. g., in Section 3.5). Although the well-known framework of *Partial Observable Markov Decision Processes* (POMDPs) (see, e. g., [32], pp. 392–393, or [43]) exceeds the amount of generality that is needed for this aim, the basic concepts will be related to POMDPs here as well, as POMDPs are a standard framework for similar scenarios.

Basic Concepts of State Transitions

Performing an action $a \in \mathbb{A}$ in a state $st := \bigwedge_{s \in S} s$ results in a *state transition* to a successor state $st' := \bigwedge_{s \in S'} s$. The perceived successor state st' may be equal to its predecessor st: If this is the case, then either the environment was not changed by the action a or the agent was not able to observe the state change (in case the environment is only partially observable for the agent). Usually, an agent's sensors should be able to reflect the relevant state changes of its environment (at least partially), otherwise meaningful reasoning will be difficult to realize.

Due to the inherent temporal character of state transitions, subsequent states can also be denoted as $st_t, st_{t+1}, ...$, where $t \in \mathbb{N} \cup \{0\}$ refers to a (discrete) point in time and $t = 0$ refers to the initial state. A state transition can then be denoted as

$$st_t \xrightarrow{a_t} st_{t+1} \tag{2.1}$$

meaning that at time t, in state st_t, the action a_t is performed and leads to the successor state st_{t+1}.

The following example further explains the agent concepts described so far in the context of a two-dimensional grid world.[3]

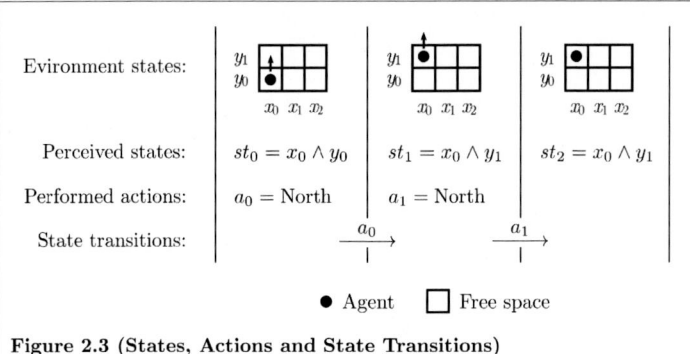

Figure 2.3 (States, Actions and State Transitions)
An agent (represented by the black circle) navigates in a tiny 3×2 grid world, starting in the southwestern corner. In its initial state $st_0 := x_0 \wedge y_0$, the agent performs the action $a_0 :=$ North, resulting in the state transition $st_0 \xrightarrow{a_0} st_1$ to the successor state $st_1 = x_0 \wedge y_1$. By performing the same action $a_1 := a_0$ again in state st_1, the agent's movement is constrained by the end of the grid world, leading to the successor state $st_2 = st_1$.

Example 2.1 (States, Actions and State Transitions) An agent in a tiny 3×2 grid world (see Figure 2.3) is equipped with two sensors to determine its x and y position. The sensor symbol sets are defined as $\mathbb{S}_x := \{x_0, x_1, x_2\}$ and $\mathbb{S}_y := \{y_0, y_1\}$ (where the southwestern corner of the grid world is assumed to be represented by x_0 and y_0). The agent is able move in the four cardinal directions and therefore its action symbol set is defined as $\mathbb{A} := \{\text{North}, \text{South}, \text{East}, \text{West}\}$. Initially, the agent is located at the southwestern corner of the grid world and its currently perceived state

---

[3] Grid worlds are traditionally used as examples in various forms in the literature, especially in the context of *Reinforcement Learning* (e. g., [62]). However, similar concepts are also used, e. g., in robotics for localization and path planning in cellular maps (see [36], Section 5.1.2 and Section 7.4.4). Also in this work, grid worlds will serve as examples in many cases.

is $st_0 := x_0 \wedge y_0$. The agent now performs the action $a_0 :=$ North, resulting in a state transition and the agent's subsequently perceived state is $st_1 = x_0 \wedge y_1$. Performing the same action $a_1 :=$ North as subsequent action again now lets the agent remain in its current state of the environment (due to the end of the grid world constraining the agent's movement). Thus the agent's subsequently perceived state $st_2 = st_1$. □

The example shown in Figure 2.3 represents a *deterministic* setting, where an action performed in a state always leads to the same subsequent state. However, state transitions can also be *non-deterministic*, i.e., performing an action in a state can lead to different subsequent states. This can be the case mainly for two reasons:

- *Non-deterministic environments*: In non-deterministic environments, the state transition is a stochastic process where the subsequent state resulting from an action can follow a certain probability distribution. Examples are gambling machines, like multi-armed bandits, where every arm has its own winning probability and thus using the arm sometimes results in a win and sometimes in a loss. Also environments involving multiple agents can be an example for non-determinism from a single agent's point of view, since the subsequent state does not only depend on the action performed by the agent, but also on the actions of all other agents in the environment.

- *Unreliable sensors*: Even if the environment itself can be considered deterministic, the values provided by the agent's sensors can be unreliable due to inaccuracy or defectiveness. Thereby, an action performed in a certain state can lead to different perceived subsequent states, even if the subsequent state is actually the same.

In many real-world applications (like in robotics, games, etc.), both kinds of non-determinism can occur and often they hardly can be distinguished by an agent.

Partial Observable Markov Decision Processes

Up to this point, some basic concepts for modeling state transitions as a result of actions performed by an agent in its environment have been considered. This subsection now considers *Partial Observable Markov Decision Processes* (POMDPs), a general framework for describing such kinds of scenarios which is widely represented in the literature (e.g., in common planning literature such as [32], or in more recent works such as [43]). Although POMDPs provide a much larger amount of generality than needed in the context of this work, they will be briefly considered and related to the concepts presented here.

Mainly according to the presentations in [32] (Chapter 16, pp. 392–393) and [43], the basic components of a decision process in the context of a fully observable system are a set of states, a set of actions and a conditional probability distribution P_{trans} for the state transitions when actions are performed. A reward distribution can determine the local short-term quality of an action performed in a state. In addition to that, in a POMDP, an agent is not able to perceive all relevant information through its sensors. For this purpose, in a POMDP, the concept of *observations* is added: An observation refers to an agent's perception of an underlying state—however, it might cover less information than actually relevant for the state. According to [32], in a POMDP, the agent is only able to access its environment through these observations. In addition to the conditional probability distribution P_{trans}, a POMDP can also comprise a conditional probability distribution P_{obs} over the observations, i.e., over what the agent observes when performing an action in a state.

While the conditional probability distribution P_{trans} over the transitions of the actual states can be considered related to the non-determinism of the environment, P_{obs} is more closely related to the reliability of the agent's sensors (see [43], p. 2, and cf. the end of the previous subsection).

However, in the remainder of this work, mostly the problem of deciding for the best action according to an agent's (learned) knowledge given a single perceived state (or observation of that state) will be considered. Thus, a simple yet effective approach for handling both kinds of non-determinism can be the counting of relative frequencies and considering the action with the maximum probability of reaching a goal given a perceived state (or observation thereof). This will lead later to the concept of *state-action sequences* (in Section 2.1.5), which provides a simple yet effective way of describing the "raw" data of an agent's behavior in its environment, while abstracting from the environment's non-determinism and the partial observability of states. In such a state-action sequence, a (complete) state will refer to what an agent is able to observe and the state-action sequence's non-determinism will be related to the agent's action selection only (i.e., whether or not the agent always decides for the same action when being provided with the same state or observation thereof).

2.1.4 Definition of an Agent

Even if it was stated at the beginning of this chapter (Section 2.1) that it is hard to find a meaningful definition of an agent (according to agent-related literature), this section makes the attempt of providing a definition of an agent that at least covers the basic needs of this work.

For this purpose, the terms of an agent's *state space*, *action space* and *state-action space* will be introduced first.

Definition 2.2 (State Space) The state space $\mathbb{S}$ of an agent with n sensors is defined as $\mathbb{S} := \mathbb{S}_1 \times ... \times \mathbb{S}_n$, where every $\mathbb{S}_i$ is a sensor symbol set containing the representations of all possible values that can be provided by the agent's i-th sensor. □

According to Definition 2.2, the state space of an agent comprises all possible states that can be distinguished by the agent through its sensors. Similarly, the agent's action space can be defined as follows:

Definition 2.3 (Action Space) The action space of a an agent is defined by the agent's action symbol set $\mathbb{A}$. □

Combining the agent's state space and its action space leads to the definition of the state-action space:

Definition 2.4 (State-Action Space) The state-action space of an agent is defined as the Cartesian product $\mathbb{S} \times \mathbb{A} = \mathbb{S}_1 \times ... \times \mathbb{S}_n \times \mathbb{A}$, where $\mathbb{S} := \mathbb{S}_1 \times ... \times \mathbb{S}_n$ is the agent's state space and $\mathbb{A}$ is the agent's action space. □

The state-action space of an agent can reveal information about the problem size of the setting in which the agent is applied. This can be important, e.g., for choosing an adequate approach for the agent's decision-making process. The size of the state-action space is usually high for many real-world problems.

With this in mind and in accordance with the considerations at the beginning of Chapter 2, an agent, which satisfies the basic needs of the concepts that will be explained in the following of this work, can be defined now as follows:

Definition 2.5 (Agent) An agent is a system that acts autonomously in an environment to fulfill its (designated) tasks by using an integrated *decision-making component* $\mathfrak{D}$ to find an *adequate way* through its state-action space $\mathbb{S} \times \mathbb{A}$. □

What still has to be clarified in the above Definition 2.5, are the term "adequate way" and the decision-making component $\mathfrak{D}$. The former usually concerns certain criteria that are expected from the resulting agent behavior. These may refer, e.g., to some optimizations (like finding the shortest path to a certain goal state) or desired behavioral properties (like "human-like" decisions or learning behavior). Besides the computational feasibility, fulfilling such criteria is one of the main challenges of developing an agent's decision-making component.

Technically, in the context of Definition 2.5, the results of the decision-making component $\mathfrak{D}$ depend at least on a currently perceived state st, for which an adequate action $a \in \mathbb{A}$ (or multiple equivalent actions) will be returned. Therefore, it can also be referred to the decision-making component as $\mathfrak{D}(st)$. Depending on the kind of the agent and on the modeling, the decision component can additionally rely on further parameters (e. g., the agent's knowledge, based on which the decisions regarding a currently perceived state st will be made—such knowledge can also be learned or adapted over time in case of an agent with learning capabilities).

Even if some considerations in this work are not directly referring to the agent's decision-making component itself, but rather to the representation of the agent's behavior *resulting* from an (possibly unknown) decision-making component: Having an approach which is able to represent an agent's behavior adequately, these representations can also be exploited for decision-making (as will be considered later in Chapter 5).

2.1.5 Agent Behavior

An agent's behavior is determined by the implementation of the agent's decision-making component $\mathfrak{D}$. The decision-making component essentially depends on the following two aspects:

- an algorithm that is capable of inferring actions for a perceived state
- the agent's knowledge to which the algorithm refers for inferring the actions.

The agent's knowledge can either (1) be provided by a knowledge engineer or it can (2) be learned by the agent itself (e. g., from training data).

In case (1), the knowledge is modeled manually using knowledge representation techniques and is usually available in a symbolic form: Symbols, each having a special meaning, e. g., a statement about the environment (like "it is raining" or "the streets are wet"), can be related to each other, e. g., by simple rules or similar concepts (like "if *it is raining*, then *the streets are wet*"). Inference algorithms in this first case must be capable of processing symbols, rules and similar concepts and—depending on the concretely used paradigm—possibly have to deal with contradictory rules, inconsistencies and the like.

2. Foundations of Learning Agents

In case (2), the agent can observe examples of states and corresponding actions, which are beneficial or disadvantageous to be performed in the respective states. The agent's knowledge will be successively built using machine learning techniques and is then usually available in a numeric form: These can be weights attached to actions, which indicate how beneficial or disadvantageous an action in a given state is, (e. g., by relative frequencies) or parameters of a function which approximates the weight distribution over the actions in a given state. Here, the inference algorithm usually deals with numeric computations and/or comparisons to retrieve the approximated distribution and to select a corresponding action based on it.

In either of the two cases, it is also possible to refrain from focusing on the agent's internal decision-making component and to describe the agent behavior *externally*, i.e., by only considering the agent's resulting behavior, without considering how it was created by the decision-making component.

Naive Approaches

As a first attempt, an agent's behavior can be described as an *action sequence*, i.e., an ordered multi-set of actions $\mathcal{A} := \{a_1, ..., a_m\}$. Every element is an action symbol of the action symbol set $\mathbb{A}$ resulting from running the agent in its environment.

Example 2.2 (Action Sequence) An agent in an 8×6 grid world (similar to the one described in Example 2.1) has to move around a water area to get from a starting point A in the southwestern corner of the grid world to a destination B in the southeastern corner of the grid world (see Figure 2.4). Its action symbol set is $\mathbb{A} := \{\text{North}, \text{South}, \text{East}, \text{West}\}$. The agent behavior can be described by an action sequence as the ordered multi-set $\mathcal{A} = \{\text{North}, \underbrace{\text{East}, ..., \text{East}}_{\text{seven times}}, \text{South}\}$. □

Unfortunately, this first approach of representing agent behavior as an action sequence suffers from several drawbacks: Besides lacking in abstraction capabilities, it does not even reveal any information about the relation of actions and states. Furthermore, it requires the set representing the actions to be ordered to preserve the meaning of the contained information.

2.1 Basic Agent Model

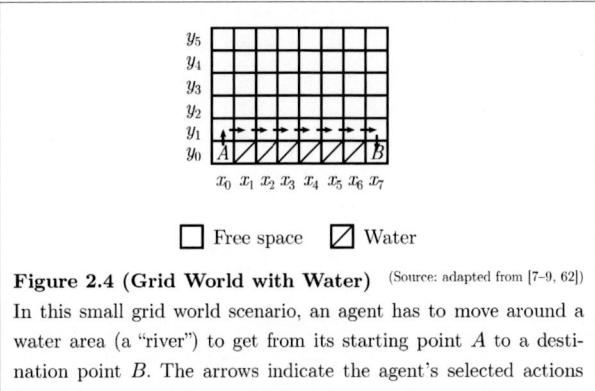

Figure 2.4 (Grid World with Water) (Source: adapted from [7–9, 62])
In this small grid world scenario, an agent has to move around a water area (a "river") to get from its starting point A to a destination point B. The arrows indicate the agent's selected actions for solving the task by considering the most direct path along the river, resulting in an action sequence.

Another rather naive approach of representing agent behavior in an environment is to describe it as a *state sequence*, i.e., an ordered multi-set of states. In the example shown in Figure 2.4, this would result in the set $\mathcal{S} := \{st_0, ..., st_9\}$ where for every state $st \in \mathcal{S}$, $st := x \wedge y$ with $x \in \mathbb{S}_x$ and $y \in \mathbb{S}_y$ being the respective elements of the agent's sensor symbol sets (i.e., $st_0 = x_0 \wedge y_0$, $st_1 = x_0 \wedge y_1$, ...). Even if this approach focuses on the agent's states for representing its behavior, it still suffers from (partly the same) obvious drawbacks: Besides also lacking in abstraction capabilities (e.g., for answering the question what the agent would do in other states not present in the state sequence), the actions performed by the agent are only represented *implicitly* through the state transitions here. As a consequence, this approach also strongly relies on the set $\mathcal{S}$ being ordered.

Representation As State-Action Pairs

Now combining the two approaches of action sequences and state sequences leads to the idea of representing agent behavior in form of (a sequence of) *state-action pairs*, where every pair indicates which action is performed in the corresponding perceived state. An agent's behavior can then be represented by a set of such state-action pairs:

Definition 2.6 (State-Action Sequence) A state-action sequence is an ordered multi-set of state-action pairs $\mathcal{SA} := \{(st_1, a_1), ..., (st_m, a_m)\}$, where every state-action pair $(st, a) \in \mathcal{SA}$ consists of a state $st := s_1 \wedge ... \wedge s_n$ (with $s_i \in \mathbb{S}_i$ being an element of the respective sensor value set) and an action $a \in \mathbb{A}$, which was performed in state st. □

Representing agent behavior as a set of state-action pairs already overcomes at least some of the drawbacks of the aforementioned approaches:

- Both states and actions are represented *explicitly*.

- By also explicitly *relating* states and actions, the set representing the state-action sequence does not even necessarily need to be ordered—at least, if one is only interested in what the agent decided for the corresponding states. (Note that this would render the state-action sequence a *state-action set*, i. e., an unordered multi-set—however, to keep the intuition of a sequence, it will be referred here to it as an ordered set, as provided by Definition 2.6.)

Nevertheless, also this approach is still lacking abstraction capabilities, since it only relates actions to specific single states. (Methods for representing agent behavior with abstraction techniques are an essential part of this work and will be presented later in Chapter 3.)

Deterministic vs. Non-Deterministic State-Action Sequences

The state-action sequence representing an agent's behavior can be either *deterministic* or *non-deterministic*. In case of a deterministic state-action sequence $\mathcal{SA}$, all state-action pairs $\mathbf{p} \in \mathcal{SA}$ with the same state also have the same action. In other words: There do not exist any two state-action pairs $\mathbf{p}_1, \mathbf{p}_2 \in \mathcal{SA}$ with their states $st_{\mathbf{p}_1}, st_{\mathbf{p}_2}$ being equal and their corresponding actions $a_{\mathbf{p}_1}, a_{\mathbf{p}_2}$ being unequal.

In case of a non-deterministic state-action sequence, the set $\mathcal{SA}$ contains state-action pairs (at least two) having the same state but different actions. This can be the case for two reasons:

- The agent's decision-making component $\mathfrak{D}(st)$ is non-deterministic in the sense that it does not always provide the same decision for the same perceived state st.

- Not all of the agent's sensors are reflected in the states of the agent's state-action sequence and therefore it seems to be that agent's decision-making component does not always provide the same decision for the same perceived state.

Both of the two cases can result in a non-deterministic state-action sequence representing the agent's behavior.

2.1.6 Knowledge-Based Agents

As already briefly mentioned in the beginning of the previous section, one possibility of designing an agent's decision-making component is that of providing a manually created knowledge base together with an adequate inference algorithm: Based on the knowledge reflected by the knowledge base, the inference algorithm can decide which action should be performed given the agent's perceptions.

By using such knowledge-based approaches, the knowledge is available *explicitly* in a symbolic form, where every symbol usually has a specific meaning. This can be, e.g., an information about the environment, like "it is raining" or "the streets are wet" as well as an action like "reduce speed". In the knowledge base, these pieces can then be related to each other, by rules (or similar concepts), e.g., "if *it is raining*, then *the streets are wet*" or "if *the streets are wet*, then *reduce speed*".

In the context of knowledge-based agents, an inference algorithm must be capable of processing such information in an efficient way. At first glance, this may sound trivial, since simple if-then-rules can be easily implemented; however—depending on the concretely used paradigm—knowledge-based approaches have to deal with contradictory rules, inconsistencies and the like. Even in simple cases, this can lead to problems, as can be seen in the following example (similar examples can be found in various forms and from various domains in the literature):

Example 2.3 (Knowledge-based Robot) According to its construction, a robot is only able to move on smooth surfaces. The robot is equipped with a sensor that is capable of recognizing different kinds of surfaces. The robot's knowledge is modeled with three rules stating that (Rule 1) a smooth surface allows for moving (Rule 2) if ice is perceived, the robot should immediately stop and (Rule 3) ice is a smooth surface. More formally, the robots knowledge base may look as follows:

$$\mathcal{KB} := \{ \underbrace{surface \to move}_{\text{Rule 1}}, \underbrace{ice \to stop}_{\text{Rule 2}}, \underbrace{ice \to surface}_{\text{Rule 3}} \}$$

The robot now perceives *ice*: According to Rule 2, it can be inferred that the robot has to stop immediately; according to Rule 3, it can be inferred that ice is a *surface* and, with that, according to Rule 1 it can be inferred that the robot should *move*. Thus, both *moving* and *stopping* will be inferred at the same time. □

Example 2.3 shows that even in simple cases, modeling knowledge is not a trivial task: Even if each of the three rules is intuitively correct if considered separately, the rules lead to contradictory inferences when put together to a knowledge base. It is obvious that these kinds of problems grow in more realistic scenarios, where the modeled knowledge is much more complex.

There are many knowledge representation paradigms that target these kinds of problems, e.g., *default logics* (by Reiter [55] or Poole [54]), *answer set programming* (ASP) [19] or *conditional knowledge bases* (with basic ideas of conditionals going back to de Finetti [23], according to [15], p. 35). Some of which provide a strong background for investigating and approximating "human-like" inference processes. However, their inference algorithms can become computational expensive when it comes to larger knowledge bases. For others, like ASP, rather efficient and ready-to-use solvers exist (e.g, CLINGO [22]), which renders them potentially suitable for designing decision-making components in the context of agent applications. Since the concepts that will be presented later in this work are geared to practical applicability (as needed, e.g, in the context of games, where even real-time inference performance may be required), especially ASP will be considered more detailed in the related work section (Section 2.3). (A comparison to ASP can also be found in [41].)

An advantage of using knowledge-based approaches for the creation of an agent's decision component is that the knowledge is available in an explicit form: By this, agent behavior can in principle be modeled in a transparent way. Nevertheless, as can be seen in Example 2.3 and as will also be shown in detail in Section 2.2, not all knowledge-based approaches are suitable for modeling larger amounts of knowledge in a comprehensible way.

2.1.7 Learning Agents and the Black Box Problem

Unlike knowledge-based agents, learning agents follow a different approach: The main idea here is that the knowledge is not provided a priori to the agent by a knowledge engineer but the agent has to learn it by itself from scratch. Such agents usually perform poorly in the beginning by following a trial-and-error principle, and successively become better over time while observing the (a priori unknown) environment. For this purpose, learning agents are usually equipped with a "special sensor" that is able to perceive a (numeric) *reward*, which provides information on how beneficial the currently perceived state is or, on how beneficial it is to perform a certain action in a perceived state, respectively. Such a reward is mostly *local*, which means that it provides information about the agent's current situation rather than providing information about its overall behavior regarding a global goal. The perceived rewards can be used to reinforce weights of state-action pairs, if the action turned out to be beneficial in the corresponding state. This finally results in a numeric representation of the learned knowledge (e. g., in form of a weight matrix). Learning agent approaches following these ideas can be roughly embraced by the term *reinforcement learning* [62].

Using a learning paradigm for an agent's decision-making component is a good choice if there is no or only few a priori knowledge about the environment available, or if the agent should be highly adaptive, e. g., in case the agent's concrete environment is not known in advance. (This can be the case, e. g., in *general video game playing artificial intelligence* (GVGAI) [53], where games to be played by an agent may be unknown in advance.[4])

One of the major challenges for such learning agents is the problem of optimizing their behavior toward a global long-term goal, while being provided with local rewards for a currently perceived state only. Therefore, it may be beneficial for an agent to decide for a locally disadvantageous action with a low local reward in a certain state (even if locally better actions are actually known for that state), to achieve a long-term goal that maximizes the global reward.[5]

Another challenge is the so-called *exploration-exploitation dilemma* (see, e. g., [62]): Having no a priori knowledge, a learning agent starts in the beginning of the learning process with random exploration of the environment, following a trial-and-error principle. As the agent collects more and more information over time about which action is beneficial in which state, the question is now at which point during the learning process the agent should stop exploring the environment and start exploiting the knowledge that was already learned: On the one hand, if the agent starts too early to exploit the learned knowledge, it can easily get stuck in a local optimum; on the other hand, if the agent starts too late to exploit the learned knowledge, the learning process becomes unnecessarily slow.

There exist several reinforcement learning algorithms today that can deal with both of the aforementioned challenges. In the following, one of the classic algorithms, *Q-learning* [68], will be outlined briefly. Even if being developed in the late eighties, this algorithm is still used nowadays, mostly combined with neural networks in the context of deep learning approaches (see, e. g., [49] for a successful recent work in the context of video games). Section 2.2, as well as several experiments later in this work, will refer to Q-learning again. Besides Q-learning, other similar algorithms exist

---

[4] This especially concerns the *learning track* of the GVGAI competition [65]; other tracks provide (partial) information to the agent in advance (e. g., the forward model of a game). Thanks to Jun.-Prof. Dr.-Ing. Alexander Dockhorn for pointing to that.

[5] A well-known problem of that kind is called the *mountain car problem* in the literature [62]: An agent driving a car in a valley has to reach a goal on the top of a hill. Since the car's motor is too weak to drive up the hill directly, the agent has to drive backwards in the wrong direction, upwards the opposite hill, to gain drive for being able to reach the goal.

(like *SARSA* [62]), which differ, e. g., in the way how weights are updated for learning. All approaches presented in this work that incorporate learning agent algorithms do not depend on a specific learning algorithm and can also be combined with other machine learning algorithms, that are not further considered here.

Q-Learning

In a common Q-learning setting (see, e. g., [62, 68]), an agent can be considered to have an n-dimensional state-space $\mathbb{S} := \mathbb{S}_1 \times ... \times \mathbb{S}_n$ (where every $\mathbb{S}_i$ is the set representing the possible values of the agent's i-th sensor, see Definition 2.2). The action space is defined by a set $\mathbb{A}$ representing the agent's possible actions (see Definition 2.3). In addition, the agent is equipped with a special sensor to perceive a local numeric reward $r(s_1, ..., s_n)$ (with $s_i \in \mathbb{S}_i$), that indicates how beneficial a state is, that is represented by the sensor values $s_1, ..., s_n$. Note that the reward is local in the sense that it only provides information about the local benefit of the state without considering its contribution to a global long-term goal (e. g., an even more beneficial goal state). The reward for performing an action a in a given state represented by $s_1, ..., s_n$ corresponds to the reward of the resulting successor state: If the agent performs an action $a \in \mathbb{A}$ in a state represented by the sensor values $s_1, ..., s_n$, then the reward for a will be equal to $r(s'_1, ..., s'_n)$, where $s'_1, ..., s'_n$ represent the sensor values of the successor state resulting from the state transition $st_t \xrightarrow{a_t} st_{t+1}$ (cf. Formula 2.1), with st_t and st_{t+1} being the states that are composed of the sensor values represented by $s_1, ..., s_n$ and $s'_1, ..., s'_n$, respectively (in line with Section 2.1.1).[6]

To be able to store which action is the best in a perceived state, the agent owns an $(n+1)$-dimensional weight matrix $Q := (q_{s_1,...,s_n,a})$ (with $s_i \in \mathbb{S}_i$, $a \in \mathbb{A}$), where every weight represents how beneficial it is to perform the action a when perceiving $s_1, ..., s_n$. Starting from a zero matrix, these weights are successively updated during the learning process, such that over time every weight $q_{s_1,...,s_n,a}$ indicates the global long-term reward that can be expected from performing action a in the state represented by $s_1, ..., s_n$. A weight is updated every time an action has been performed, when the corresponding reward is perceived, according to the update rule (cf. [68])

$$q'_{s_1,...s_n,a} := \underbrace{(1-\alpha) \cdot q_{s_1,...s_n,a}}_{\text{old knowledge}} + \underbrace{\alpha \cdot (r(s_1,...,s_n) + \gamma \cdot \max_{a' \in \mathbb{A}} q_{s'_1,...,s'_n,a'})}_{\text{new information}} \qquad (2.2)$$

where $q'_{s_1,...,s_n,a}$ is the new weight, $q_{s_1,...,s_n,a}$ is the old weight, α is the *learning rate* and γ is the *discount factor*.

---

[6] Note that in a more general setting, it is also imaginable that the reward additionally depends on a performed action. Thanks to Dr. Peter Dauscher for pointing to that.

When updating a weight, the learning rate α determines how much of the new information gained from the perceived reward is adopted for the new weight. The discount factor γ determines the degree to which the knowledge about future states is considered: The higher γ is chosen, the more extensively the benefit of future states will be considered in the newly incorporated information (due to $\max_{a' \in \mathbb{A}} q_{s_1,...s_n,a'}$ referring to the best action that can be performed in the subsequent state according to the so far learned matrix Q).

Furthermore, a Q-learning algorithm usually incorporates an *exploration probability* ϵ: This probability determines in how many cases the agent chooses a random action instead of choosing the best one according to the so far learned Q-matrix. The exploration probability plays an important role, since (if $\epsilon > 0$) it allows a learning agent to try out and learn something new, even if it gained already a certain amount of knowledge about the environment. By this, it prevents the agent from getting stuck in local optima. The exploration probability is closely related to the exploration-exploitation dilemma mentioned at the beginning of the Q-learning section and finding adaptive solutions for this parameter is part of learning agent research. In very basic agent models, ϵ is usually a low constant or it is set to a high value in the early beginning of the agent's learning phase (when the agent does not yet know anything about its environment) and it is then successively discounted when the agent gains more knowledge over time.

Example 2.4 (Learning Agent in a Grid World) An agent in a grid world (similar to the one from Example 2.2) has to learn to get from a starting point A to a destination point B, by avoiding a region of water in the South of the scenario. The agent has two sensors to determine its x and y position and is able to perform actions from the set $\mathbb{A} := \{\text{North}, \text{South}, \text{East}, \text{West}\}$. The cells of the grid world represent the states having a corresponding local reward distribution and the destination cell B represents the terminal state of the environment that causes a learning episode to end (see Figure 2.5). Using a Q-learning approach, the agent starts with random exploration of the environment. Over time, the agent behavior gets more and more accurate and finally converges to the optimal behavior. □

2. Foundations of Learning Agents

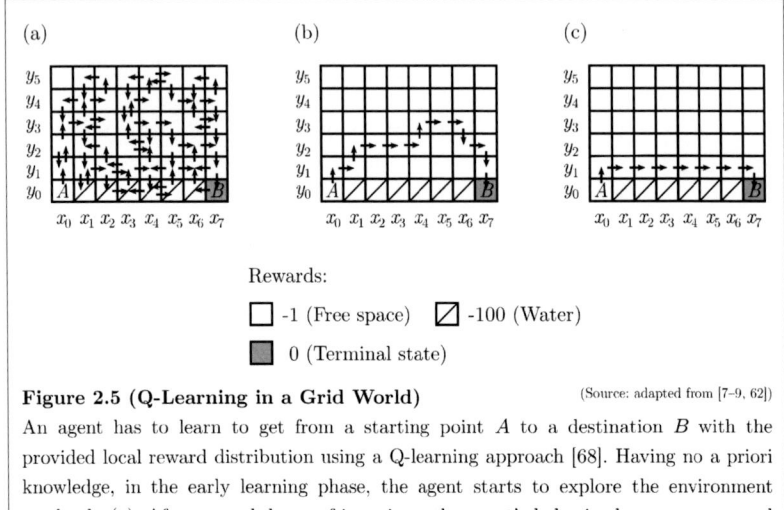

Figure 2.5 (Q-Learning in a Grid World) (Source: adapted from [7–9, 62])
An agent has to learn to get from a starting point A to a destination B with the provided local reward distribution using a Q-learning approach [68]. Having no a priori knowledge, in the early learning phase, the agent starts to explore the environment randomly (a). After several dozen of iterations, the agent's behavior becomes more and more accurate (b). Finally, the agent behavior converges to the optimum (c).

Neural Networks As Function Approximators

One drawback of the classic Q-learning approach (and similar approaches) is that of the matrix representation of the weights, whose growing number quickly becomes unhandy with increasing problem size. To overcome this issue, a successful approach is to consider the Q matrix as a function $f\colon \mathbb{S}_1 \times \ldots \times \mathbb{S}_n \times \mathbb{A} \to \mathbb{R}$ that returns the corresponding weight for a state-action pair and to learn an approximation of that function using a neural network. By this, the weight matrix Q can usually be represented with much less weights: If modeled adequately, the number of weights needed for the network can be much smaller than the number of weights that would be needed for Q. Approaches of this kind have been implemented, e. g., for learning video games only from observing the pixel matrix of the screen and considering the game score as reward [49].

Black Box Problem

Besides the function f being approximated (which in fact works very well in many practical applications), a real drawback of using a neural network as function approximator is that the learned knowledge will be represented by the weights of the neural network instead of the weights being directly attached to state-action pairs. By this, the learned knowledge contained in the weights gets a very implicit character and thereby becomes inaccessible to humans—even in case of small-sized problems. This is one manifestation of what is called the *black box problem* of neural networks in the literature.

2.2 Another "Black Box": Comprehensible Representation of Agent Behavior

As presented in Section 2.1.6, agent behavior can be described by rules that indicate which actions are performed by the agent in its perceived states. Since neural networks (and other machine learning approaches) can lack in transparency, a rule-based approach seems to be an obvious way of representing agent behavior more transparently, since the rules of the agent's decisions are accessible in an explicit form (in contrast to vectors and matrices of numeric weights, which are common representation schemes for several machine learning approaches).

However, even in smaller scenarios, representing agent behavior as simple rules, like

$$if\ X\ then\ Y$$

or, more formally,

$$X \to Y$$

does not naturally result in representations that are easy to comprehend by humans. Whereas the black box problem of neural network approaches is well-known and considered in current machine learning research (e.g., in the context of tasks related to image recognition), the "black box" problem of representing agent behavior in a comprehensible and human-readable way is less present.

Example 2.5 (A Further "Black Box" Problem) Again, a learning agent in a grid world (as in Example 2.4) is considered: The agent learns to get from a starting point A to the destination B, avoiding a region of water in the South of the scenario (see Figure 2.5). Learning is realized by using a basic Q-learning approach [68] (see Section 2.1.7) with a weight update according to Formula (2.2) and the local rewards being distributed as provided in Figure 2.5. By this means, the agent learns a weight for each possible state-action pair, which indicates the long-term global benefit of performing the action in the state.[7] After several dozen of iterations, the agent behavior converges to the optimal behavior (as shown in Figure 2.5)—*but how can be described what the agent learned in fact?* □

As a first naive approach to answer the question resulting from Example 2.5, simply all rules that can be created directly from the weighted state-action pairs can be provided (see Figure 2.6). Even if the rules shown in Figure 2.6 represent the knowledge of the agent's learned behavior *completely*, the representation is obviously far from being comprehensible—especially if considering the simplicity of the task.

To tackle these kinds of issues, one of the central ideas that will be followed in this work is that of representing knowledge on several levels of abstraction: Higher levels reflect the represented knowledge in a rougher, more heuristic way, whereas lower levels reflect the knowledge more concretely, by providing *exceptions* to the knowledge on the higher levels. On the one hand, this seems to be in line with generalization and conditionalization capabilities of human thinking (i. e., adding conditional exceptions to what is supposed to be known), which can be observed in psychological experiments (e. g, in [27], pp. 210–211).[8] On the other hand, it is also close to ideas from default logic, like *justifications* (Reiter [55]) or the *default negation* known from answer set programming (ASP) [19], while at the same time being less tightly coupled to logic, which might potentially be of interest, e. g., when being used in interdisciplinary working environments.

2.3 Related Approaches

Knowledge representation approaches usually are a good choice when it comes to the explicit representation of knowledge (in contrast to the implicit representation of numerical methods as described at the end of Section 2.1.7). However, the previous section (Section 2.2) also showed that the simple use of rules (even if being complete) does not necessarily lead to a satisfying representation, both regarding compactness and (as a consequence) readability and comprehensibility for humans.

---

[7] Note that the learning paradigm is not of major interest here and could be replaced by any other approach (with or without neural network as function approximator) that is capable of learning the task in form of weighted state-action pairs, where the highest weight indicates the best action for a provided state.

[8] The study in [27] especially expatiates on the negative effects of (over-)generalization and conditionalization in human thinking. However, it also shows that these techniques are intuitively used by humans for building models, e. g., when trying to comprehend unknown tasks.

$x_0 \wedge y_0 \to$ East $[-82.49]$	$x_1 \wedge y_5 \to$ West $[-4.15]$	$x_3 \wedge y_5 \to$ South $[-3.69]$	$x_5 \wedge y_5 \to$ North $[-3.16]$
$x_0 \wedge y_0 \to$ North $[-5.65]$	$x_2 \wedge y_0 \to$ East $[-10.00]$	$x_3 \wedge y_5 \to$ West $[-3.73]$	$x_5 \wedge y_5 \to$ South $[-3.18]$
$x_0 \wedge y_0 \to$ South $[-5.69]$	$x_2 \wedge y_0 \to$ North $[-2.82]$	$x_4 \wedge y_0 \to$ East $[-10.00]$	$x_5 \wedge y_5 \to$ West $[-3.19]$
$x_0 \wedge y_0 \to$ West $[-5.70]$	$x_2 \wedge y_0 \to$ South $[-10.00]$	$x_4 \wedge y_0 \to$ North $[-2.00]$	$x_6 \wedge y_0 \to$ East $[0.00]$
$x_0 \wedge y_1 \to$ East $[-5.19]$	$x_2 \wedge y_0 \to$ West $[-19.10]$	$x_4 \wedge y_0 \to$ South $[-10.00]$	$x_6 \wedge y_0 \to$ North $[-0.15]$
$x_0 \wedge y_1 \to$ North $[-5.20]$	$x_2 \wedge y_1 \to$ East $[-4.09]$	$x_4 \wedge y_0 \to$ West $[-10.00]$	$x_6 \wedge y_0 \to$ South $[-10.00]$
$x_0 \wedge y_1 \to$ South $[-5.24]$	$x_2 \wedge y_1 \to$ North $[-4.10]$	$x_4 \wedge y_1 \to$ East $[-2.71]$	$x_6 \wedge y_0 \to$ West $[-27.25]$
$x_0 \wedge y_1 \to$ West $[-5.20]$	$x_2 \wedge y_1 \to$ South $[-72.75]$	$x_4 \wedge y_1 \to$ North $[-2.87]$	$x_6 \wedge y_1 \to$ East $[-1.00]$
$x_0 \wedge y_2 \to$ East $[-4.82]$	$x_2 \wedge y_1 \to$ West $[-4.20]$	$x_4 \wedge y_1 \to$ South $[-69.27]$	$x_6 \wedge y_1 \to$ North $[-1.49]$
$x_0 \wedge y_2 \to$ North $[-4.84]$	$x_2 \wedge y_2 \to$ East $[-4.08]$	$x_4 \wedge y_1 \to$ West $[-3.01]$	$x_6 \wedge y_1 \to$ South $[-52.17]$
$x_0 \wedge y_2 \to$ South $[-4.83]$	$x_2 \wedge y_2 \to$ North $[-4.10]$	$x_4 \wedge y_2 \to$ East $[-3.11]$	$x_6 \wedge y_1 \to$ West $[-1.52]$
$x_0 \wedge y_2 \to$ West $[-4.88]$	$x_2 \wedge y_2 \to$ South $[-4.14]$	$x_4 \wedge y_2 \to$ North $[-3.24]$	$x_6 \wedge y_2 \to$ East $[-1.84]$
$x_0 \wedge y_3 \to$ East $[-4.55]$	$x_2 \wedge y_2 \to$ West $[-4.15]$	$x_4 \wedge y_2 \to$ South $[-3.13]$	$x_6 \wedge y_2 \to$ North $[-1.87]$
$x_0 \wedge y_3 \to$ North $[-4.56]$	$x_2 \wedge y_3 \to$ East $[-4.03]$	$x_4 \wedge y_2 \to$ West $[-3.12]$	$x_6 \wedge y_2 \to$ South $[-1.83]$
$x_0 \wedge y_3 \to$ South $[-4.54]$	$x_2 \wedge y_3 \to$ North $[-4.06]$	$x_4 \wedge y_3 \to$ East $[-3.30]$	$x_6 \wedge y_2 \to$ West $[-2.08]$
$x_0 \wedge y_3 \to$ West $[-4.57]$	$x_2 \wedge y_3 \to$ South $[-4.08]$	$x_4 \wedge y_3 \to$ North $[-3.32]$	$x_6 \wedge y_3 \to$ East $[-2.38]$
$x_0 \wedge y_4 \to$ East $[-4.38]$	$x_2 \wedge y_3 \to$ West $[-4.10]$	$x_4 \wedge y_3 \to$ South $[-3.33]$	$x_6 \wedge y_3 \to$ North $[-2.48]$
$x_0 \wedge y_4 \to$ North $[-4.37]$	$x_2 \wedge y_4 \to$ East $[-3.98]$	$x_4 \wedge y_3 \to$ West $[-3.31]$	$x_6 \wedge y_3 \to$ South $[-2.39]$
$x_0 \wedge y_4 \to$ South $[-4.34]$	$x_2 \wedge y_4 \to$ North $[-4.05]$	$x_4 \wedge y_4 \to$ East $[-3.39]$	$x_6 \wedge y_3 \to$ West $[-2.44]$
$x_0 \wedge y_4 \to$ West $[-4.36]$	$x_2 \wedge y_4 \to$ South $[-4.03]$	$x_4 \wedge y_4 \to$ North $[-3.37]$	$x_6 \wedge y_4 \to$ East $[-2.75]$
$x_0 \wedge y_5 \to$ East $[-4.24]$	$x_2 \wedge y_4 \to$ West $[-4.02]$	$x_4 \wedge y_4 \to$ South $[-3.40]$	$x_6 \wedge y_4 \to$ North $[-2.82]$
$x_0 \wedge y_5 \to$ North $[-4.29]$	$x_2 \wedge y_5 \to$ East $[-3.96]$	$x_4 \wedge y_4 \to$ West $[-3.41]$	$x_6 \wedge y_4 \to$ South $[-2.73]$
$x_0 \wedge y_5 \to$ South $[-4.30]$	$x_2 \wedge y_5 \to$ North $[-3.94]$	$x_4 \wedge y_5 \to$ East $[-3.45]$	$x_6 \wedge y_4 \to$ West $[-2.75]$
$x_0 \wedge y_5 \to$ West $[-4.29]$	$x_2 \wedge y_5 \to$ South $[-3.95]$	$x_4 \wedge y_5 \to$ North $[-3.44]$	$x_6 \wedge y_5 \to$ East $[-2.98]$
$x_1 \wedge y_0 \to$ East $[-19.04]$	$x_2 \wedge y_5 \to$ West $[-3.98]$	$x_4 \wedge y_5 \to$ South $[-3.44]$	$x_6 \wedge y_5 \to$ North $[-2.95]$
$x_1 \wedge y_0 \to$ North $[-2.76]$	$x_3 \wedge y_0 \to$ East $[-10.00]$	$x_4 \wedge y_5 \to$ West $[-3.42]$	$x_6 \wedge y_5 \to$ South $[-2.89]$
$x_1 \wedge y_0 \to$ South $[-19.02]$	$x_3 \wedge y_0 \to$ North $[-0.70]$	$x_5 \wedge y_0 \to$ East $[-10.00]$	$x_6 \wedge y_5 \to$ West $[-2.88]$
$x_1 \wedge y_0 \to$ West $[-2.87]$	$x_3 \wedge y_0 \to$ South $[-10.00]$	$x_5 \wedge y_0 \to$ North $[-1.58]$	$x_7 \wedge y_1 \to$ East $[-0.57]$
$x_1 \wedge y_1 \to$ East $[-4.68]$	$x_3 \wedge y_0 \to$ West $[-10.00]$	$x_5 \wedge y_0 \to$ South $[-19.01]$	$x_7 \wedge y_1 \to$ North $[-0.95]$
$x_1 \wedge y_1 \to$ North $[-4.73]$	$x_3 \wedge y_1 \to$ East $[-3.44]$	$x_5 \wedge y_0 \to$ West $[-10.09]$	$x_7 \wedge y_1 \to$ South $[0.00]$
$x_1 \wedge y_1 \to$ South $[-47.43]$	$x_3 \wedge y_1 \to$ North $[-3.62]$	$x_5 \wedge y_1 \to$ East $[-1.90]$	$x_7 \wedge y_1 \to$ West $[-1.01]$
$x_1 \wedge y_1 \to$ West $[-4.85]$	$x_3 \wedge y_1 \to$ South $[-27.14]$	$x_5 \wedge y_1 \to$ North $[-2.36]$	$x_7 \wedge y_2 \to$ East $[-1.05]$
$x_1 \wedge y_2 \to$ East $[-4.49]$	$x_3 \wedge y_1 \to$ West $[-3.69]$	$x_5 \wedge y_1 \to$ South $[-52.56]$	$x_7 \wedge y_2 \to$ North $[-1.15]$
$x_1 \wedge y_2 \to$ North $[-4.53]$	$x_3 \wedge y_2 \to$ East $[-3.61]$	$x_5 \wedge y_1 \to$ West $[-2.04]$	$x_7 \wedge y_2 \to$ South $[-1.00]$
$x_1 \wedge y_2 \to$ South $[-4.55]$	$x_3 \wedge y_2 \to$ North $[-3.68]$	$x_5 \wedge y_2 \to$ East $[-2.53]$	$x_7 \wedge y_2 \to$ West $[-1.29]$
$x_1 \wedge y_2 \to$ West $[-4.53]$	$x_3 \wedge y_2 \to$ South $[-3.67]$	$x_5 \wedge y_2 \to$ North $[-2.70]$	$x_7 \wedge y_3 \to$ East $[-1.89]$
$x_1 \wedge y_3 \to$ East $[-4.35]$	$x_3 \wedge y_2 \to$ West $[-3.70]$	$x_5 \wedge y_2 \to$ South $[-2.55]$	$x_7 \wedge y_3 \to$ North $[-2.08]$
$x_1 \wedge y_3 \to$ North $[-4.34]$	$x_3 \wedge y_3 \to$ East $[-3.67]$	$x_5 \wedge y_2 \to$ West $[-2.63]$	$x_7 \wedge y_3 \to$ South $[-1.87]$
$x_1 \wedge y_3 \to$ South $[-4.36]$	$x_3 \wedge y_3 \to$ North $[-3.72]$	$x_5 \wedge y_3 \to$ East $[-2.87]$	$x_7 \wedge y_3 \to$ West $[-1.87]$
$x_1 \wedge y_3 \to$ West $[-4.38]$	$x_3 \wedge y_3 \to$ South $[-3.65]$	$x_5 \wedge y_3 \to$ North $[-2.91]$	$x_7 \wedge y_4 \to$ East $[-2.53]$
$x_1 \wedge y_4 \to$ East $[-4.24]$	$x_3 \wedge y_3 \to$ West $[-3.74]$	$x_5 \wedge y_3 \to$ South $[-2.90]$	$x_7 \wedge y_4 \to$ North $[-2.53]$
$x_1 \wedge y_4 \to$ North $[-4.21]$	$x_3 \wedge y_4 \to$ East $[-3.69]$	$x_5 \wedge y_3 \to$ West $[-2.92]$	$x_7 \wedge y_4 \to$ South $[-2.50]$
$x_1 \wedge y_4 \to$ South $[-4.24]$	$x_3 \wedge y_4 \to$ North $[-3.71]$	$x_5 \wedge y_4 \to$ East $[-3.09]$	$x_7 \wedge y_4 \to$ West $[-2.49]$
$x_1 \wedge y_4 \to$ West $[-4.20]$	$x_3 \wedge y_4 \to$ South $[-3.67]$	$x_5 \wedge y_4 \to$ North $[-3.12]$	$x_7 \wedge y_5 \to$ East $[-2.81]$
$x_1 \wedge y_5 \to$ East $[-4.12]$	$x_3 \wedge y_4 \to$ West $[-3.81]$	$x_5 \wedge y_4 \to$ South $[-3.05]$	$x_7 \wedge y_5 \to$ North $[-2.75]$
$x_1 \wedge y_5 \to$ North $[-4.12]$	$x_3 \wedge y_5 \to$ East $[-3.72]$	$x_5 \wedge y_4 \to$ West $[-3.06]$	$x_7 \wedge y_5 \to$ South $[-2.80]$
$x_1 \wedge y_5 \to$ South $[-4.16]$	$x_3 \wedge y_5 \to$ North $[-3.69]$	$x_5 \wedge y_5 \to$ East $[-3.17]$	$x_7 \wedge y_5 \to$ West $[-2.77]$

Figure 2.6 (A "Black Box" by Learned Rules)
The figure shows all 188 rules that can be easily created from the weighted state-action pairs learned by the agent in Example 2.5 using a basic Q-learning approach [68]. (Note that for state $x_7 \wedge y_0$ no rules are provided, since this is the terminating goal state.) The attached weights are the original weights learned by the Q-learning algorithm after several dozen of iterations. As an example, in the starting state $x_0 \wedge y_0$, the best action according to the weights will be North and the worse action by far will be East (since this would lead the agent directly into the water, cf. Figure 2.5). The rules could be easily searched by an inference algorithm to infer which action is the best for a given state (e. g., the one with the highest weight). However, it is obvious that even if the learned behavior is simple, the provided rules are hard to comprehend by humans.

This section discusses different existing approaches that are related to the ideas presented in this work. The outlined approaches will comprise machine learning and clustering techniques to gain structural insights into state-action sequences resulting from learned agent behavior (Section 2.3.1), eligible approaches to represent knowledge learned by agents in a comprehensible way (Section 2.3.2) and a brief overview over learning and hybrid agent models, focusing on the context of games (Section 2.3.3).

2.3.1 Learning Approaches for Structural Insights

Numerous machine learning approaches exist that can be used in the context of agents. Reinforcement learning with neural networks used as function approximators (see Section 2.1.7) in conjunction with deep learning techniques seem to be one of the most popular and successful approaches these days (see, e.g., [49]). However, even for smaller problems, these approaches usually result in large numerical representations that do not allow for gaining insights into the structural relations induced by the underlying learning problem (e.g., which of an agent's percepts are important for making certain decisions).

In contrast, Bayesian networks (and other probabilistic network approaches) (see, e.g., [17], Section 8.2.2) are well-suited to reflect structural dependencies among certain sensors and, moreover, due to their graphical representation, they can be read rather easily (as long as the number of nodes, i.e., the number of an agent's sensors, is not too large). However, although dedicated methods exist that are able to learn the network's structure as well [30], usually the structure is provided in advance to learn the induced conditional probability tables from data. Moreover, the structural knowledge is represented in a graph-model and not in the form of rules. The structural knowledge is also reflected on a sensor-level and not on the level of sensor values, as it will be the case for the approaches presented here (in Chapter 3). This renders it hard to infer specific aspects of an agent's behavior from the Bayesian network's graph-representation, without also considering the corresponding conditional probability tables.

Decision trees provide the concept of a *hierarchical* representation, which can be read top-down to gain an overview over the data of the underlying learning problem. This can render them a suitable approach, even for higher-dimensional problems, as it is the case for agents having a larger amount of sensors. In [39], decision trees have been successfully applied in the context of a Q-learning agent. However, a decision tree learns a hierarchical representation that primarily focuses on which *sensors* are most relevant for splitting the sensory data toward finding good decisions. In contrast, the approaches that will be presented here learn a hierarchical representation, that provides information about which *sensor values* are most important for making good decisions. As it is the case for many other graph-based approaches, both for Bayesian networks and for decision trees, the comprehensibility and interpretability—even if being much better than, e. g., for neural networks—may decrease when it comes to problems with a large number of nodes (as it is often the case for real-world problems).

An approach from the reinforcement learning domain that involves the idea of *hierarchical abstraction* can be found in [63]. There, reinforcement learning is interweaved with a hierarchical structure providing information about different abstraction levels of primitive actions and higher-level tasks. Such a hierarchical structure can be considered a decomposition of the underlying learning problem, which can help to reduce the state-action space (unlike the approach that will be presented in this work, where rules are represented hierarchically for being able to generalize over sensory percepts and actions).

A well-known approach in the context of learning rule-like knowledge from data is the APRIORI algorithm by Agrawal et al. [1]. This algorithm can be applied e. g., in the context of recommender systems to learn *association rules* like

"People that buy *seeds and flower soil* usually also buy *watering cans*."

Such rules are accompanied by *confidence* values, that are similar to the rule weights learned by the approaches that will be presented here (Section 3.4 and Section 3.5). However, the APRIORI algorithm does not learn a complete knowledge base that comprises rules together with their exceptions. It will later be adapted to improve the knowledge base extraction approach presented in Section 3.4.

To be able to create symbolic knowledge from continuous sensory data as well, a technique based on k-means clustering (see [61] for an overview) will be used. As a representative from the field of *unsupervised learning*, it serves well for detecting clusters of values in case sensors are providing continuous data (e. g., a temperature sensor). All values belonging to a found cluster can then be associated with a symbolic sensor value. This approach can also be used in the same way for handling continuous action spaces. Moreover, it can be used to reduce the number of sensors (in case the number of sensors is high), by separating the sensors into two clusters (if possible), of which only the one containing the most relevant sensors will be further considered. (More details on this will be provided in Section 3.5.3).

2.3.2 Comprehensible Representations for Knowledge Learned by Agents

Once having gained some structural insights into the nature of a problem, an interesting question is, what renders a knowledge representation approach eligible for representing such learned knowledge in the context of agents—especially for applications in games?

One of the most important properties of modern machine learning approaches, like neural networks and deep learning (as used, e. g., in [49] in the context of agents), is the ability to *generalize* (i. e, to be able to make good decisions also on similar or even unknown states). Thus, *generalization* can be considered an essential property of a knowledge representation approach, to be considered eligible for learned knowledge. Moreover, for agent applications in the context of games (which will be extensively considered in this work), but also for other agent applications (e. g., in robotics), *efficiency* plays an important role (especially concerning *reasoning*).

Modern machine learning techniques in the context of agents are able to deal with high-dimensional state-action spaces and thus the results (i. e., the relation between percepts and actions) usually cannot be expected to be described easily in a compact and human readable way. This can result in a confusingly large amount of unstructured knowledge (as could be see already before in the context of a low-dimensional problem in Figure 2.6).

A well-known concept from Reiter's *default logic* [55], that can help to reduce the number of rules in an agent's knowledge base, is that of *defaults*: In Reiter's default logic, a default is a special rule that is not always applicable when its premise is satisfied, but requires additional assumptions, called *justifications*, to be consistent (i. e., not to be falsified). By this means, instead of creating one single rule for each case of a large amount of possible cases (which obviously would result in a large amount of rules), a default rule can be created that covers most of the cases. The remaining (exceptional) cases can then be excluded through the default rule's justifications and further rules are only needed to cover the remaining exceptional cases. This usually results in much less rules.

In *answer set programming* (ASP) [19], a similar mechanism is provided by a special negation operator called *default negation* (*not*), in addition to a common ("strict") negation operator ($\neg$). In case a rule's premise comprises a default negation *not a*, either the negation of a must be explicitly known or there must be no information about a to satisfy the rule's premise. In contrast, if a rule's premise depends on $\neg a$, then the rule's premise can only be satisfied if the negation of a is explicitly known. Also this approach can be easily exploited to reduce the number of rules for describing agent behavior, by creating a rule whose premise includes default negations to exclude it from being applied in the exceptional cases and by adding further rules that only handle these exceptional cases.

Both the concept of *defaults* and that of *default negation* can be attributed some kind of generalization capabilities: Since it is possible with these concepts to construct rules that *usually* apply, except in some specific cases (e. g., when certain specific sensor values are perceived by an agent), such rules can also cover a priori unknown cases (e. g., when new or unknown states are perceived).

Referring to the idea of generalization, one possibility for tackling the problem of representing an agent's knowledge about a higher-dimensional state-action space in a *comprehensible* way is to rely the agent's knowledge base more on default-like rules and as few as possible on rather specific rules. This can result in a more compact and thereby more comprehensible representation of the agent's knowledge. However, since an answer set program can be considered a set of rules, there is no explicit order among the rules regarding their specificity. This can be a limiting factor regarding readability and comprehensibility, as more general rules need to explicitly exclude the more specific cases, by making use of default negations in their premises. The following example of a small answer set program that demonstrates this can be found in [8] and in similar form in [41]:

Example 2.6 (Default Negation for Generalization) This example considers the agent behavior that was learned in the grid world in Figure 2.5. The agent is equipped with two sensors to determine its x and y position and can perform the actions $\mathbb{A} := \{\text{North}, \text{South}, \text{East}, \text{West}\}$ (see also Example 2.4). Using a Q-learning (or similar) approach, the agent learned to get from the starting point A in the southwestern corner of the scenario to the destination B in the southeastern corner of the scenario, avoiding the "river" in the south. The knowledge how to get best from A to B (which is contained in the multi-dimensional matrix Q after learning), can be expressed by the following answer set program $\mathcal{P}^Q$, making use of default negation:[9]

$$\mathcal{P}^Q := \{\text{East} \leftarrow not\ y_0, not\ x_7.,$$
$$\text{North} \leftarrow y_0.,$$
$$\text{South} \leftarrow x_7.\}$$

At its starting point A, the agent perceives x_0 and y_0, thus the rule North $\leftarrow y_0$. will be the only rule that can be applied and the action "North" will be concluded (the rule South $\leftarrow x_7$. is not applicable due to x_7 not being known, and the rule

---

[9] Note that in answer set programs, rules are traditionally written starting from the conclusion (head) to the premise (tail) and are terminated by a dot (as usually also the case for other logic programs; see, e. g., [14], p. 287, for an overview).

East ← $not\ y_0, not\ x_7$. is not applicable, since y_0 is perceived and it requires either y_0 not to be known or $\neg y_0$ to be known). In the following seven states, where y_1 will be perceived, the rule East ← $not\ y_0, not\ x_7$. will be applied (since both y_0 and x_7 do not occur here) and finally, when x_7 is perceived, South ← x_7. will be applied (and East ← $not\ y_0, not\ x_7$. will not, since it requires either x_7 not to be known or $\neg x_7$ to be known).

$\mathcal{P}^Q$ also shows generalization capabilities, in case another state that is not part of the state-action sequence from A to B is perceived: If, e. g., x_4 and y_3 is perceived by the agent, then "East" will be concluded; any perceived state comprising x_7, will result in the conclusion "South". □

The rule-based approaches mentioned here do not comprise any weights, e. g., for reflecting more accurately what has been learned from data (i. e., how strong or important certain rules are, according to the data from which they were learned).

A generalization of the default-and-exception-rules idea will be presented later in Chapter 3, which allows for representing rules on several levels of abstraction and which is tailored to the needs of learning such rules from sensory data. In this approach, every rule can be considered an exception to a more general rule on a more general abstraction level. For the approach, also an efficient reasoning algorithm will be provided.

Unlike *ranked default theories*, where defaults can be prioritized (see [45] for an overview), the generalization aspect will be represented more explicitly here with a strong focus on straight-forward readability of the represented knowledge. Moreover, the approach presented here additionally incorporates weights to the rules, which can be considered an "interface" to machine learning approaches, when learning such representations from data.

2.3.3 Learning and Hybrid Agent Models for Games

Besides Tesauro's classic backgammon player TD-GAMMON from the nineties (see, e. g., [64]), both the more recent success by DEEPMIND's go player ALPHAGO [60] and its derivatives as well as the work by Mnih et al. [49] showed that the research for intelligent agents in games made huge progress (see also Section 1.1). Thus, a question might be, whether there is still room for further research in this field today?

While many of the existing approaches tackle the problem of optimizing a single game, in this work also an agent model will be considered, that is able to learn multiple a priori unknown games. Optimizing a single game has already been shown

2.3 Related Approaches

to work well, e. g., in [49, 60, 64] (among others), whereas learning multiple and a priori unknown games is a younger discipline—especially in the context of highly diverse and dynamic real-time games, as in *general video game artificial intelligence* (GVGAI) [53] research. Also motivated by strong time constraints in this context (the learning track rules of the GVGAI competition [65] prior to 2018 limit the playing time to a maximum of 5 minutes and allow only 40 milliseconds for decision-making, according to [5], see also Footnote 4 on page 43), especially models are of interest here, that do not rely on hundreds of thousands of training runs, but are able to perform in near real-time, both regarding *learning* and *reasoning*. The ability of an agent to quickly learn and adapt to unknown games, without requiring an extensively large amount of training time, still leaves a lot of room for improvement.

Existing agent models can be roughly distinguished into the following two categories, along the lines of the *planning track* and the *learning track* of the GVGAI competition (cf. [5]):

- Agent models for the planning track: Agents of the planning track are provided with a *forward model* of a (a priori unknown) game (i. e., a model that allows for forward simulations of the game to extrapolate possible future game states). Agent models in the context of this track must be able to handle and exploit such forward models for making meaningful decisions or creating plans (i. e., action sequences to reach a desired state). For these purposes, common and successfully used algorithms are breadth-first search or *monte carlo tree search* (MCTS) [21]. Furthermore, as discussed in [5], *genetic algorithms* may be used in the context of planning track agent models to evolve eligible action sequences as plans. A successful representative of a planning track agent is YOLOBOT (see [53], Section 2.3), which uses a combined approach also involving MCTS.

- Agent models for the learning track: In contrast to the planning track, agent models in the context of the learning track do not have direct access to a game's forward model. This means, that agents based on these models must learn on their own about the environment and the game mechanics by observing the state transitions resulting from their actions. One possibility to tackle this challenge is to use reinforcement learning techniques similar to that being described in Section 2.1.7. However, since an agent may be trained in levels different from those in which it will be used or evaluated later, this would require the agent to be trained anew every time it is put into another level (even if it is a level of the same game): Even if the game mechanics may remain the same, the anatomy of the level (or further parameters of the environment) may change, rendering the weights of a learned Q-matrix or an approximating neural network improper. Following [5], the approach described by İlhan and

Etaner-Uyar, which combines MCTS with a SARSA reinforcement learning approach, seems to have a lower performance when it comes to short training times. As also pointed out in [5], a randomly behaving agent was still one of the most successful agents in the learning track of the GVGAI competition rounds of the years 2018 and 2019, which shows that there is a lot of room for further research in this field.

Another example of a hybrid agent model in the context of a video game from the recent years is [31], which incorporates sub-symbolic and symbolic approaches: It has been published nearly the same time as the first publication [7] related to the work that is presented here, with both results independently indicating that there is a huge potential for incorporating sub-symbolic and symbolic approaches in the context of learning agents.[10] However, in contrast to the approach that will be presented toward the end of this work (Section 5.2), the primary scope of [31] is not that of *general* video game playing, since only one kind of game is considered there.

2.4 Summary

This chapter presented the basics that are needed throughout this work. It thereby contributed the definitions around the concept of an agent as considered in this work as well as preliminary ideas and fundamental problems of learning agents. Moreover it provided the motivation of the concepts that will be described in the upcoming chapters by also considering related approaches (Section 2.3).

In the context of learning agents in games, approaches for gaining formal knowledge that provides structural insights into the agent behavior and/or the underlying problem, seem to be rarely considered. From knowledge representation, well-established ideas like *default rules* are known. However, these approaches can be limited in human-readability, comprehensibility and efficiency—especially when it comes to larger amounts of knowledge learned by agents, or in case of high-dimensional data (i.e., agents having a large number of sensors).

To create hybrid machine learning/knowledge representation agent models for games, efficient practical approaches are required, that are able to deal with strong time constraints, both for learning and reasoning. The following chapters will tackle these issues.

---

[10] The work [7] has been published as a peer-reviewed paper on the 29th of September in 2016, whereas a first version of [31] appeared as a preprint on arXiv.org on the 18th of September in 2016; a second version appeared there on the 1st of October of the same year.

3. Knowledge Base Extraction

This chapter explains the concepts of *exception-tolerant hierarchical knowledge bases*[11] (HKBs), a comprehensible approach for representing knowledge compactly as rules with exceptions. The HKBs developed in the context of this work were originally designed for the representation of knowledge learned by agents, independently from an underlying machine learning technique. Due to the arrangement of rules on several levels of abstraction, larger portions of knowledge can be read top-down on an adequate level of abstraction.

In recent years, HKBs have been developed including learning algorithms to learn HKBs from data, an efficient reasoning algorithm and a revision approach. The latter was especially geared to the needs of *general video game playing artificial intelligence* (GVGAI): In this context, if an agent has to learn to play different a priori unknown video games, it may also face belief revision problems (e. g., when being confronted with new slightly different levels of the same game). Furthermore, in [41], HKBs have been compared to *answer set programming* (ASP) [19].

Over the years, HKBs have successfully been used in several applications. The applications comprise:

- materialization of knowledge learned by agents [8],
- discovery and exploitation of heuristics in unknown environments to accelerate the learning process of an agent [9],
- measurement of subjectively experienced strategic depth in games [11], and
- learning of approximated forward models in video games [5, 26].

(These applications will be considered in Chapter 4 and Chapter 5.)

Furthermore, HKBs and related applications have been considered in several other works, especially by researchers in the field of *computational intelligence in games*, e. g., in [28, 29, 47]. In Kuhn [42], HKBs were also used to extract and exploit knowledge about human intuitions for solving job-shop problems, e. g., by improving genetic algorithms with the extracted knowledge bases. HKBs have also stimulated bachelor's and master's theses [12, 40] and contributed to other's PhD research [25].

---

[11] Thanks to my PhD supervisor Prof. Dr. Gabriele Kern-Isberner for having the idea of adding the term "exception-tolerant" to the name in order to distinguish it from a different approach by Borgida and Etherington [18].

3. Knowledge Base Extraction

Several results of HKBs from the papers [9, 26] have also been outlined in the chapter "Learning in GVGAI" (Chapter 5) of the recently published *book on GVGAI* [53].

In this chapter, foundations and formal definitions for HKBs are provided, mostly following [8] (Section 3.1). After that, an efficient reasoning algorithm for HKBs is described, which was proposed in an earlier publication by Apeldoorn and Kern-Isberner [7] (Section 3.2). HKBs are introduced as a tool for knowledge engineering (Section 3.3) and two basic algorithms and one advanced algorithm for learning HKBs in the context of agents are provided (Section 3.4 and Section 3.5); the latter was published in a more recent paper by Apeldoorn, Hadidi and Panholzer [6]. (Details about contributions are provided in the bibliographic remarks, Section 3.7.)

3.1 Definition of HKBs

This section provides the basic definitions needed for HKBs. It starts from the preliminary definition of a deterministic state-action sequence in Section 3.1.1 and closes at the end of Section 3.1.2 with the central definitions for HKBs, according to [8] (and several other papers making use of these definitions, e.g., [5, 9, 11]).

For this purpose, the agent model described in Section 2.1 is considered and briefly summarized here again: According to the model, an agent is equipped with n sensors and can perform a fixed number of different actions. Thus, the agent's discrete state space is defined as $\mathbb{S} := \mathbb{S}_1 \times ... \times \mathbb{S}_n$, where every $\mathbb{S}_i$ is a sensor symbol set representing all possible values of the agent's i-th sensor. The agent's action symbol set $\mathbb{A}$ represents all possible actions of the agent. Every action $a \in \mathbb{A}$ performed in a state $st := s_1 \wedge ... \wedge s_n$ with $s_i \in \mathbb{S}_i$ leads to a successor state st' (see sections 2.1.1 to 2.1.5 for details).

3.1.1 From Non-Deterministic to Deterministic State-Action Sequences

Based on the agent model from Section 2.1, the agent behavior in an environment can be represented by a *state-action sequence*, as defined in Definition 2.6 from Section 2.1.5. For non-deterministic environments (as explained already earlier, at the end of Section 2.1.5), a state-action sequence $\mathcal{SA}$ may contain pairs $\mathbf{p}, \mathbf{q} \in \mathcal{SA}$ with $\mathbf{p} := (st_\mathbf{p}, a_\mathbf{p})$, $\mathbf{q} := (st_\mathbf{q}, a_\mathbf{q})$, where $st_\mathbf{p} = st_\mathbf{q}$ and $a_\mathbf{p} \neq a_\mathbf{q}$. For reasons of simplification, in the following, many considerations will refer to *deterministic* state-action sequences instead, which are defined as follows:

3.1 Definition of HKBs

Definition 3.1 (Deterministic State-Action-Sequence) A deterministic state-action sequence is a state-action sequence $\mathcal{SA}^* := \{(st_1, a_1), ..., (st_m, a_m)\}$, where for every two pairs $\mathbf{p}, \mathbf{q} \in \mathcal{SA}^*$, $st_\mathbf{p} = st_\mathbf{q}$ implies that $a_\mathbf{p} = a_\mathbf{q}$. □

For a better understanding of deterministic and non-deterministic state-action sequences, Figure 2.5 from Section 2.1.7 can be considered here again: Figure 2.5 (a), shows a non-deterministic state-action sequence (with multiple outgoing arrows from a single grid cell), whereas Figure 2.5 (b) and (c) show deterministic state-action sequences (with at most one outgoing arrow per grid cell).

To represent agent behavior in a non-deterministic environment, a deterministic state-action sequence $\mathcal{SA}^*$ can be created from a state-action sequence $\mathcal{SA}$ by keeping only those pairs $\mathbf{p} \in \mathcal{SA}$ with the best action $a_{st}^{\max}$ given a state st, i.e., those $\mathbf{p} \in \mathcal{SA}$ with $a_\mathbf{p} = a_{st}^{\max} := \arg\max_{a \in \mathbb{A}} P(a|st)$ (cf. Table of Notations).[12] Such a deterministic state-action sequence can then be considered the representation of the best or "most common" actions for every state of the environment.

3.1.2 Rules and HKBs

The basic idea of an HKB is to represent a (deterministic) state-action sequence $\mathcal{SA}^*$ (see Definition 2.6 and Definition 3.1) in a *compact way*, which also allows for *generalization*. This can be achieved by trying to incorporate only a few of the agent's sensors (and sensor values) to express the knowledge contained in $\mathcal{SA}^*$. For this purpose, within an HKB, the knowledge is organized on several levels of abstraction, where the topmost level contains the most general rule(s) (with empty premise(s)) and the bottommost level contains the most specific rules (corresponding to the state-action pairs contained in $\mathcal{SA}^*$). Every rule on a lower abstraction level can define an *exception* to a more general rule on a higher abstraction level of the HKB. To be able to define HKBs more formally, at first, two basic kinds of rules have to be distinguished (based on the definition of complete states and partial states, Definition 2.1), mainly following the corresponding definition provided in [8] (and preliminary considerations from [7]):

---

[12] If $\arg\max_{a \in \mathbb{A}}$ is not unique, i.e., every $a \in A \subseteq \mathbb{A}$ is leading to the same maximum conditional probability/relative frequency $P(a|st)$, one $a \in A$ can be chosen randomly.

Definition 3.2 (Complete Rule/Generalized Rule) *Complete rules* and *generalized rules* are of the form $p \to a\ [w]$ (i.e., "if p is known, then a can be concluded"), where the premise p is either a *complete state* (in case of a *complete rule*) or a *partial state* (in case of a *generalized rule*), the conclusion $a \in \mathbb{A}$ represents an action of the agent's action symbol set $\mathbb{A}$ and $w \in \mathbb{R}$ is the rule's weight (indicating the "strength" of the rule).[13] □

Thus, with complete rules, actions can be concluded from a complete state and with generalized rules, actions can be concluded from a partial state. Based on that (still following [8]), an HKB can now be defined as follows:

Definition 3.3 (Exception-Tolerant Hierarchical Knowledge Base) An *exception-tolerant hierarchical knowledge base* (HKB) is defined as an ordered set $\mathcal{KB} := \{R_1, ..., R_{n+1}\}$ of $n+1$ *rule sets*, with n being the number of state space dimensions (i.e., the number of an agent's sensors). Every (non-empty) set $R_{j<n+1} \in \mathcal{KB}$ contains *generalized rules* and the set $R_{n+1} \in \mathcal{KB}$ (when being non-empty) contains *complete rules*, such that every premise $p_\rho := \bigwedge_{s \in S_\rho} s$ of a rule $\rho \in R_j$ (with S_ρ being the rule's *premise set*) is of length $|S_\rho| = j - 1$. □

Furthermore, in the context of HKBs, the terms *exception* and *needed exception* will be of importance and are therefore provided here by the following definitions, originating from [7, 8]:[14]

Definition 3.4 (Exception) A rule $\rho \in R_{j>1}$ is an *exception* to a rule $\tau \in R_{j'<j}$ with premise $p_\tau := \bigwedge_{s \in S_\tau} s$ and action a_τ as conclusion, if the *premise set* $S_\tau \subset S_\rho$ and $a_\rho \neq a_\tau$. □

Definition 3.5 (Needed Exception) A rule $\rho \in R_{j>1}$ is a *needed exception* to a rule $\tau \in R_{j'<j}$, with premise $p_\tau := \bigwedge_{s \in S_\tau} s$, action a_τ as conclusion and weight w_τ, if it is an *exception* and no other rule $\upsilon \in R_{j'}$ exists with premise $p_\upsilon := \bigwedge_{s \in S_\upsilon} s$ and action a_υ as conclusion, where $S_\upsilon \subset S_\rho$, $a_\upsilon = a_\rho$ and weight $w_\upsilon > w_\tau$. □

---

[13] Note that when learning HKBs from data (as, e.g., in [8] or later in Section 3.4), the weights of the rules are usually in $[0;1]$. Nevertheless, when using HKBs as a knowledge engineering tool, in principle, no such constraints exist (even if it might be useful to limit the weights to a certain range).

[14] Note that the definitions provided here are slightly more general than those provided in [8], since here, a rule $\rho \in R_{j>1}$, is also considered an exception to a rule $\tau \in R_{j'<j}$, if $j - j' > 1$.

The following example illustrates how knowledge can be compactly represented as an HKB by consequently exploiting the concept of rules and exceptions.

Example 3.1 (HKB for an Agent in a Grid World) In this example, an agent in a grid world is considered again (similar to Example 2.2 and Example 2.4): The agent moves from a starting point A to a destination point B by avoiding a large area in the middle of the grid world (see the left side of Figure 3.1). Also here, the agent is equipped with two sensors to determine its x and y position in the environment (i. e., its state-space is $\mathbb{S} := \mathbb{S}_x \times \mathbb{S}_y$, with $\mathbb{S}_x := \{x_0, ..., x_7\}$ and $\mathbb{S}_y := \{y_0, ..., y_5\}$) and the agent is able to perform actions from the set $\mathbb{A} := \{\text{North}, \text{South}, \text{East}, \text{West}\}$.

The right side of Figure 3.1 shows an HKB that describes the agent behavior indicated by the arrows on the left side of Figure 3.1. Starting from the most general rule $\top \rightarrow$ East [0.41] on the topmost level R_1, the HKB can be read top down in the following way (the indentations indicate the level on which the rules are located):

"*Usually go to east;*   (according to $\top \rightarrow$ East)
   except when x_0 is perceived, go to north, or,   (according to $x_0 \rightarrow$ North)
   when x_7 is perceived, go to south;   (according to $x_7 \rightarrow$ South)
     except when x_0 and y_5 are perceived, go to east."
                                               (according to $x_0 \wedge y_5 \rightarrow$ East)

The rule $x_0 \wedge y_5 \rightarrow$ East [1.0] on level R_3 serves as a "second order" exception here, since it is an exception to the rule $x_0 \rightarrow$ North [0.83], which is in turn an exception to the topmost rule $\top \rightarrow$ East [0.41] on level R_1 (according to Definition 3.4). The rule $x_0 \wedge y_5 \rightarrow$ East [1.0] is also a *needed exception* here (see Definition 3.5). □

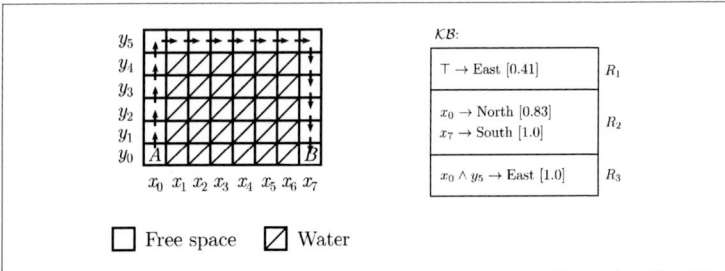

Figure 3.1 (HKB for an Agent in a Grid World)   (Source: adapted from [11])
On the left, arrows indicate an agent's movement in a grid world from a starting point to a destination around a "lake". On the right, an HKB $\mathcal{KB}$ represents the agent behavior compactly and comprehensively (in contrast to Figure 2.6). The rule weights are the conditional relative frequencies of the concluding actions given the premises, e. g., $P(\text{North} \,|\, x_0) = \frac{5}{6} \approx 0.83$. (See also Example 3.1.)

3.2 Reasoning for HKBs

Reasoning and the process of retrieving inferences from a knowledge base have a long tradition in AI research—especially in those fields of knowledge representation that are closely related to logic. However, many strongly logic-based reasoning approaches are limited in their efficiency (and even feasibility!) and when it comes to practical applications, an eligible reasoning approach should be able to provide appropriate inference results in near real-time. Regarding practical aspects (especially in the context of robotics), Hertzberg, Lingemann and Nüchter write in their book [36], pp. 307–308 (2012, Springer Vieweg, translated from German):

> "A good inference approach only yields true consequences from provided knowledge, and that as efficient as possible. [...] (Correct and complete inference in propositional logic is only possible with NP-complete approaches, first order logic is even undecidable—both are no properties that can be considered useful for an efficient inference approach.)"

The reasoning algorithm that will be described here, is able to efficiently provide inferences that exploit the knowledge contained in an HKB at its best. The algorithm relies on an HKB (representing the current knowledge of an agent) and one or more piece(s) of supposedly evident information (i. e., the agent's currently perceived sensor values). Such a reasoning algorithm was first introduced in [7], where it was used for an experimental study on agents improving their learning performance by exploiting knowledge represented by HKBs, which were extracted from the agents' experiences during their learning process. Meanwhile, the algorithm has been proven useful in several further applications (e. g., [5, 6, 9]); some of which are relying on (near) real-time capability.

More concretely, closely following [7], a reasoning algorithm $\Re(\mathcal{KB}, st)$ will be described here, that takes an HKB $\mathcal{KB} := \{R_1, ..., R_{n+1}\}$ (where R_1 contains the most general rule(s) and R_{n+1} contains the most specific rules, i. e., the *complete rules*) and the current perceived state st of the agent as input and that outputs a set $A \subseteq \mathbb{A}$ of inferred actions. The set A usually contains only one single action—only in case multiple equivalent rules with the same maximum weight and different conclusions exist on a level R_j, more than one action can be contained in A.

When a state $st := s_1 \wedge ... \wedge s_n$ is perceived, the reasoning algorithm searches for the most specific rules ρ whose premises are satisfied by s and which have the maximum weight among all satisfied rules on the same level of abstraction (i. e., rules ρ with premise $p_\rho := \bigwedge_{s' \in S_\rho} s'$ where S_ρ is a subset of the set $S := \{s_1, ..., s_n\}$ and no other rule σ exists with premise $p_\sigma := \bigwedge_{s' \in S_\sigma} s'$ where $S_\sigma \subseteq S$ and $w_\sigma > w_\rho$).

3.2 Reasoning for HKBs

The action(s) contained in A will then be returned by $\Re$ (in case of $|A| > 1$, the returned actions are equally good and an agent may select randomly among them). Algorithm 3.1 formalizes the described reasoning algorithm.

Input: Exception-tolerant hierarchical knowledge base $\mathcal{KB}$, state $st := s_1 \wedge ... \wedge s_n$
Output: Set $A \subseteq \mathbb{A}$ of actions inferred from $\mathcal{KB}$ for state st

```
01    % Initialize the set of all partial states of the given state st,
02    % the inferred actions A and index j
03    S := {s₁,...,sₙ}
04    A := ∅
05    j := |KB|
06
07    % Search for most specific rules whose premise is satisfied by
08    % the given state st with maximum weight among all satisfied rules
09    while A = ∅ and j > 1 do
10        R := Rⱼ ∈ KB
11        for each ρ ∈ R do
12            if Sρ ⊆ S and ∄σ ∈ R: Sσ ⊆ S, wσ > wρ then
13                A := A ∪ {aρ}
14            end if
15        end for
16        j := j - 1
17    end while
```

Algorithm 3.1 (Reasoning on HBKs) (Source: adapted from [7])

The algorithm $\Re(\mathcal{KB}, st)$ searches the HKB $\mathcal{KB}$ upwards, starting on the most specific level R_{n+1}, for the first rule(s) whose premise(s) is/are satisfied by the given state st. It returns a set $A \subseteq \mathbb{A}$ of actions by using the rule(s) with the maximum weight among the found most specific rule(s). (The algorithm can also be implemented easily in a slightly modified form for additionally returning the rules that are used for creating A.)

Example 3.2 (Reasoning in a Grid World) This example considers again the HKB $\mathcal{KB}$ for the agent in the grid world scenario shown in Figure 3.1: For the starting state $st_0 := x_0 \wedge y_0$, the reasoning algorithm $\Re$ (Algorithm 3.1) starts searching on level R_3, where only the rule $x_0 \wedge y_5 \rightarrow$ East $[1.0]$ is located, whose premise is not satisfied by st_0 (since $\{x_0, y_5\} \nsubseteq \{x_0, y_0\}$; cf. line 12 of Algorithm 3.1). Thus, the algorithm continues searching on level R_2, where it finds the rule $x_0 \rightarrow$ North $[0.83]$, whose premise is satisfied (since $\{x_0\} \subseteq \{x_0, y_0\}$). Since there isn't any other rule with a higher weight on level R_2 and a premise satisfied by the state st_0, the result will be $\Re(\mathcal{KB}, st_0) = \{\text{North}\}$ and thus the action "North" can be concluded for state st_0. For another state $st_1 := x_0 \wedge y_5$ (the northwestern corner of the grid world), the result will be $\Re(\mathcal{KB}, st_1) = \{\text{East}\}$ (due to the only rule on level R_3 being directly found by the reasoning algorithm). For a third state $st_2 := x_3 \wedge y_5$, the reasoning algorithm will fall back to the most general rule on the level R_1 and thus the result will be $\Re(\mathcal{KB}, st_2) = \Re(\mathcal{KB}, st_1) = \{\text{East}\}$. □

The reasoning algorithm described here turns out to be rather efficient in practice: By searching an HKB upwards for one or more firing rule(s), usually only *a part* of the rules contained in the HKB has to be considered. Only in case a given state is not covered by any of the rules on the levels $R_{j>1}$, the algorithm has to search through all rules on all levels of the HKB, until it falls back to the most general level R_1.

However, this does not have much impact on the overall performance of the algorithm, since, in practice, if the reasoning algorithm frequently has to fall back to upper levels of the HKB (or even to the topmost level R_1), this means in general that there are only a few rare exceptional cases occurring in the agent's environment— which in turn means that the HKB will most likely be "shallow", only comprising a few levels with few exceptions. Thus, even if it happens frequently in this case that the algorithm has to consider a large portion (or all) of the rules contained in the HKB, the number of rules that have to be considered will be quite low.

Or, vice versa: Assuming an environment with only a few regularities and hence with many exceptional cases occurring, a corresponding HKB will most likely comprise many levels with a lot of exceptions to reflect this properly. However, in such an environment, exceptional cases will be more common and thus, it will happen much more often that the reasoning algorithm finds the corresponding rule(s) on the lower levels, without considering larger portions of rules on the upper levels of the HKB.

3.3 HKBs for Knowledge Engineering

An HKB (as defined in Section 3.1) can be used as a modeling tool for agent behavior. An interesting question is, whether an HKB is able to model *every* possible behavior of an agent in an n-dimensional state-space, i.e., whether it is always possible to find an HKB as a model for any deterministic state-action sequence $\mathcal{SA}^*$.

As a first approach, a simple answer to this question can be provided by considering a trivial HKB $\mathcal{KB}_{trivial}$, where all levels $R_{j<n+1}$ are empty and the bottommost level R_{n+1} contains exactly one *complete rule* $\rho_{\mathbf{p}}$ for each state-action pair $\mathbf{p} := (st_{\mathbf{p}}, a_{\mathbf{p}}) \in \mathcal{SA}^*$. For such an HKB, the reasoning algorithm $\mathfrak{R}$ would obviously return the correct conclusions $a_{\mathbf{p}}$ for every state $st_{\mathbf{p}}$ of a pair $\mathbf{p} \in \mathcal{SA}^*$, i.e., $\forall \mathbf{p} \in \mathcal{SA}^*: \mathfrak{R}(\mathcal{KB}_{trivial}, st_{\mathbf{p}}) = \{a_{\mathbf{p}}\}$.

However, this immediately leads to the more elaborate question, whether the representation as an HKB has any benefits over the representation of the agent behavior as a state-action sequence. More concretely: Is it always possible to find an HKB $\mathcal{KB}$ that completely represents the knowledge contained in $\mathcal{SA}^*$, with at most as many rules as the total number of state-action pairs in $\mathcal{SA}^*$ and which *generalizes* better than $\mathcal{SA}^*$? The following proposition provides an answer to this question.

Proposition 3.1 (Knowledge Engineering Properties of HKBs) For every deterministic state-action sequence $\mathcal{SA}^*$, an HKB $\mathcal{KB}$ can be found

(1) that represents $\mathcal{SA}^*$ *completely* (i.e., $\forall \mathbf{p} \in \mathcal{SA}^*$: $\Re(\mathcal{KB}, st_\mathbf{p}) = a_\mathbf{p}$),

(2) is at least as *compact* as $\mathcal{SA}^*$ (i.e., $|\bigcup_{R \in \mathcal{KB}} R| \leq |\mathcal{SA}^*|$) and

(3) that *generalizes* $\mathcal{SA}^*$ (i.e., $\Re(\mathcal{KB}, st)$ can also provide conclusions for states st not contained in any pairs of $\mathcal{SA}^*$).

Proof Starting from a deterministic state-action sequence $\mathcal{SA}^*$, following the above preliminary considerations, an HKB $\mathcal{KB} := \mathcal{KB}_{trivial}$ can be easily constructed with all levels $R_{j<n+1} \in \mathcal{KB}$ being empty and with one complete rule $\rho_\mathbf{p} := st_\mathbf{p} \to a_\mathbf{p} \, [w_\rho]$ (with an arbitrary weight w_ρ) on level R_{n+1} for every pair $\mathbf{p} := (st_\mathbf{p}, a_\mathbf{p}) \in \mathcal{SA}^*$.

For such a trivial HKB, according to Algorithm 3.1, the reasoning algorithm $\Re(\mathcal{KB}, st_\mathbf{p})$ will obviously provide the correct conclusion $a_\mathbf{p}$ for every $\mathbf{p} \in \mathcal{SA}^*$, by finding the corresponding rule $\rho_\mathbf{p}$ on the bottommost level R_{n+1} for any given state $st_\mathbf{p}$, which satisfies property (1).

Now, it can be assumed that for an arbitrarily selected state-action pair $\mathbf{p}' \in \mathcal{SA}^*$, the corresponding rule $\rho_{\mathbf{p}'}$ is moved to the topmost level R_1 by simply replacing its premise with $\top$. For the resulting HKB $\mathcal{KB}'$, the reasoning algorithm $\Re(\mathcal{KB}', st_\mathbf{p})$ will then still provide the correct conclusions for every $\mathbf{p} \neq \mathbf{p}'$, since these rules remain unchanged on the bottommost level R_{n+1}.

For $\mathbf{p}'$, no rule will be found now by $\Re(\mathcal{KB}', st_{\mathbf{p}'})$ on level R_{n+1} anymore and thus $\Re(\mathcal{KB}', st_{\mathbf{p}'})$ will fallback to rule $\rho_{\mathbf{p}'} \in R_1$ (according to Algorithm 3.1), which also results in the correct conclusion $a_{\mathbf{p}'}$. Due to the rule $\rho_{\mathbf{p}'}$ (with premise $\top$) being located on the topmost level R_1 now, $\Re(\mathcal{KB}', st)$ will also fallback to $\rho_{\mathbf{p}'}$ for any other state st and thus will also be able to infer conclusions from $\mathcal{KB}'$ for states st that are not contained in any pairs of $\mathcal{SA}^*$, which satisfies property (3).

Since level $R_{n+1} \in \mathcal{KB}$ was initially filled with one rule per state-action pair, with all other levels being empty, and only one rule was moved to level R_1, it still holds for $\mathcal{KB}'$ that $|\bigcup_{R \in \mathcal{KB}'} R| = |\bigcup_{R \in \mathcal{KB}} R| = |\mathcal{SA}^*|$, which satisfies property (2).

In case there are further rules on level R_{n+1} with the same concluding action $a_{\mathbf{p}'}$, then all these rules can be removed now from level R_{n+1} without losing the *completeness property* (property (1)), since $\Re(\mathcal{KB}', st)$ will also fall back to the topmost rule $\rho_{\mathbf{p}'} \in R_1$ for all states st of the pairs in $\mathcal{SA}^*$ for which the corresponding action is equal to $a_{\mathbf{p}'}$. Thus, in this case, it even holds that $|\bigcup_{R \in \mathcal{KB}'} R| < |\mathcal{SA}^*|$. □

It is now easily imaginable that the rule-exception principle can be also exploited on the intermediate levels $R_{1<j<n+1} \in \mathcal{KB}$ to gain even more compact representations, which reflect the inherent logic of the data contained in a state-action sequence $\mathcal{SA}^*$. Such an HKB then also has more accurate generalization capabilities, since $\mathfrak{R}(\mathcal{KB}, st)$ can fall back to the *next more general* rule on a level $R_{1<j<n+1}$ that fits well for the state st (instead of falling back to the most general rule on level R_1).

After having shown that HKBs can be used as a knowledge engineering tool to represent deterministic state-action sequences in a more compact and generalizing way, a further interesting questions is, how compact representations can be learned automatically from (deterministic) state-action sequences. Different algorithms for that will be presented later in this chapter (Section 3.4 and Section 3.5).

3.4 Basic Knowledge Base Extraction Approaches

This section introduces basic ideas and some first basic approaches for learning HKBs from data. The task of automatically retrieving a knowledge base from data—especially from data representing agent behavior in form of a state-action sequence (see Section 2.1.5)—mainly comprises two aspects:

- extracting a knowledge base that represents the knowledge *adequately*, and
- providing a representation of the knowledge that is *transparent* and *easily accessible* to the reader.

HKBs have eligible properties to satisfy these aspects for the following reasons:

- The knowledge can be represented *compactly* by exploiting the generalization possibilities of HKBs together with the concept of exceptions: Rules that cover a larger amount of the data represented by the HKB can be located on higher, more general levels, whereas the rules representing some rare cases contained in the data can be located on the lower, more specific levels.

- Due to the knowledge being organized on several levels of abstraction, HKBs can be read top-down to the desired degree of detail. By this, the reader can easily get an overview over the data represented by the HKB without the need for considering rules that are only covering some rare cases (which seems to be in line with some central properties of human thinking; see the last paragraph of Section 2.2, p. 48).

- The knowledge represented by an HKB is extensively transparent, since usually only one single rule fires when reasoning is performed for a provided state (see Algorithm 3.1 and Example 3.2).

- Being only loosely coupled to logic, HKBs are *easy to read* and therefore also *accessible to people not having expertise in logic* (see [41] for a study of the comprehensibility of HKBs). This is perhaps one of the strongest features of HKBs, which allows for applying the following approaches in interdisciplinary working environments (see, e. g., [6]).[15]

Retrieving knowledge bases from data has numerous applications and can be used, e. g, to explain what a learning agent has learned [6, 8], to represent how human agents solve problems [11, 42] or how an agent's environment works (i. e., the *forward model* of the environment) [5, 26], among others.

3.4.1 Basic Ideas

To retrieve a knowledge base in the context of an agent, the knowledge that is implicitly contained in a plain state-action pair representation of the agent's behavior (i. e., a state-action sequence, see Section 2.1.5 or a Q-matrix, see Section 2.1.7) will be extracted and adequately represented in form of an HKB. For this purpose, some basic *representation criteria* will be determined at first, that provide some intuitions on how the knowledge represented by the HKB should look like (according to [7]):

- Criterion 1: *adequately relevant* (the knowledge should be restricted to the relevant parts only)

- Criterion 2: *adequately generic* (equivalent or even better, more general knowledge should be preferred over more specific knowledge)

While the first criterion ensures that irrelevant rules not related to the original data will not be included in a resulting HKB, the second criterion aims at providing a *compact* representation by ensuring that more general rules with shorter premises are preferred over more specific ones, where possible. Furthermore, by this means, the

---

[15] Being affiliated to a multi-disciplinary research institute with researchers from biostatistics, epidemiology, physics and other disciplines, the author was able to experience good receptions of the approaches by researchers from different fields.

resulting HKB will have better generalization opportunities, since rules that are more general cover larger pieces of the agent's state space (cf. Section 3.3).

These criteria form the base of the following approaches.

3.4.2 A Preliminary Algorithm

In this section, a first approach to extract a knowledge base from a learning agent is provided. Although the algorithm has some obvious drawbacks (which will be discussed at the end of this section), it was successfully used in various applications in the past (e. g., [5, 7, 9, 11, 26, 42]) and may serve as a base for understanding the more elaborate approaches.

The algorithm takes a (multi-dimensional) weight matrix $Q := (q_{s_1,...,s_n,a})$ as input (with $s_i \in \mathbb{S}_i, a \in \mathbb{A}$), i. e., a weighted state-action pair representation, which contains a learned weight for every state-action pair of the agent's state-action space. The weights could be learned by any machine learning approach that fits the needs of the task to be learned (e. g., reinforcement learning approaches like Q-learning and the like, see Section 2.1.7). The algorithm returns an HKB $\mathcal{KB}$ which reflects the learned knowledge contained in Q. If one is only interested in the knowledge about the best weighted state-action pairs contained in Q (i. e., the best learned behavior), only the best state-action pairs with the highest weight given a state can be considered here, ignoring the weights of all other state-action pairs.

Following [7, 8], the HKB extraction algorithm performs the following steps:

(1) *Normalization of weights*:
Every weight $w_{\text{raw}} \in Q := (q_{s_1,...,s_n,a})$ is normalized over the action dimension to a weight[16]

$$w := \frac{w_{\text{raw}} - \min_{a \in \mathbb{A}} (q_{s_1,...,s_n,a})}{\max_{a \in \mathbb{A}} (q_{s_1,...,s_n,a}) - \min_{a \in \mathbb{A}} (q_{s_1,...,s_n,a})}$$

(2) *Creation of rule sets*:
All generalized rules (i.e., all rules $\bigwedge_{i \in I} s_i \to a \ [w]$ with $s_i \in \mathbb{S}_i$ and with set $I \subset \{1, ..., n\}$, where n is the number of state space dimensions) are created by aggregating an average weight $\bar{w}$ over all missing state space dimensions (i. e., over those state space dimensions $\mathbb{S}_i$ of which no sensor value symbol is contained in the premise of the respective rule). (See Example 3.3 for a more detailed explanation of the aggregation mechanism.) The resulting rules will be

---

[16] Note that the provided formula here corrects the corresponding formula of the original work [7]. Thanks to Manuel Feilen for pointing to the erroneous formula in [7].

grouped according to their generality into the different sets $R_1, ..., R_{n+1}$ of the HKB (where R_1 contains the most general rules and R_{n+1} contains the most specific rules, i.e., the complete rules; see Definition 3.2). The complete rules are derived directly from the Q-matrix.

(3) *Removal of worse rules*:
This step follows the intuition of restricting the resulting HKB to the relevant knowledge only (which corresponds to Criterion 1, see Section 3.4.1): In all sets R_j, a rule $\rho \in R_j$ is removed, if another rule $\sigma \in R_j$ exists with the same partial state as premise and a higher weight. In other words: on every level of the HKB only the best rules for a given partial state are kept.

(4) *Removal of worse more specific rules*:
The intuition here is to prefer better/equivalent general over more specific knowledge where eligible (corresponding to Criterion 2, Section 3.4.1): In all sets $R_{j>1}$, a rule $\rho \in R_j$ with premise $p_\rho := \bigwedge_{s \in S_\rho} s$, conclusion a_ρ and weight w_ρ is removed, if a more general rule $\sigma \in R_{j'<j}$ exists with premise $p_\sigma = \bigwedge_{s \in S_\sigma} s$, premise set $S_\sigma \subset S_\rho \subseteq \{s_1, ..., s_n\}, |S_\rho| = j - 1$ and with weight $w_\sigma \geq w_\rho$.

(5) *Removal of too specific rules*:
In this step, the intuition is to prefer general over specific knowledge, if the more specific knowledge is not necessarily needed or relevant (which corresponds to both Criterion 1 and 2 that are provided in Section 3.4.1). In all sets $R_{j>1}$, a rule $\rho \in R_j$ with premise $p_\rho := \bigwedge_{s \in S_\rho} s$ and conclusion a_ρ is removed, if a more general rule $\sigma \in R_{j'<j}$ exists with the same action $a_\sigma = a_\rho$ as conclusion, premise $p_\sigma := \bigwedge_{s \in S_\sigma} s$ with premise set $S_\sigma \subset S_\rho \subseteq \{s_1, ..., s_n\}, |S_\rho| = j - 1$ and with rule ρ not being a *needed exception* to a rule $\tau \in R_{j-1}$ (see Definition 3.5).

(6) *Optional filter steps*:
Optionally, filters may be applied to filter out further rules which are helpful to explain the knowledge contained in Q, but which are not needed for reasoning later (e.g., since they are never firing given the states contained in Q, or since other rules exist on the same level of abstraction which would lead to the same result when reasoning is performed on the extracted knowledge base).

After these steps, the HKB comprises all sets $R_j \neq \emptyset$ with the extracted rules representing the knowledge contained in the learned weights of Q. Algorithm 3.2 summarizes the algorithm.

3. Knowledge Base Extraction

```
Input:    Multi-dimensional weight matrix Q
Output:   Exception-tolerant hierarchical knowledge base KB^Q
```
```
01   % Normalization; according to Step (1)
02   normalize( Q )
03
04   % Initial creation of the rule sets; according to Step (2)
05   R^Q := {R_1, ..., R_{n+1}}   % Ordered set of rule sets
06
07   % Removal of worse rules; according to Step (3)
08   for each R ∈ R^Q do
09       for each ρ ∈ R do
10           if ∃σ ∈ R: p_σ = p_ρ, w_σ > w_ρ then
11               R := R \ {ρ}
12           end if
13       end for
14   end for
15
16   % Removal of worse more specific rules; according to Step (4)
17   for j := 2 to n + 1 do
18       R := R_j ∈ R^Q
19       for each ρ ∈ R do
20           if ∃σ ∈ R_{j'<j}: S_σ ⊂ S_ρ, w_σ ≥ w_ρ then
21               R := R \ {ρ}
22           end if
23       end for
24   end for
25
26   % Removal of too specific rules; according to Step (5)
27   for j := 2 to n + 1 do
28       R := R_j ∈ R^Q
29       for each ρ ∈ R do
30           if ∃σ ∈ R_{j'<j}: a_σ = a_ρ, S_σ ⊂ S_ρ and
31              (∄τ ∈ R_{j-1}: a_ρ ≠ a_τ, S_τ ⊂ S_ρ or
32              ∃υ ∈ R_{j-1}: a_υ = a_ρ, S_υ ⊂ S_ρ, w_υ > w_τ) then
33               R := R \ {ρ}
34           end if
35       end for
36   end for
37
38   % Perform optional filter steps; according to Step (6)
39   filter( R^Q )
40
41   KB^Q := {R ∈ R^Q | R ≠ ∅}
```

Algorithm 3.2 (Preliminary Knowledge Base Extraction) (Source: based on [7])
The algorithm starts with Step (1) by normalizing the weights of the matrix Q to be in $[0,1]$. Afterwards, the sets R_j are initially filled with all possible rules by aggregating the weights according to Step (2). After that, the three main steps of the algorithm, Step (3) to Step (5), successively remove the *worse rules*, the *worse more specific rules* and the *too specific rules*. Finally, some optional filter steps may remove further unneeded rules (e.g., those that are not needed to infer the best actions for the respective complete states in Q).

In the following, two examples will be provided: The first example (Example 3.3) originally stems from [7] and helps to understand more detailed how the aggregation of the weights contained in the matrix Q is realized in Step (2) of the algorithm.

After that, a complete example of extracting a knowledge base from an agent's behavior in the context of a simple game will be provided in Example 3.4.

Example 3.3 (Aggregation of Weights) Assuming an agent with a 2-dimensional state space $\mathbb{S} := \mathbb{T} \times \mathbb{U}$ with $\mathbb{T} := \{t_1, t_2\}$ and $\mathbb{U} := \{u_1, u_2\}$ and a (normalized) matrix $Q := (q_{t,u,a})$ of weights learned with an arbitrary machine learning approach. Then the following ten generalized rules are created according to the second step of the preliminary HKB extraction algorithm (assuming that the agent's state space has been explored completely before, such that all possible states are known in Q):

$$\left.\begin{array}{l} \top \to a_1\,[\bar{w}_1] \quad \text{with} \quad \bar{w}_1 = \dfrac{1}{4}\sum_{t\in\mathbb{T},u\in\mathbb{U}} q_{t,u,a_1} \\[6pt] \top \to a_2\,[\bar{w}_2] \quad \text{with} \quad \bar{w}_2 = \dfrac{1}{4}\sum_{t\in\mathbb{T},u\in\mathbb{U}} q_{t,u,a_2} \end{array}\right\} \text{most general rules}$$

$$\left.\begin{array}{l} t_1 \to a_1\,[\bar{w}_3] \quad \text{with} \quad \bar{w}_3 = \tfrac{1}{2}\sum_{u\in\mathbb{U}} q_{t_1,u,a_1} \\ t_1 \to a_2\,[\bar{w}_4] \quad \text{with} \quad \bar{w}_4 = \tfrac{1}{2}\sum_{u\in\mathbb{U}} q_{t_1,u,a_2} \\ t_2 \to a_1\,[\bar{w}_5] \quad \text{with} \quad \bar{w}_5 = \tfrac{1}{2}\sum_{u\in\mathbb{U}} q_{t_2,u,a_1} \\ t_2 \to a_2\,[\bar{w}_6] \quad \text{with} \quad \bar{w}_6 = \tfrac{1}{2}\sum_{u\in\mathbb{U}} q_{t_2,u,a_2} \\ u_1 \to a_1\,[\bar{w}_7] \quad \text{with} \quad \bar{w}_7 = \tfrac{1}{2}\sum_{t\in\mathbb{T}} q_{t,u_1,a_1} \\ u_1 \to a_2\,[\bar{w}_8] \quad \text{with} \quad \bar{w}_8 = \tfrac{1}{2}\sum_{t\in\mathbb{Z}} q_{t,u_1,a_2} \\ u_2 \to a_1\,[\bar{w}_9] \quad \text{with} \quad \bar{w}_9 = \tfrac{1}{2}\sum_{t\in\mathbb{T}} q_{t,u_2,a_1} \\ u_2 \to a_2\,[\bar{w}_{10}] \quad \text{with} \quad \bar{w}_{10} = \tfrac{1}{2}\sum_{t\in\mathbb{T}} q_{t,u_2,a_2} \end{array}\right\} \text{more specific rules}$$

$\square$

Example 3.4 (Basic Knowledge Base Extraction) In this example, an agent has to navigate a horse from a starting point to a trophy in a two-dimensional horse race game. The state space is provided by $\mathbb{S} := \mathbb{S}_x \times \mathbb{S}_y$ (with sets $\mathbb{S}_x := \{x_0, ..., x_5\}$ and $\mathbb{S}_y := \{y_0, ..., y_5\}$) and the action space is provided by the action symbol set $\mathbb{A} := \{\text{Left}, \text{Right}, \text{Up}, \text{Down}, \text{Jump}\}$, allowing the agent to navigate and jump over hurdles (see Figure 3.2). The agent behavior results in the state-action sequence $\mathcal{SA} = \{(x_0 \wedge y_2, \text{Right}), (x_1 \wedge y_2, \text{Down}), (x_1 \wedge y_1, \text{Right}), (x_2 \wedge y_1, \text{Right}), (x_3 \wedge y_1, \text{Jump}), (x_4 \wedge y_1, \text{Right})\}$ that is indicated by the red arrow in Figure 3.2.

3. Knowledge Base Extraction

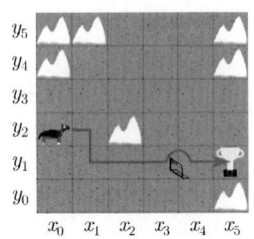

Figure 3.2 (Horse Racing Game) (Source: a. f. exhibit software by the author for Z Quadrat GmbH) An agent has to control a horse to reach a trophy by navigating or jumping. The arrow indicates the agent's behavior.

The extraction of a knowledge base to represent the agent behavior is realized by Algorithm 3.2: After transforming $\mathcal{SA}$ to a sparse Q-matrix by starting from a zero matrix and setting the corresponding weights of all state-action pairs contained in $\mathcal{SA}$ to 1, the algorithm starts with Step (1) by normalizing the weights (which does not have any effect here, since the matrix Q only contains zeros and ones at this point). After that, in Step (2), the algorithm creates all possible rules with a weight > 0, which results in the following initial rule sets on the different levels of the HKB (rules to be removed in the next step are shaded gray):

$\top \to$ Right $[\frac{4}{6}]$	
$\top \to$ Jump $[\frac{1}{6}]$	
$\top \to$ Down $[\frac{1}{6}]$	
$y_1 \to$ Right $[\frac{3}{4}]$	$x_1 \to$ Right $[\frac{1}{2}]$
$y_1 \to$ Jump $[\frac{1}{4}]$	$x_1 \to$ Down $[\frac{1}{2}]$
$y_2 \to$ Right $[\frac{1}{2}]$	$x_2 \to$ Right $[1]$
$y_2 \to$ Down $[\frac{1}{2}]$	$x_3 \to$ Jump $[1]$
$x_0 \to$ Right $[1]$	$x_4 \to$ Right $[1]$
$x_0 \wedge y_2 \to$ Right $[1]$	$x_2 \wedge y_1 \to$ Right $[1]$
$x_1 \wedge y_2 \to$ Down $[1]$	$x_3 \wedge y_1 \to$ Jump $[1]$
$x_1 \wedge y_1 \to$ Right $[1]$	$x_4 \wedge y_1 \to$ Right $[1]$

Note that the rule weights $\neq 1$ are denoted in fractions here to outline the relation to the relative frequencies of the agent's performed actions: Since the matrix Q is initially created from the state-action sequence $\mathcal{SA}$ by only setting the corresponding weights of all state-action pairs contained in $\mathcal{SA}$ to 1, a rule's weight corresponds to the relative frequency of the actions given the (partial) state here.

After that, in Step (3) of the algorithm, all *worse (or equivalent) rules* are removed, i.e., only those rules having a maximum weight for a given (partial) state are kept (by convention, if two rules are equally good by having equal weights, the preceding one according to the alphabetical order of their concluding actions will be kept): On the topmost level (R_1), only the rule with the conclusion Right is kept, since this is the overall most frequent action here. On the next more specific level (R_2), the rule $y_1 \to$ Jump is removed, since Jump is a less frequent action than Right for the partial state y_1. For the partial state y_2, the rules $y_2 \to$ Right and $y_2 \to$ Down have equal weights and therefore are equally good, thus, by convention, the rule $y_2 \to$ Right will be removed since Down precedes Right according to the alphabetical order. The same applies for the rules of the partial state x_1. This results in the following rule sets:

$\top \to$ Right [$\frac{4}{6}$]	
$y_1 \to$ Right [$\frac{3}{4}$]	$x_2 \to$ Right [1]
$y_2 \to$ Down [$\frac{1}{2}$]	$x_3 \to$ Jump [1]
$x_0 \to$ Right [1]	$x_4 \to$ Right [1]
$x_1 \to$ Down [$\frac{1}{2}$]	
$x_0 \land y_2 \to$ Right [1]	$x_2 \land y_1 \to$ Right [1]
$x_1 \land y_2 \to$ Down [1]	$x_3 \land y_1 \to$ Jump [1]
$x_1 \land y_1 \to$ Right [1]	$x_4 \land y_1 \to$ Right [1]

In Step (4), the *worse (or equivalent) more specific rules* are removed, i.e., those rules, for which a more general rule with a higher weight exists: On level R_2, this affects the rules $y_2 \to$ Down and $x_1 \to$ Down, since these rules have a lower weight than the weight of the more general rule $\top \to$ Right on the level R_1. On the most specific level R_3, this affects, e.g., the rule $x_0 \land y_2 \to$ Right, since the rule $x_0 \to$ Right is more general (due to $\{x_0\} \subset \{x_0, y_2\}$) and is equally good according to its weight. The same applies for the rules in the right column of level R_3, for all of which a more general rule on level R_2 with an equal weight can be found. Thus, the resulting rules sets are as follows:

$\top \to$ Right [$\frac{4}{6}$]	
$y_1 \to$ Right [$\frac{3}{4}$]	$x_3 \to$ Jump [1]
$x_0 \to$ Right [1]	$x_4 \to$ Right [1]
$x_2 \to$ Right [1]	
$x_1 \land y_2 \to$ Down [1]	
$x_1 \land y_1 \to$ Right [1]	

Finally, in Step (5), all *too specific rules* are removed, i.e., all unnecessary rules, for which a more general rule with the same conclusion exists (and which is not needed as an exception on the preceding more general level, cf. Definition 3.5). This removes, e.g., the rule $y_1 \to$ Right on level R_2, since the most general rule $\top \to$ Right already provides the same conclusion, but generalizes better. Similarly, this applies to all other rules on the levels R_2 and R_3 with the action Right as conclusion. This results in the final HKB:

$\top \to$ Right $[\frac{4}{6}]$
$x_3 \to$ Jump $[1]$
$x_1 \wedge y_2 \to$ Down $[1]$

An additional filter step would not have any effect here.

The resulting HKB represents the knowledge of the agent behavior indicated by the (red) arrow in Figure 3.2 compactly and can be read from top to bottom (i. e., from general to more specific) as follows:

"Usually go to the right;
except when x_3 is perceived, jump;
except when x_1 and y_2 are perceived, go down."

Moreover, the reasoning algorithm (Algorithm 3.1) can be applied to every state of the initial state-action sequence $\mathcal{SA}$ to infer the correct action for each state contained in $\mathcal{SA}$. □

Example 3.4 shows that the algorithm presented in this section is able to create compact knowledge bases with multiple abstraction levels, which explain the structure of the underlying problem and its solution well in an easy and comprehensible way. However, even if the presented algorithm has been used successfully (in this or in slightly modified forms) in several applications like [5, 7, 9, 11, 26, 42], it still has some major drawbacks:

- In the worst case, the maximum number of rules calculated for an n-dimensional state space on the j-th level R_j in Step (2) of the algorithm is

$$c_{\max}(j) = |\mathbb{A}| \cdot \sum_{\substack{\mathbf{S} \subseteq \mathfrak{S} \\ |\mathbf{S}| = j-1}} \prod_{\mathbb{S} \in \mathbf{S}} |\mathbb{S}|$$

where $\mathfrak{S} := \{\mathbb{S}_1, ..., \mathbb{S}_n\}$ is the set of all sensor symbol sets (cf. [11], Definition 5). The *total* maximum number of rules $\hat{c}_{\max}$ calculated on all levels in Step (2) of the algorithm is

$$\hat{c}_{\max} = \sum_{j=1}^{n+1} c_{\max}(j) = |\mathbb{A}| \cdot \sum_{j=1}^{n+1} \sum_{\substack{\mathbf{S} \subseteq \mathfrak{S} \\ |\mathbf{S}| = j-1}} \prod_{\mathbb{S} \in \mathbf{S}} |\mathbb{S}| \qquad (3.1)$$

Thus, the number of rules that are initially created (and later partly removed by the removal strategies) grow drastically with the number of sensor symbol sets (see the inner product of Formula (3.1)). This bad runtime behavior has been overcome in the past in [5, 26], by calculating several HKBs from smaller sub-spaces of the state-action space and later merging the resulting HKBs to a complete HKB again. However, a more proper and intuitive solution would be to exclude unneeded rules as soon as possible in the calculation process. A corresponding improvement will be presented in Section 3.4.3.

- Another drawback, that is related to the problem of bad runtime behavior, lies in the disadvantageous calculation order: Since the principle idea of the algorithm is to successively filter out all unneeded rules on all levels of the created HKB, the algorithm cannot be aborted for quickly getting good intermediate results, if one is only interested in a rougher representation of the knowledge.

- The third drawback is that the algorithm suffers from a lack of transparency: Even if it has already been shown in numerous applications that the algorithm provides proper and useful results, it is not quite clear that a resulting HKB reflects the knowledge contained in the Q-matrix (or the state-action sequence from which the matrix was created) well in any case. This is mainly due to the removal strategies in Step (3) to Step (5) (line 7–36 of Algorithm 3.2) not being directly associated with the ideas of the reasoning algorithm (Algorithm 3.1). Furthermore, starting directly from a Q-matrix as input additionally contributes to the nontransparent character of the algorithm. A lack of transparency can be a serious problem for such an algorithm, especially when being used in critical applications (e. g., medical applications). In Section 3.5 a more elaborate knowledge retrieval algorithm will be provided that overcomes this drawback.

The following section will especially tackle the first mentioned drawback.

3.4.3 Incorporating the APRIORI Algorithm

This section incorporates the APRIORI algorithm by Agrawal et al. [1] into the preliminary HKB extraction approach introduced in the previous section (Algorithm 3.2) to prevent considering all rules in Step (2) of Algorithm 3.2. This will be achieved by replacing Step (2) of Algorithm 3.2 with (an adapted form of) the APRIORI algorithm, according to [8].

Usually, one is interested in a compact representation that properly reflects the knowledge contained in the weights of the learned matrix $Q := (q_{s_1,\ldots,s_n,a})$. Since the decision making from such a Q-matrix is determined by the highest weight of an

3. Knowledge Base Extraction

action given a state, the corresponding state-action pairs are considered the most relevant portion of Q here. For this purpose, a set of state-action pairs $\mathcal{SA}^Q$ will be created from Q, such that for every state-action pair $\mathbf{p} \in \mathcal{SA}^Q$ with $\mathbf{p} := (st_\mathbf{p}, a_\mathbf{p})$, the action $a_\mathbf{p}$ is the one with the highest weight in Q given the state $st_\mathbf{p} := s_1 \wedge ... \wedge s_n$ (with $s_i \in \mathbb{S}_i$), i.e., $a_\mathbf{p} := \arg\max_{a \in \mathbb{A}} q_{s_1,...,s_n,a}$. (Note that $\mathcal{SA}^Q$ does not necessarily need to be ordered here.)

To meet the set-theoretic aspects of the original APRIORI algorithm, in the following, $S_\mathbf{p} := \{s_1, ..., s_n\}$ will be used to denote a complete state $st_\mathbf{p} := \bigwedge_{s \in S_\mathbf{p}} s$ belonging to a state-action pair $\mathbf{p} \in \mathcal{SA}^Q$ as set (cf. Section 2.1.1).

Closely following [8], an adaption of the APRIORI algorithm can now be described, which replaces Step (2) of Algorithm 3.2 to initially fill the rule sets $R_1, ..., R_{n+1}$:

Given the set $\mathcal{SA}^Q$ of (the best) state-action pairs, the adapted APRIORI algorithm starts with short premises having a minimum support $supp_{\min}$ (i.e., those partial states that are contained to some extent in $\mathcal{SA}^Q$). The premises are then successively extended to longer premises by keeping only those premises that are still having at least the minimum support of $supp_{\min}$. According to [8], also referring to the considerations of the APRIORI algorithm as presented in [14] (p. 148), the support of a premise p_ρ with corresponding premise set $S_\rho \subseteq \{s_1, ..., s_n\}$ is calculated as

$$supp(S_\rho) := \frac{|\{\mathbf{p} \in \mathcal{SA}^Q \mid S_\rho \subseteq S_\mathbf{p}\}|}{|\mathcal{SA}^Q|}$$

and the weight w_ρ of a corresponding rule ρ of the form $p_\rho \to a_\rho\ [w_\rho]$ with premise set S_ρ is calculated as the confidence

$$conf(\rho) := \frac{|\{\mathbf{p} \in \mathcal{SA}^Q \mid S_\rho \subseteq S_\mathbf{p}, a_\rho = a_\mathbf{p}\}|}{|\{\mathbf{p} \in \mathcal{SA}^Q \mid S_\rho \subseteq S_\mathbf{p}\}|}$$

More detailed, still following [8], the adapted APRIORI algorithm takes a set of state-action pairs $\mathcal{SA}^Q$ as input and outputs an initial ordered set of rule sets with potentially eligible and relevant rules $\mathcal{R}^Q := \{R_1, ..., R_{n+1}\}$ by proceeding as follows:

(1) Create set R_1 and add all rules ρ with an empty premise p_ρ, $a_\rho \in \mathbb{A}$ and $w_\rho := conf(\rho) > 0$.

(2) Create a set of premise sets $\mathcal{S}_1$ and add all (ordered) premise sets S_ρ of length $|S_\rho| = 1$ with support $supp(S_\rho) \geq supp_{\min}$.

(3) Create set R_2 and add for all premise sets $S_\rho \in \mathcal{S}_1$ all rules ρ with $p_\rho := \bigwedge_{s \in S_\rho}$, $a_\rho \in \mathbb{A}$ and $w_\rho := conf(\rho) > 0$.

(4) Set $k := 2$.

(5) Create the set $\mathcal{S}_k$ of premise sets of length k. Combine every two premise sets $S_\rho, S_\sigma \in \mathcal{S}_{k-1}$ having the first $k-1$ elements in common to create a new premise set $S_\tau := S_\rho \cup S_\sigma$.[17] Add the new combined premise set S_τ to $\mathcal{S}_k$ if

- all $(k-1)$-elementary subsets of S_τ occur in sets of $\mathcal{S}_{k-1}$ and,
- $supp(S_\tau) \geq supp_{\min}$.

(6) Create set R_{k+1} and add for all premise sets $S_\rho \in \mathcal{S}_k$ all rules ρ with $p_\rho := \bigwedge_{s \in S_\rho}$, $a_\rho \in \mathbb{A}$ and $w_\rho := conf(\rho) > 0$.

(7) Set $k := k + 1$.

(8) If $k \leq n$, continue with Step (5).

After performing these steps, the rule sets contained in $\mathcal{R}^Q$ are initially filled with preselected rules that are potentially relevant for the knowledge base to be extracted, given a minimum support of $supp_{\min}$. By selecting $supp_{\min} > 0$, the preselection will be done in a rougher, more heuristic way. This can speed up the knowledge retrieval even more, at the cost of accidentally skipping rules of potential interest.

Given a minimal support $supp_{\min}$, due to the completeness of the original APRIORI algorithm (cf. [14], p. 152), no premises are dropped too early if they could be of potential interest later. In the adaption of the algorithm used here, rules with a confidence of 0 are also not included in the initial rule sets $R_1, ..., R_n$. However, this does not break the completeness of the APRIORI algorithm, since only the rules for the final R_j sets are skipped (and not the corresponding premises based on which the APRIORI algorithm is performed).

Example 3.5 (Knowledge Base Extraction and Adapted APRIORI) The grid world scenario from Example 2.4 (see Figure 2.5) is considered again here, where an agent with state space $\mathbb{S} := \mathbb{S}_x \times \mathbb{S}_y$ (with $\mathbb{S}_x := \{x_0, ..., x_7\}$ and $\mathbb{S}_y := \{y_0, ..., y_5\}$) and action space $\mathbb{A} := \{\text{North}, \text{East}, \text{South}, \text{West}\}$ learns to get from a starting point A to a destination B with a common Q-learning approach. Using the adapted version of the APRIORI algorithm as Step (2) of Algorithm 3.2, an HKB will be extracted now from the agent's learned Q-matrix to compactly represent the knowledge about the *best behavior* learned by the agent (see Figure 2.5 (c)). Since only the knowledge about the best behavior is of interest here, the set of the corresponding state-action

---

[17] An additional performance gain may be achieved here in practice since (in contrast of the original APRIORI algorithm) only those pairs of sets that do not have any sensor values of the same sensor value set in common have to be considered for combination.

3. Knowledge Base Extraction

pairs $\mathcal{SA}^Q = \{(x_0 \wedge y_0, \text{North}), (x_0 \wedge y_1, \text{East}), ..., (x_7 \wedge y_1, \text{East}), (x_7 \wedge y_1, \text{South})\}$ will be created at first from the agent's learned Q-matrix.

Starting from the state-action pairs $\mathcal{SA}^Q$, that belong to the agent's best behavior, the adapted APRIORI algorithm is performed with $supp_{\min} := 0$, to initially fill the ordered set of rule sets $\mathcal{R}^Q$ with potential relevant rules. After that, $\mathcal{R}^Q$ contains the following rules on the different levels of the nascent HKB (rules to be removed in the next step are shaded gray):

$\top \rightarrow$ East [0.778]	
$\top \rightarrow$ South [0.111]	
$\top \rightarrow$ North [0.111]	
$y_0 \rightarrow$ North [1.0]	$x_2 \rightarrow$ East [1.0]
$y_1 \rightarrow$ East [0.875]	$x_3 \rightarrow$ East [1.0]
$y_1 \rightarrow$ South [0.125]	$x_4 \rightarrow$ East [1.0]
$x_0 \rightarrow$ East [0.5]	$x_5 \rightarrow$ East [1.0]
$x_0 \rightarrow$ North [0.5]	$x_6 \rightarrow$ East [1.0]
$x_1 \rightarrow$ East [1.0]	$x_7 \rightarrow$ South [1.0]
$x_0 \wedge y_0 \rightarrow$ North [1.0]	$x_6 \wedge y_1 \rightarrow$ East [1.0]
$x_7 \wedge y_1 \rightarrow$ South [1.0]	$x_5 \wedge y_1 \rightarrow$ East [1.0]
$x_2 \wedge y_1 \rightarrow$ East [1.0]	$x_4 \wedge y_1 \rightarrow$ East [1.0]
$x_1 \wedge y_1 \rightarrow$ East [1.0]	$x_3 \wedge y_1 \rightarrow$ East [1.0]
$x_0 \wedge y_1 \rightarrow$ East [1.0]	

Step (3) of Algorithm 3.2 now removes all worse (or equivalent) rules (as in Example 3.4, by convention, if two rules are equally good by having equal weights, the preceding one according to the alphabetical order of their conclusions will be kept): On the topmost level R_1, $\top \rightarrow$ South and $\top \rightarrow$ North are removed (due to having the same premise with lower weights than $\top \rightarrow$ East); on level R_2, $y_1 \rightarrow$ South is removed (due to $y_1 \rightarrow$ East having a higher weight) and $x_0 \rightarrow$ North is removed (due to the conclusion of $x_0 \rightarrow$ East alphabetically preceding North). After that, $\mathcal{R}^Q$ contains the following rules:

$\top \rightarrow$ East [0.778]	
$y_0 \rightarrow$ North [1.0]	$x_3 \rightarrow$ East [1.0]
$y_1 \rightarrow$ East [0.875]	$x_4 \rightarrow$ East [1.0]
$x_0 \rightarrow$ East [0.5]	$x_5 \rightarrow$ East [1.0]
$x_1 \rightarrow$ East [1.0]	$x_6 \rightarrow$ East [1.0]
$x_2 \rightarrow$ East [1.0]	$x_7 \rightarrow$ South [1.0]
$x_0 \wedge y_0 \rightarrow$ North [1.0]	$x_6 \wedge y_1 \rightarrow$ East [1.0]
$x_7 \wedge y_1 \rightarrow$ South [1.0]	$x_5 \wedge y_1 \rightarrow$ East [1.0]
$x_2 \wedge y_1 \rightarrow$ East [1.0]	$x_4 \wedge y_1 \rightarrow$ East [1.0]
$x_1 \wedge y_1 \rightarrow$ East [1.0]	$x_3 \wedge y_1 \rightarrow$ East [1.0]
$x_0 \wedge y_1 \rightarrow$ East [1.0]	

3.4 Basic Knowledge Base Extraction Approaches

Now, all worse (or equivalent) more specific rules are removed by Step (4) of Algorithm 3.2: On level R_2, $x_0 \rightarrow$ East is removed (due to the more general rule $\top \rightarrow$ East on level R_1 having a higher weight); on level R_3, $x_0 \wedge y_0 \rightarrow$ North is removed (due to $y_0 \rightarrow$ North on level R_2 being more general and having an equal weight) and all other rules on level R_3 that are shaded gray are removed, since a more general rule for the respective x-coordinates with an equal weight can be found on level R_2. After this step, $\mathcal{R}^Q$ contains the following rules:

$\top \rightarrow$ East [0.778]	
$y_0 \rightarrow$ North [1.0]	$x_4 \rightarrow$ East [1.0]
$y_1 \rightarrow$ East [0.875]	$x_5 \rightarrow$ East [1.0]
$x_1 \rightarrow$ East [1.0]	$x_6 \rightarrow$ East [1.0]
$x_2 \rightarrow$ East [1.0]	$x_7 \rightarrow$ South [1.0]
$x_3 \rightarrow$ East [1.0]	
$x_0 \wedge y_1 \rightarrow$ East [1.0]	

Finally, Step (5) of Algorithm 3.2 removes the too specific rules: On level R_2, all rules with conclusion East are removed (due to $\top \rightarrow$ East on level R_1 providing the same conclusion while being more general); on level R_3, $x_0 \wedge y_1 \rightarrow$ East is removed for the same reason. This results in the final HKB $\mathcal{KB}^Q = \mathcal{R}^Q$:

$\top \rightarrow$ East [0.778]
$y_0 \rightarrow$ North [1.0]
$x_7 \rightarrow$ South [1.0]

The resulting HKB $\mathcal{KB}^Q$ compactly represents the knowledge of the learned agent behavior shown in Figure 2.5c, stating:

> *"Usually go to east;*
> *except when y_0 is perceived, go to north, or,*
> *when x_7 is perceived, go to south."*

It can be easily verified here that the reasoning algorithm (Algorithm 3.1) will infer the corresponding correct actions for each state from the original state-action sequence $\mathcal{SA}^Q$. □

The incorporation of the adapted APRIORI algorithm already drastically speeds up the knowledge retrieval process by avoiding the initial creation of all possible rule sets. Furthermore, it provides the possibility to even further improve the runtime behavior by choosing $supp_{\min} > 0$, resulting in less accurate "more heuristic" HKBs, where weaker rules representing rare exception can potentially be missing. However, this motivates the need for a more advanced knowledge base extraction algorithm, that is both rather efficient and complete, while at the same time overcoming the two remaining drawbacks mentioned at the end of Section 3.4.2: The possibility of interrupting the knowledge retrieval process at any time for immediately getting rougher preliminary representations and the ability of being transparent throughout the whole extraction process to increase the confidence in the resulting HKBs.

3.5 Advanced Knowledge Base Extraction

This section presents a knowledge base extraction algorithm that overcomes the drawbacks of the aforementioned preliminary approaches from Section 3.4, while at the same time being more *transparent*. The approaches described here are also suitable for higher-dimensional state spaces. The descriptions will partly follow [6].

In contrast to the algorithms from Section 3.4.2 and Section 3.4.3, the main algorithm described here will follow a different approach: Instead of creating initial rule sets that are successively reduced by different filtering strategies, the presented algorithm fills an HKB from top to bottom until it completely explains the data from which it was created. This guarantees that the resulting HKB will be complete, in the sense that the correct actions can be inferred for every state of the original input sequence.

In the following, the main algorithm will be introduced at first (Section 3.5.1). After that, it will be shown, that HKBs produced by the algorithm always completely represent the data from which they are created (Section 3.5.2). This is followed by extensions that allow for creating HKBs from numeric sensor data (Section 3.5.3) and for preselecting sensors to handle higher-dimensional data (Section 3.5.4).

3.5.1 Advanced HKB Extraction Algorithm

The algorithm for efficiently extracting an HKB starts from a deterministic state-action sequence $\mathcal{SA}^*$ (see Definition 3.1), i.e., a state-action sequence, where no two state-action pairs $\mathbf{p} := (st_\mathbf{p}, a_\mathbf{p})$, $\mathbf{q} := (st_\mathbf{q}, a_\mathbf{q})$ in $\mathcal{SA}^*$ exist with states $st_\mathbf{p} = st_\mathbf{q}$ and actions $a_\mathbf{p} \neq a_\mathbf{q}$. Thus, according to such a deterministic state-action sequence, the action to be selected for a complete state is always the same. This may sound limiting, since in real applications, state-action sequences are usually not supposed to be deterministic. However (as it was already mentioned earlier in Section 3.1.1), a deterministic state-action sequence $\mathcal{SA}^*$ can be easily obtained from a non-deterministic state-action sequence $\mathcal{SA}$ by keeping only those pairs $\mathbf{p} \in \mathcal{SA}$ with the most frequent action given a state, i.e.,

$$\mathcal{SA}^* := \{(st_\mathbf{p}, a_\mathbf{p}) \in \mathcal{SA} \mid a_\mathbf{p} = \arg\max_{a \in \mathbb{A}} P(a|st_\mathbf{p})\} \qquad (3.2)$$

(if $\arg\max_{a \in \mathbb{A}}$ is not unique here, i.e., every $a \in A \subseteq \mathbb{A}$ is leading to the same maximum $P(a|st_\mathbf{p})$, one $a \in A$ is chosen randomly).

Furthermore, it is assumed that the possible actions are known in advance. If this is not the case, the set of possible actions $\mathbb{A}$ can be inferred from the original state-action sequence $\mathcal{SA}$ by selecting all distinct actions that appear in $\mathcal{SA}$. (Note that this does not necessarily lead to an agent's original action space, since not all of the agent's possible actions necessarily occur in $\mathcal{SA}$).

Following the explanations from [6], the general idea of the algorithm is, to add on each level of an initially empty HKB those rules that cover as many state-action pairs of $\mathcal{SA}^*$ as possible, starting with the topmost level R_1. On each of the more specific levels, further rules are then successively added as exceptions to the rules of the previous level(s), until the HKB covers all state-action pairs of $\mathcal{SA}^*$—i.e., until the reasoning algorithm (see Algorithm 3.1) infers for every state-action pair $\mathbf{p} \in \mathcal{SA}^*$ the corresponding action $a_\mathbf{p}$ from the state $s_\mathbf{p}$.

More concretely, after rendering the input state-action sequence deterministic according to Formula (3.2) (if necessary), which results in the input sequence $\mathcal{SA}^*$, and after creating the set of possible actions $\mathbb{A}$ from $\mathcal{SA}$ (if it is not a priori known), the algorithm proceeds as follows:

(1) In the first step, the best most general rule $\top \to a_\rho$ $[w_\rho]$ with an empty premise is created, whose concluding action a_ρ has a relative frequency $P(a_\rho)$ that is maximal in $\mathcal{SA}^*$ among all actions. The rule's weight is set to $w_\rho := P(a_\rho)$, the rule is added to the first rule set R_1 and R_1 is added as topmost level to the nascent HKB $\mathcal{KB}$.

(2) Subsequently, the set $\mathcal{SA}^-$ of all remaining state-action pairs that are currently not covered by $\mathcal{KB}$ are calculated (i.e., those pairs $\mathbf{p} := (st_\mathbf{p}, a_\mathbf{p})$ for which the reasoning algorithm $\mathfrak{R}$ (see Algorithm 3.1) cannot infer the correct action $a_\mathbf{p}$ from the state $st_\mathbf{p}$).

(3) The counter indicating the current calculated level of $\mathcal{KB}$ is initialized by $j := 1$.

(4) The fourth step represents the first part of the algorithm's main loop:

- If the set $\mathcal{SA}^-$ of all remaining state-action pairs is empty, the algorithm terminates here and returns the current HKB $\mathcal{KB}$.

3. Knowledge Base Extraction

- Otherwise (if $\mathcal{SA}^-$ is not empty), rules for the remaining state-action pairs $\mathbf{p} := (st_\mathbf{p}, a_\mathbf{p})$ in $\mathcal{SA}^-$ are added to the new level R_{j+1} by iterating over $\mathcal{SA}^-$: A rule with conclusion $a_\mathbf{p}$ is created for each subset $S_\mathbf{p}^j \subseteq S_\mathbf{p}$ of length j of a state set $S_\mathbf{p}$ associated with a state $st_\mathbf{p}$ (see Definition 2.1). Note that the weight of a rule ρ is calculated as $w_\rho := P(\bigwedge_{s \in S_\mathbf{p}^j} s \wedge a_\rho)$ here and will later (in Step (6)) be set to $w_\rho := P(a_\rho | \bigwedge_{s \in S_\mathbf{p}^j} s)$. (An explanation for that will be provided at the end of the stepwise description of the algorithm.)

(5) In the fifth step, all unused rules on the new calculated (bottommost) level R_{j+1} are removed, by keeping only those rules that are used by the reasoning algorithm $\mathfrak{R}$ (Algorithm 3.1) to infer the actions $a_\mathbf{p}$ from the states $st_\mathbf{p}$ for all state-action pairs $\mathbf{p} := (st_\mathbf{p}, a_\mathbf{p})$ in $\mathcal{SA}^*$—i.e., only those rules are remaining that have the highest weight among all rules firing given a state. (This step resembles Step (3) of Algorithm 3.2 or Criterion 1 in Section 3.4.1, respectively.)

(6) The sixth step adapts the weights of all rules from $w_\rho := P(\bigwedge_{s \in S_\mathbf{p}^j} s \wedge a_\rho)$ to $w_\rho := P(a_\rho | \bigwedge_{s \in S_\mathbf{p}^j} s)$ (see Step (4)).

(7) Subsequently, the set $\mathcal{SA}^-$ of all remaining state-actions pairs that are currently not covered by $\mathcal{KB} \cup \{R_{j+1}\}$ are calculated again (similar to Step (2)).

(8) The eighth step removes all unused rules on *all* levels of the HKB $\mathcal{KB} \cup \{R_{j+1}\}$, i.e., those rules that became superfluous either due to the newly added rules on the level R_{j+1} in Step (4) or due to the adaption of the weights in Step (5). (This step resembles to Step (4) and Step (5) of Algorithm 3.2 or Criterion 2 in Section 3.4.1, respectively.)

(9) Finally, level R_{j+1} is added to $\mathcal{KB}$, the counter indicating the current calculated level is increased by 1 and the algorithm proceeds with Step (4).

Note that in Step (4) of the algorithm, the weight of a rule ρ is at first calculated as $w_\rho := P(\bigwedge_{s \in S_\mathbf{p}^j} s \wedge a_\rho)$. This follows the intuition that overall more frequent occurrences of $\bigwedge_{s \in S_\mathbf{p}^j} s \wedge a_\rho$ in $\mathcal{SA}$ have a more "default-like" character and should therefore be considered on the more general levels of the HKB $\mathcal{KB}$. (Contrariwise, less frequent occurrences of $\bigwedge_{s \in S_\mathbf{p}^j} s \wedge a_\rho$ should rather be considered exceptions on the more specific levels of $\mathcal{KB}$). By setting the weights to $P(\bigwedge_{s \in S_\mathbf{p}^j} s \wedge a_\rho)$ here, it is later possible to keep the "strongest" rules according to the overall relative frequency, by considering the rules used by the reasoning algorithm $\mathfrak{R}$ to infer the correct action (which selects the rules according to the maximum weight in case the premise of multiple premises is satisfied by a provided state). Later on, in Step (6), the rule weights are adapted to $w_\rho := P(a_\rho | \bigwedge_{s \in S_p^j} s)$, since, in the end, it should be easy to comprehend from the resulting HKB $\mathcal{KB}$ how strong a rule ρ is to infer the correct action a_ρ when knowing a (partial) state $\bigwedge_{s \in S_p^j} s$, rather than considering the overall occurrences of $\bigwedge_{s \in S_p^j} s \wedge a_\rho$ in $\mathcal{SA}$. (The latter information is then represented anyway by the level on which the rule is located, following the above intuition.) This also conforms to the representation of the preliminary algorithms from Section 3.4.2 and Section 3.4.3. Algorithm 3.3 shows a formalization of the algorithm.

Example 3.6 (Advanced HKB Extraction) This example considers again the horse race game introduced in Example 3.4. Again, the agent has to navigate the horse from its starting point to the trophy. As in Example 3.4, the agent's state space is provided by $\mathbb{S} := \mathbb{S}_x \times \mathbb{S}_y$ (with $\mathbb{S}_x := \{x_0, ..., x_5\}$ and $\mathbb{S}_y := \{y_0, ..., y_5\}$) and its action space is provided by the set $\mathbb{A} := \{\text{Left}, \text{Right}, \text{Up}, \text{Down}, \text{Jump}\}$, allowing the agent to navigate and to jump over hurdles (see Figure 3.2). Also in this example here, the extraction algorithm will be applied to the state-action sequence $\mathcal{SA} := \{(x_0 \wedge y_2, \text{Right}), (x_1 \wedge y_2, \text{Down}), (x_1 \wedge y_1, \text{Right}), (x_2 \wedge y_1, \text{Right}), (x_3 \wedge y_1, \text{Jump}), (x_4 \wedge y_1, \text{Right})\}$ that is indicated by the (red) arrow in Figure 3.2.

The input state-action sequence $\mathcal{SA}$ is already deterministic (since all state-action pairs have different states and hence no pairs can exist having the same state but different actions). Thus, the algorithm will be called with $\mathcal{SA}^* := \mathcal{SA}$ as input. Furthermore, the set of possible actions $\mathbb{A}$ is already known and does not need to be created from $\mathcal{SA}$.

Starting from an empty HKB $\mathcal{KB} := \emptyset$, in the first step, the overall best rule with an empty premise is added to the topmost level R_1 of the HKB, resulting in the following $\mathcal{KB}$:

$$\top \to \text{Right } [\tfrac{4}{6}]$$

(Similar to Example 3.4, also here rule weights $\neq 1$ are denoted in fractions to outline that the weights represent the (conditional) relative frequencies of the agent's performed actions.)

Subsequently, the set of remaining state-action pairs $\mathcal{SA}^-$ is calculated (Step (2)), which comprises all state-action pairs for which the reasoning algorithm $\mathfrak{R}(\mathcal{KB}, st_\mathbf{p})$ does not provide the correct conclusion $a_\mathbf{p}$ (where $\mathcal{KB}$ is the current HKB, $st_\mathbf{p}$ is the state and $a_\mathbf{p}$ is the corresponding action of a state-action pair $\mathbf{p} \in \mathcal{SA}$). Here, the reasoning algorithm already provides the correct conclusion for all state-action pairs with action Right. Thus, the only two state-action pairs that remain from the input sequence $\mathcal{SA}^*$ are:

3. Knowledge Base Extraction

```
Input:   Deterministic set of state-action pairs SA*
Output:  HKB KB
01   % Create and add the most general rule
02   a_ρ := arg max_{a∈A} P(a)
03   w_ρ := P(a_ρ)
04   R_1 := {⊤ → a_ρ [w_ρ]}
05   KB := {R_1}
06
07   % Get remaining state-action pairs not covered by the current KB
08   SA⁻ := {p ∈ SA* | {a_p} ≠ ℜ(KB, ⋀_{s∈S_p} s)}
09
10   j := 1
11   while SA⁻ ≠ ∅ do
12
13       % Create rules of the HKB's next level to cover as much
14       % state-action pairs as possible
15       R_{j+1} := ∅
16       for each p ∈ SA⁻ do
17           for each S_p^j ⊂ S_p do   % S_p^j is a subset of S_p of length j
18
19               % Create new rule
20               s_ρ := ⋀_{s∈S_p^j} s
21               a_ρ := a_p
22               w_ρ := P(⋀_{s∈S_p^j} s ∧ a_ρ)   % is adapted to P(a_ρ | ⋀_{s∈S_p^j} s) in lines 36-39
23               ρ := s_ρ → a_ρ [w_ρ]
24
25               % Add rule if it does not exist yet
26               if ρ ∉ R_{j+1} then
27                   R_{j+1} := R_{j+1} ∪ {ρ}
28               end if
29           end for
30       end for
31
32       % Remove unused rules on the bottom most level of the HKB
33       % (delete all worse (i.e., less frequent) rules)
34       R_{j+1} := R_{j+1} \ {ρ ∈ R_{j+1} | ∄p ∈ SA*: ρ fires to infer {a_p} = ℜ(KB ∪ {R_{j+1}}, ⋀_{s∈S_p} s)}
35
36       % Adapt rule weights
37       for each ρ ∈ R_{j+1} do
38           w_ρ := P(a_ρ | ⋀_{s∈S_p^j} s)
39       end for
40
41       % Get remaining state-action pairs not covered by the current KB
42       SA⁻ := {p ∈ SA* | {a_p} ≠ ℜ(KB ∪ {R_{j+1}}, ⋀_{s∈S_p} s)}
43
44       % Remove unused rules on all levels of the HKB
45       % (delete rules that became superfluous either due to the new rules on
46       % level R_{j+1} or due to the adaption of the weights)
47       for each R ∈ KB do
48           R := R \ {ρ ∈ R | ∄p ∈ SA*: ρ fires to infer {a_p} = ℜ(KB ∪ {R_{j+1}}, ⋀_{s∈S_p} s)}
49       end for
50
51       KB := KB ∪ {R_{j+1}}
52       j := j + 1
53   end while
```

Algorithm 3.3 (Advanced Extraction of HKBs)   (Source: adapted from [6])

Rules are created on a level R_j to cover as many state-action pairs as possible. All remaining pairs are then considered on the next level R_{j+1} until all pairs are covered by KB.

$$\mathcal{SA}^- := \{(x_1 \wedge y_2, \text{Down}), (x_3 \wedge y_1, \text{Jump})\}$$

After setting the counter that indicates the current level of the HKB to $j := 1$ (Step (3)), rules with a premise of length $j = 1$ are added to level R_{j+1} (Step (4)). After this step, $\mathcal{KB} \cup R_2$ looks as follows (also here, rules to be removed in the next are shaded gray again):

$\top \to \text{Right } [\frac{4}{6}]$	
$x_1 \to \text{Down } [\frac{1}{6}]$	$x_3 \to \text{Jump } [\frac{1}{6}]$
$y_2 \to \text{Down } [\frac{1}{6}]$	$y_1 \to \text{Jump } [\frac{1}{6}]$

Note that, at this point, the rule weights on level R_2 represent the relative frequencies of a rule's premise together with the concluding action in the input sequence $\mathcal{SA}^*$, rather than the *conditional* relative frequencies of the concluding action *given* the premise. (E.g., for rule $x_1 \to \text{Down}$, x_1 and the action Down occur together in one of the six state-action pairs in $\mathcal{SA}^*$). By this, rules whose premise-action-combination appears more frequently in $\mathcal{SA}^*$ are kept on the more general levels of the HKB, whereas rules, whose premise-action-combination appears less frequent, will be represented as exceptions on the more specific levels (cf. the description in Step (4) of the algorithm).

In Step (5), the unused rules are now removed, i.e., those rules that either provide a wrong conclusion or that do not fire at all when applying the reasoning algorithm $\mathfrak{R}$ to each state of the state-action pairs in $\mathcal{SA}^*$. If multiple rules with the same conclusion are firing for a provided state, one of them can be chosen randomly (by convention, in the following, the preceding one according to the alphabetical order of its premise will be selected). Here, for $(x_1 \wedge y_2, \text{Down}) \in \mathcal{SA}^*$, both rules $x_1 \to \text{Down}$ and $y_2 \to \text{Down}$ fire, thus, by convention, $x_1 \to \text{Down}$ is selected (since x_1 precedes y_2 according to the alphabetical order). For $(x_3 \wedge y_1, \text{Jump}) \in \mathcal{SA}^*$, the rule $x_3 \to \text{Jump}$ is selected for the same reason. For all other pairs in $\mathcal{SA}^*$, the rules on level R_2 will either not provide the correct conclusion or will not fire at all. After removing the unused rules on level R_2 and after adapting the remaining rules' weights on that level to the conditional relative frequencies $P(a_\rho | \bigwedge_{s \in S_\mathbf{p}^j} s)$ (Step (6)), $\mathcal{KB} \cup \{R_2\}$ looks as follows:

$\top \to \text{Right } [\frac{4}{6}]$
$x_1 \to \text{Down } [\frac{1}{2}]$
$x_3 \to \text{Jump } [1]$

Now, the set of remaining state-action pairs $\mathcal{SA}^-$ is calculated again (Step (7)), resulting in only one pair not covered by $\mathcal{KB} \cup \{R_2\}$ (i.e., for which $\mathfrak{R}(\mathcal{KB}, st_\mathbf{p})$ does not provide the corresponding conclusion $\{a_\mathbf{p}\}$):

$$\mathcal{SA}^- := \{(x_1 \wedge y_1, \text{Right})\}$$

After removing all unused rules on all levels of $\mathcal{KB} \cup \{R_2\}$ (Step (8))—which will not have any effect here, since all of the three rules fire at least once when applying $\mathfrak{R}$ to the states of the state-action pairs in $\mathcal{SA}^*$—the newly calculated level R_2 is added to the HKB $\mathcal{KB} := \mathcal{KB} \cup \{R_2\}$ and the counter indicating the current level is increased to $j := 2$.

In the next iteration, rules with premises of length $j = 2$ are added to level R_{j+1} (Step (4)), resulting in a single rule added for the one remaining state-action pair $(x_1 \wedge y_1, \text{Right}) \in \mathcal{SA}^-$. After this, $\mathcal{KB} \cup \{R_3\}$ looks as follows:

$\top \to \text{Right}\ [\frac{4}{6}]$
$x_1 \to \text{Down}\ [\frac{1}{2}]$
$x_3 \to \text{Jump}\ [1]$
$x_1 \wedge y_1 \to \text{Right}\ [1]$

In this iteration, no more changes are made to $\mathcal{KB} \cup \{R_3\}$ in Step (5) to Step (8) and the set of remaining pairs $\mathcal{SA}^-$ will be empty at the end of the iteration:

- Since the premise of the only rule added on the bottommost level R_3 reflects a complete state, it will definitely be used (Step (5)).

- The weights will not be changed, due to $P(\bigwedge_{s \in S_\mathbf{p}^j} s \wedge a_\rho) = 1 = P(a_\rho | \bigwedge_{s \in S_\mathbf{p}^j} s)$ on the bottommost level with $j = 2$ (Step (6)).

- The set of remaining pairs will be empty, since for each state $st_\mathbf{p}$ of a state-action pair $\mathbf{p} \in \mathcal{SA}^*$, only the corresponding action $a_\mathbf{p}$ will be inferred by the reasoning algorithm $\mathfrak{R}$, i.e., $\forall \mathbf{p} \in \mathcal{SA}^*: \mathfrak{R}(\mathcal{KB} \cup \{R_3\}, st_\mathbf{p}) = \{a_\mathbf{p}\}$ (Step (7)).

- Since each rule of $\mathcal{KB}$ provides at least once the correct action $a_\mathbf{p}$ for a state of a pair $\mathbf{p} \in \mathcal{SA}^*$, no further rules are removed on all levels of $\mathcal{KB}$ (Step (8)).

Finally, in Step (9), R_3 is added to $\mathcal{KB}$ and j is increased again by 1. Since $\mathcal{SA}^-$ is empty now (due to Step (7)), the algorithm terminates, returning the final $\mathcal{KB}$, that states:

"Usually go to the right;
   except when being in a state x_1 then go down, or,
   except when being in a state x_3 then jump;
      except if being in state $x_1 \wedge y_1$ then go to the right."

Also in the example shown here, it can be easily seen that the reasoning algorithm $\mathfrak{R}$ (Algorithm 3.1) will infer the corresponding actions correctly from each state of a state-action pair from the original deterministic state-action sequence $\mathcal{SA}^*$. □

Example 3.6 shows, that the algorithm is straightforward and easy to follow by creating exceptions, exceptions of exceptions ("2nd-order exceptions"), etc. on each level, starting on the more general levels with the rules that cover the most of the state-action-pairs.

Remarkably, the resulting HKB differs from the one that was created in the Example 3.4 for the same scenario and the same agent behavior: In general, HKBs produced by Algorithm 3.3 have the potential of being a bit less compact than the ones produced by Algorithm 3.2. This is because Algorithm 3.3 calculates the HKB from top to bottom (i.e., from general to more specific knowledge) and thereby is not able to find optimizations that rely on certain more specific rules found later on the more specific levels: Although, Algorithm 3.3 is able to *remove* more general rules due to more specific rules found later in the creation process (see lines 44–49), it is not able to *create* rules on more general levels in dependence of rules found on the lower levels (which would allow for creating an overall more compact HKB). However, the ability of creating an HKB straightforward from top to bottom renders the algorithm much more efficient in practice, since it can be interrupted after any iteration, resulting in a rougher still meaningful HKB, instead of always relying on calculating the HKB as a whole.

3.5.2 Completeness of the Approach

An important question is now, whether Algorithm 3.3 is *complete*, in the sense that for an arbitrary deterministic state-action sequence $\mathcal{SA}^*$, a corresponding HKB $\mathcal{KB}$ will be provided by the algorithm, such that for each state-action pair $\mathbf{p} \in \mathcal{SA}^*$ with $\mathbf{p} := (st_\mathbf{p}, a_\mathbf{p})$, the reasoning algorithm $\mathfrak{R}$ (Algorithm 3.1) will return the corresponding action $a_\mathbf{p}$ for state $st_\mathbf{p}$, i.e., $\forall \mathbf{p} \in \mathcal{SA}^*: \mathfrak{R}(\mathcal{KB}, st_\mathbf{p}) = \{a_\mathbf{p}\}$. This question will be answered by the following proposition:

3. Knowledge Base Extraction

Proposition 3.2 (Completeness of Algorithm 3.3) For every deterministic state-action sequence $\mathcal{SA}^*$, Algorithm 3.3 provides an HKB $\mathcal{KB}$ that represents the knowledge contained in $\mathcal{SA}^*$ *completely*, i.e., $\forall \mathbf{p} \in \mathcal{SA}^*$: $\Re(\mathcal{KB}, st_\mathbf{p}) = \{a_\mathbf{p}\}$.

Proof Algorithm 3.3 obviously only terminates if $\mathcal{SA}^-$ is empty (see line 11—no further break or return commands are contained in the algorithm). Thus, to show that Proposition 3.2 holds, it will be argued in the following that

(i) at the end of each iteration, it holds that $\forall \mathbf{p} \in \mathcal{SA}^*$: $\Re(\mathcal{KB}, st_\mathbf{p}) = \{a_\mathbf{p}\}$ if $\mathcal{SA}^-$ is empty, and

(ii) that, at some point, there will be an iteration, where $\mathcal{SA}^-$ is guaranteed to be empty at the end (i.e., the algorithm is guaranteed to terminate).

For the first part (i):

Before the algorithm's main loop—which is considered the 0-*th iteration* of the HKB to be learned in the following—a single rule ρ with an empty premise is added to the topmost level of $\mathcal{KB}$ (in Step (1)) and, subsequently (in Step (2)), $\mathcal{SA}^-$ is assigned a subset of the state-action pairs of $\mathcal{SA}^*$ for which $\Re(\mathcal{KB}, st_\mathbf{p}) \neq \{a_\mathbf{p}\}$. After Step (2), since there is only one rule in $\mathcal{KB}$, only two cases exist here: If all state-action pairs in $\mathcal{SA}^*$ have the same action $a_\mathbf{p} = a_\rho$, it holds that $\forall \mathbf{p} \in \mathcal{SA}^*$: $\Re(\mathcal{KB}, st_\mathbf{p}) = \{a_\mathbf{p}\}$ and $\mathcal{SA}^-$ is empty. Otherwise (if not all state-action pairs in $\mathcal{SA}^*$ have the same action), only one action can be covered by the only rule in $\mathcal{KB}$ and it does not hold that $\forall \mathbf{p} \in \mathcal{SA}^*$: $\Re(\mathcal{KB}, st_\mathbf{p}) = \{a_\mathbf{p}\}$ and $\mathcal{SA}^-$ is not empty. Thus, it holds here that $\mathcal{SA}^-$ is empty if and only if it holds that $\forall \mathbf{p} \in \mathcal{SA}^*$: $\Re(\mathcal{KB}, st_\mathbf{p}) = \{a_\mathbf{p}\}$.

In the algorithm's *main loop*, the only step that modifies the set of remaining state-action pairs $\mathcal{SA}^-$ is Step (7) (lines 41–42). In that step, $\mathcal{SA}^-$ is assigned a subset of all state-action pairs of $\mathcal{SA}^*$ for which $\Re(\mathcal{KB} \cup \{R_{j+1}\}, st_\mathbf{p}) \neq \{a_\mathbf{p}\}$. Since this is the only step modifying $\mathcal{SA}^-$ and since this step is executed in every iteration of the main loop without any conditions, after this step, $\mathcal{SA}^-$ is empty if and only if it holds that $\forall \mathbf{p} \in \mathcal{SA}^*$: $\Re(\mathcal{KB} \cup \{R_{j+1}\}, st_\mathbf{p}) = \{a_\mathbf{p}\}$.

Subsequently, Step (8) (lines 44–49) potentially removes unused rules on all levels of $\mathcal{KB} \cup \{R_{j+1}\}$: Since only *unused* rules are removed here (i.e., those rules that were not involved in any of the correct conclusions $\Re(\mathcal{KB} \cup \{R_{j+1}\}, st_\mathbf{p}) = \{a_\mathbf{p}\}$ in Step (7)), this does not affect the statement that $\mathcal{SA}^-$ is empty if and only if it holds that $\forall \mathbf{p} \in \mathcal{SA}^*$: $\Re(\mathcal{KB} \cup \{R_{j+1}\}, st_\mathbf{p}) = \{a_\mathbf{p}\}$.

Step (9) of the algorithm (line 51) guarantees that level R_{j+1} is added to $\mathcal{KB}$, since it is executed in every iteration of the main loop without any conditions.

Thus, it holds that at the end of every iteration $\forall \mathbf{p} \in \mathcal{SA}^*$: $\Re(\mathcal{KB}, st_\mathbf{p}) = \{a_\mathbf{p}\}$ if (and only if) $\mathcal{SA}^-$ is empty.

For the second part (ii):

To show that there will be an iteration, at the end of which $\mathcal{SA}^-$ is guaranteed to be empty, it will be shown that

(ii-a) at the end of the n-th iteration (where n is number of sensors), $\mathcal{SA}^-$ is guaranteed to be empty, and that

(ii-b) the algorithm will necessarily reach the n-th iteration or $\mathcal{SA}^-$ was empty before (or is empty in the same iteration).

The second part (ii-b) can be shown easily and will be considered first:

Two cases can be distinguished here: $n = 0$ and $n > 0$. If $n = 0$, the 0-th iteration (before the main loop) is the n-th iteration and thus (ii-b) holds. Otherwise (if $n > 0$), at the end of the 0-th iteration, either the termination condition of the algorithm's main loop is satisfied, i.e., $\mathcal{SA}^-$ is empty, and thus (ii-b) holds, or the first iteration will subsequently start by entering the main loop (line 11), with j being initialized to 1 before. In the main loop, until the termination condition is satisfied, the counter j is increased by 1 in *every further iteration* according to line 52. This is guaranteed, since it is the only line modifying j and it is executed without any conditions and no break/return (or other jump commands) that could skip this line are contained in the main loop. Thus, it is ensured that the n-th iteration, where $j = n$, is either reached at some point, or the termination condition of the main loop must have been satisfied before, which is that $\mathcal{SA}^-$ is empty. In any of the cases, (ii-b) holds.

The first part (ii-a) (i.e., at the end of the n-th iteration, $\mathcal{SA}^-$ is guaranteed to be empty), holds for the following reasons:

If the 0-th iteration already represents the n-th iteration, then the agent that created $\mathcal{SA}^*$ must have had zero sensors and thus the states of the state-action pairs contained in $\mathcal{SA}^*$ do not comprise any sensor values (i.e., $\forall \mathbf{p} \in \mathcal{SA}^*$: $st_\mathbf{p} = \top$). Due to $\mathcal{SA}^*$ being deterministic, all pairs contained in $\mathcal{SA}^*$ have the same action $a_\mathbf{p}$, which is the one of the conclusion of the only rule added on the topmost level in Step (1) of the algorithm (lines 1–5). Thus, all actions contained in $\mathcal{SA}^*$ must be covered by this rule. Since in Step (2) (in line 8), $\mathcal{SA}^-$ is assigned a subset of all state-action pairs $\mathbf{p} := (st_\mathbf{p}, a_\mathbf{p})$ of $\mathcal{SA}^*$ for which $\Re(\mathcal{KB}, st_\mathbf{p}) \neq \{a_\mathbf{p}\}$, $\mathcal{SA}^-$ will be assigned the empty set here, before the 0-th iteration ends by initializing j with 1. The case that the 0-th iteration does not represent the n-th iteration will be considered in the following.

3. Knowledge Base Extraction

The only step that modifies $\mathcal{SA}^-$ in the algorithm's main loop is Step (7) (line 42). There, $\mathcal{SA}^-$ is assigned a subset of all state-action pairs $\mathbf{p} := (st_{\mathbf{p}}, a_{\mathbf{p}})$ of $\mathcal{SA}^*$ for which $\mathfrak{R}(\mathcal{KB} \cup \{R_{j+1}\}, st_{\mathbf{p}}) \neq \{a_{\mathbf{p}}\}$. Thus, it must be shown here that in the n-th iteration, just before Step (7), it holds that $\forall \mathbf{p} \in \mathcal{SA}^*: \mathfrak{R}(\mathcal{KB} \cup \{R_{j+1}\}, st_{\mathbf{p}}) = \{a_{\mathbf{p}}\}$, since in this case, $\mathcal{SA}^-$ will be assigned the empty set. Since it is the only step that modifies $\mathcal{SA}^-$ in the main loop, $\mathcal{SA}^-$ will remain empty until the end of the iteration, i.e., until the end of the current run of the main loop. Furthermore, it is guaranteed that Step (7) (line 42) is executed in *every iteration* of the main loop, since it has no conditions and no break/return (or other jump commands) are contained in the algorithm (cf. (ii-b)).

To show this, it will be started at the beginning of the algorithm's main loop: In Step (4) (lines 13–30), in the n-th iteration, since $j = n$ (according to (ii-b)), only *complete rules* (with *complete states* as premises) are added to the bottommost level R_{n+1} for each *distinct* state-action pair $\mathbf{p} \in \mathcal{SA}^-$. Thus, at the end of Step (4), R_{n+1} contains one complete rule of the form $st_{\mathbf{p}} \to a_{\mathbf{p}}$ [1] for each distinct state-action pair $\mathbf{p} \in \mathcal{SA}^-$ with $\mathbf{p} := (st_{\mathbf{p}}, a_{\mathbf{p}})$. Since $\mathcal{SA}^-$ is always a subset of the deterministic input set $\mathcal{SA}^*$ (according to Step (7)), $\mathcal{SA}^-$ must also be deterministic (i.e., all pairs $\mathbf{p} \in \mathcal{SA}^-$ with the same state $st_{\mathbf{p}}$ have the same action $a_{\mathbf{p}}$) and it is thereby guaranteed here that there is exactly one rule for each distinct state action pair $\mathbf{p} \in \mathcal{SA}^-$ providing the conclusion $a_{\mathbf{p}}$ for the state $st_{\mathbf{p}}$ (according to Algorithm 3.1, which always uses the best most specific rule). Thus, at the end of Step (4), in the n-th iteration, where $j = n$, it holds that $\forall \mathbf{p} \in \mathcal{SA}^-: \mathfrak{R}(\mathcal{KB} \cup \{R_{j+1}\}, st_{\mathbf{p}}) = \{a_{\mathbf{p}}\}$.

Due to the rules contained in R_{n+1} being *complete* rules with *complete* states as premises and due to $\mathcal{SA}^-$ being *deterministic*, none of the rules added to R_{n+1} will fire for a complete state of a pair $\mathbf{p} \in \mathcal{SA}^* \setminus \mathcal{SA}^-$. Thus, if for any $\mathbf{p} \in \mathcal{SA}^* \setminus \mathcal{SA}^-$ it held in the $(n-1)$-th iteration (where $j = (n-1)$) that $\mathfrak{R}(\mathcal{KB} \cup \{R_{j+1}\}, st_{\mathbf{p}}) = \{a_{\mathbf{p}}\}$, then this must still hold in the n-th iteration. Thus, at the end of Step (4), it holds that $\forall \mathbf{p} \in \mathcal{SA}^*: \mathfrak{R}(\mathcal{KB} \cup \{R_{j+1}\}, st_{\mathbf{p}}) = \{a_{\mathbf{p}}\}$.

The subsequent Step (5) (lines 32–34) removes all rules on level R_{n+1} that do not fire for any state of the pairs contained in $\mathcal{SA}^*$. Since only *unused* rules are removed here, after Step (5), it still holds that $\forall \mathbf{p} \in \mathcal{SA}^*: \mathfrak{R}(\mathcal{KB} \cup \{R_{j+1}\}, st_{\mathbf{p}}) = \{a_{\mathbf{p}}\}$.

In Step (6) (lines 36–39), in the n-th iteration (where $j = n$, according to (ii-b)), the weights of the rules $\rho \in R_{n+1}$ are adapted from $w_\rho := P(\bigwedge_{s \in S_{\mathbf{p}}^n} s \wedge a_\rho)$ to conditional probabilities $w_\rho := P(a_\rho | \bigwedge_{s \in S_{\mathbf{p}}^n} s)$. Since all rules on the final level R_{n+1} are complete rules, the state in the conditional part is a complete state and due to $\mathcal{SA}^*$ being deterministic, it holds that $P(\bigwedge_{s \in S_{\mathbf{p}}^n} s) = 1$. With this, it is

$$P(a_\rho | \bigwedge_{s \in S_\mathbf{p}^n} s) = \frac{P(\bigwedge_{s \in S_\mathbf{p}^n} s \wedge a_\rho)}{1} = P(\bigwedge_{s \in S_\mathbf{p}^n} s \wedge a_\rho)$$

and thus, no changes are made in this step. Thus, at the end of Step (6), it still holds that $\forall \mathbf{p} \in \mathcal{SA}^*$: $\Re(\mathcal{KB} \cup \{R_{j+1}\}, st_\mathbf{p}) = \{a_\mathbf{p}\}$.

As a consequence, the subsequent Step (7) will assign the empty set to $\mathcal{SA}^-$ in the n-th iteration and $\mathcal{SA}^-$ will remain empty until the end of the iteration (as argued in the second paragraph of (ii-a)).

By now having shown that (i) and (ii) hold, it is ensured that (latest) after the n-th iteration, Algorithm 3.3 will return a complete knowledge model for a deterministic input state-action sequence $\mathcal{SA}^*$, such that $\forall \mathbf{p} \in \mathcal{SA}^*$: $\Re(\mathcal{KB}, st_\mathbf{p}) = \{a_\mathbf{p}\}$. □

Note that, even if the $\mathcal{SA}^-$ is guaranteed to be empty at the end of Algorithm 3.3 (as has been shown in part (ii) here), this does not necessarily mean that $|\mathcal{SA}^-|$ will decrease monotonically after every iteration (depending on the inherent structure contained in the data to which the algorithm is applied).[18]

3.5.3 Learning HKBs from Numeric Data

All of the aforementioned approaches only work for discrete sensor data, where each sensor value is represented by an element of the respective sensor symbol set. In practice, data provided by sensors (and also action data!) may of course be numeric as well, and can even be (nearly) continuous. For discrete numeric sensors (e.g., a light sensor of a robot, that is able to distinguish a certain fixed number of shades of gray), a naive approach would be, to simply associate each numeric sensor value with a corresponding symbol, e.g., $\mathbb{S}_{\text{light}} := \{\text{grayShade1}, \text{grayShade2}, \text{grayShade3}, ...\}$ (with $|\mathbb{S}_{\text{light}}|$ being equal to the fixed number of shades of gray, which the sensor is able to distinguish). However, if the number of different numeric values increases (and especially in the case of (nearly) continuous sensor values), it is obvious that the naive approach is not always feasible. Furthermore, too fine-grained sensor symbol sets may result in reduced generalization capabilities of an HKB.

This section briefly outlines a more advanced technique for handling numeric sensor data. The main idea is to use a clustering approach for creating a sensor symbol set from the numeric data of a sensor. Each cluster found in the sensor data then corresponds to one sensor symbol, resulting in a sensor symbol set. By mapping each value of the numeric data to the sensor symbols (according to their association

---

[18] Thanks to Chung Shing Rex Ha for fruitful discussions, which helped pointing that out.

with the clusters), results for each numeric value in a corresponding sensor symbol. The resulting symbols can then appear in the state-action sequence that serves as an input to one of the knowledge base extraction algorithms that were presented in the previous sections.

The question is now, how to determine an eligible number of clusters (i.e., the number of distinct sensor symbols) for the numeric data provided by a sensor?

To answer this question, basically two cases can be distinguished:

- If additional information is available about the sensor or its data, then it may be desirable to determine the (maximum) number of clusters manually in advance (e.g., in case the sensor's purpose implies that the data should be represented by a specific number of sensor symbols).

- Otherwise, if nothing is known about the sensor or the sensor data, the number of clusters (i.e., the number sensor symbols used to represent the data) should be determined automatically.

In the following, the multi-set $\mathbb{D}^{\text{raw}}$ denotes the raw numeric input data that was collected by an agent's sensor. The set $\mathbb{S}_\mathbb{D}$ represents the sensor symbol set that will be created from $\mathbb{D}^{\text{raw}}$, and $\mathbb{D}$ denotes the resulting output multi-set that will be created from $\mathbb{D}^{\text{raw}}$ by replacing each numeric value of $\mathbb{D}^{\text{raw}}$ with a symbol from $\mathbb{S}_\mathbb{D}$. Furthermore, the value $d_{\max}$ denotes a predefined maximum number of clusters (which in the second of the above cases can be assumed to be equal to $|\mathbb{D}^{\text{raw}}|$, since this would be the maximum number of clusters, with each cluster containing exactly one single value).

A compact eligible clustering for $\mathbb{D}^{\text{raw}}$, can now be found by simply performing the following steps (covering both of the aforementioned cases with $d_{\max} := |\mathbb{D}^{\text{raw}}|$ for the second case):

(1) Starting with a minimum number of two clusters, the current number of clusters d will be set to $d := 2$. (Note that the case of one cluster is not further considered here, since this would result in a single sensor symbol, rendering the corresponding sensor useless for distinguishing states. In the special case that $\forall v_1, v_2 \in \mathbb{D}^{\text{raw}}: v_1 = v_2$, a single cluster can immediately be returned.)

(2) A *k-means clustering* (see, e.g., [61]) with $k := d$ is performed on $\mathbb{D}^{\text{raw}}$: Besides the number of clusters d and the multi-set $\mathbb{D}^{\text{raw}}$, the k-means clustering also needs the initial *centroids* as input, representing the (initial) mean values of each cluster. The l-th initial centroid c_l^{init} (where $l = 1$ refers to the first centroid) is calculated here as

$$c_l^{\text{init}} := \min(\mathbb{D}^{\text{raw}}) + (l-1) \cdot \frac{\max(\mathbb{D}^{\text{raw}}) - \min(\mathbb{D}^{\text{raw}})}{d-1}$$

By this means, the initial centroids are distributed *equidistantly* over the range of values of $\mathbb{D}^{\text{raw}}$ here (with the minimum referring to the first and the maximum referring to the last initial centroid). The values contained in $\mathbb{D}^{\text{raw}}$ are then assigned to the clusters (using a nearest neighbor metric) and the centroids are updated afterwards. The process is iterated, until none of the clusters is changed anymore. The k-means clustering then results in the clusters containing the assigned values and also provides the final centroids.

(3) If none of the clusters returned by the k-means clustering from the previous step is empty, then each cluster will now be associated with a sensor symbol. This results in the sensor symbol set $\mathbb{S}_\mathbb{D}$. The mapping of each value $v \in \mathbb{D}^{\text{raw}}$ to the sensor symbol of $\mathbb{S}_\mathbb{D}$ that represents the cluster to which v belongs then results in the multi-set $\mathbb{D}$.

Otherwise (if one of the clusters returned by the k-means clustering is empty), it will be immediately stopped here, returning $\mathbb{D}$ with the assignment from the *previous* iteration. (Note that this case cannot occur in the first iteration where $d = 2$, except for the special case that $\forall v_1, v_2 \in \mathbb{D}^{\text{raw}} \colon v_1 = v_2$, as described already at the end of Step (1). This ensures that the returned $\mathbb{D}$ will always have a valid assignment in the end.)

(4) If $d < d_{\max}$, then d will be increased by 1 and it is proceeded with Step (2). Otherwise, $\mathbb{D}$ is returned with the *current* assignment of sensor symbols.

After having performed these steps on a data set $\mathbb{D}^{\text{raw}}$, the resulting set $\mathbb{D}$ contains for each numeric value $v \in \mathbb{D}^{\text{raw}}$ a corresponding symbol of $\mathbb{S}_\mathbb{D}$ representing the cluster to which the value belongs. (Note that instead of k-means clustering, also other clustering techniques could be imaginable here.)

In practice, the clusters' centroids can be attached as annotations to the respective symbol names of the corresponding $s \in \mathbb{S}_\mathbb{D}$. This results in a good intuition on what is represented by a symbol (while at the same time rendering the symbol names unique, as stipulated at the beginning of Section 2.1.1). In the same way, also the number of clusters and the represented cluster sizes can be helpful annotations to comprehensibly represent the meaning of symbols learned from numeric data. For annotating these information, in the following, a naming scheme of the form

$$\text{name}\,(\,c\,)\,/\,C\,(\,p\,) \tag{3.3}$$

will be used for such learned symbols, where *name* is the name of the symbol that represents the cluster, $c := c_l$ is the cluster's (final) centroid, $C := |\mathbb{S}_\mathbb{D}|$ is the total

3. Knowledge Base Extraction

number of clusters, and p is the cluster's size (i.e., the percentage of values of the set $\mathbb{D}^{\text{raw}}$ that is covered by the cluster). Such an annotated symbol name then states that the symbol *name* represents a cluster around the centroid c, covering p percent of the data. If the number of the represented cluster is also of importance here, then a numbering can simply be added as suffix to each name (as done for the shades of gray in the light sensor example at the beginning of this section, i.e., grayShade1, grayShade2, grayShade3, ...) to additionally include this information.

Note that the described approach can also be applied in the same way to numeric action data (e.g., in case of a (nearly) continuous action space).

The following example demonstrates the learning of an HKB from both numeric sensor and numeric action data.

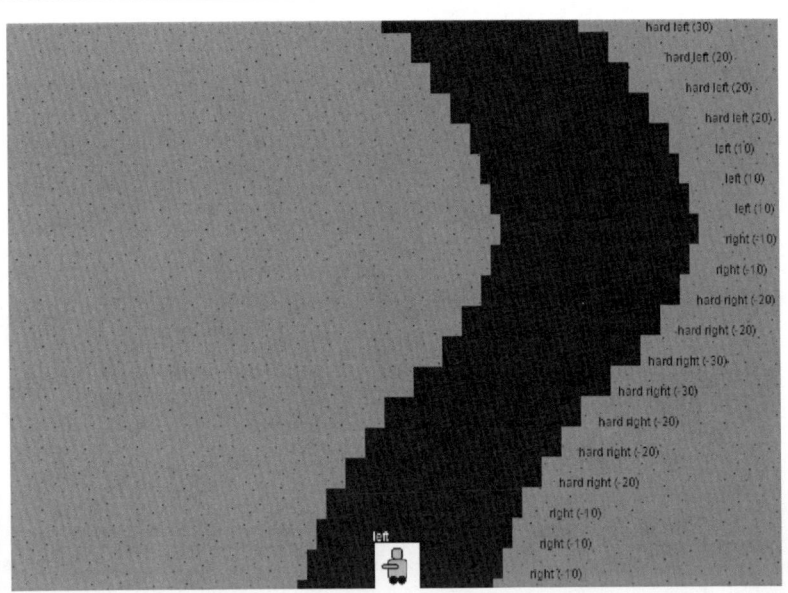

Figure 3.3 (Road Following Task) (Source: a. f. teaching software by the author used for Z Quadrat GmbH)
In this simulation originally developed for educational purposes in *fuzzy logic* (for a brief introduction to fuzzy logic see, e.g., [14], Chapter 13, especially Section 13.3.1), a robot has to follow a road. The robot perceives its position in the form of a numeric value in the range $[-20, 20]$, which represents its deviation to the left/right from the road's center. The robot can perform steering actions in the range $[-20, 20]$, i.e., the amount of steering to the left/right. The robot's current position is shown above the robot. On the right of each road segment, the curvature is indicated.

Example 3.7 (Fuzzy-Controlled Robot) A (simulated) robot has to follow an unknown road (see Figure 3.3). Its one-dimensional numeric state space is provided by its position on the road in the range $[-20, 20]$, where -20 refers to the leftmost and 20 refers to the rightmost deviation from the road's center. Its numeric action space is provided by the robot's steering, which is also in the range $[-20, 20]$, where -20 refers to the maximum steering to the left and 20 refers to the maximum steering to the right. To elegantly master the task using smooth steering actions, the robot uses a *fuzzy controller* (see [36], Section 7.3 for a similar task) with five triangular fuzzy sets for the input state (farLeft, left, center, right, farRight) and five for the output steering action (HardLeft, Left, Straight, Right, HardRight). Running the robot now in this scenario results in a raw data sequence, similar to a state-action sequence (cf. Definition 2.6), where both states and actions consist of numeric values. The raw data sequence can therefore be considered a "quasi-state-action sequence", where the first element of each pair refers to the robot's state (its position) and the second element to the steering action:

$$\mathcal{D}_{\text{robot}} = \{(-2.00, 2.41), (-3.60, 3.86), (-2.80, 3.17), (-4.20, 4.36), ...\}$$

(The values are rounded to two digits here; the full length of the raw data sequence considered in this example is $|\mathcal{D}_{\text{robot}}| = 90$.)

From $\mathcal{D}_{\text{robot}}$, the numeric data set $\mathbb{D}_{\text{pos}}^{\text{raw}}$ for the robot's states and $\mathbb{D}_{\text{steer}}^{\text{raw}}$ for its actions are obtained (where both sets are supposed to be *ordered* in the sense that the order of values as provided by $\mathcal{D}_{\text{robot}}$ is preserved).

Now, the described clustering approach is applied to both sets $\mathbb{D}_{\text{pos}}^{\text{raw}}$ and $\mathbb{D}_{\text{steer}}^{\text{raw}}$, with a predefined maximum number of clusters $d_{\max} := 5$. The learned symbols associated with the clusters are then named according to the fuzzy sets of the robot's fuzzy controller, resulting in the sensor symbol set $\mathbb{S}_{\mathbb{D}_{\text{pos}}}$ and the action symbol set $\mathbb{A}_{\mathbb{D}_{\text{steer}}}$.

This leads to the sets $\mathbb{D}_{\text{pos}}$ and $\mathbb{D}_{\text{steer}}$, which resemble to the sets $\mathbb{D}_{\text{pos}}^{\text{raw}}$ and $\mathbb{D}_{\text{steer}}^{\text{raw}}$ with each numeric value being replaced by a corresponding symbol of the respective sets $\mathbb{S}_{\mathbb{D}_{\text{pos}}}$ and $\mathbb{A}_{\mathbb{D}_{\text{steer}}}$. Since the data sets are both supposed to preserve the order of values as provided by $\mathcal{D}_{\text{robot}}$ (see above), a proper state-action sequence can now easily be constructed from $\mathbb{D}_{\text{pos}}$ and $\mathbb{D}_{\text{steer}}$, where the numeric values are replaced by the learned symbols:

3. Knowledge Base Extraction

$$\begin{aligned}\mathcal{SA}_{\text{robot}} = \{&(\text{center}(0.23)/5(43\%), \text{Right}(4.44)/5(18\%)), \\ &(\text{left}(-6.06)/5(18\%), \text{Right}(4.44)/5(18\%)), \\ &(\text{center}(0.23)/5(43\%), \text{Right}(4.44)/5(18\%)), \\ &(\text{left}(-6.06)/5(18\%), \text{Right}(4.44)/5(18\%)), \\ &...\}\end{aligned}$$

(Also here, except for the percentage values, the values are rounded to two digits; the naming of the learned symbols of $\mathcal{SA}_{\text{robot}}$ conforms to the scheme provided in (3.3).)

Finally, Algorithm 3.3 is run on $\mathcal{SA}_{\text{robot}}$, which results in the HKB provided in Figure 3.4.

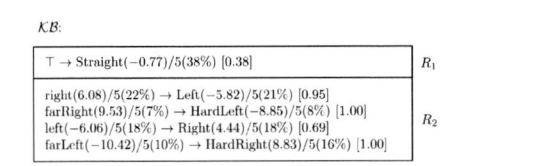

Figure 3.4 (HKB for Fuzzy-Controlled Road Following)
The HKB $\mathcal{KB}$ learned in the context of Example 3.7 comprises five rules. The naming of the rules' symbols follows the scheme in (3.3). The rule on the first level R_1 states that, usually, the robot has to steer straight (which resembles to a steering value of ≈ -0.77, according to the data of the example). The learned action symbol "Straight" represents one of five clusters, which covers 38% of the data. The level R_2 provides exceptions to the rule on level R_1 for cases where the robot perceives a position "right", "farRight", "left" or "farLeft" on the road. These four rules resemble to the relation of the input/output fuzzy sets of the robot's fuzzy controller.

As can be seen in Figure 3.4, the resulting HKB well reflects the input/output fuzzy sets of the robot's fuzzy controller used to navigate the robot on the road and can be easily read as follows:

"Usually steer straight (about -0.77),
  except when right (about 6.08), then steer left (about -5.82), or,
  except when far right (about 9.53), then hard left (about -8.85), or,
  except when left (about -6.06), then right (about 4.44), or,
  except when far left (about -10.42), then hard right (about 8.83)."

□

3.5.4 Handling Higher-Dimensional Data

Although the more advanced knowledge base extraction algorithm presented in Section 3.5.1 (Algorithm 3.3) is already much faster, it can still run into performance issues when it comes to higher-dimensional data (e.g., agents having hundreds of sensors). To cope with this, a possible approach is the preselection of sensors, since oftentimes only a small subset of the sensors is relevant for making adequate decisions. The question now is, which of an agent's sensors can be easily omitted without running a too high risk of ignoring relevant information?

To answer this question (similar as in Section 3.5.3), again two cases can be distinguished here:

- If there is a priori information available about the sensor data and/or the task to be learned, it might be eligible to predetermine the number $n' < n$ of sensors to be preselected in advance.

- Otherwise (if no such a priori information is available), the algorithm should be able to predetermine the number of sensors on its own.

If a preselection of the relevant sensors has to be performed, in both cases, the sensors will be ordered at first, according to their *potential relevance* for an HKB. This relevance is determined from the average relation of the distinct sensor values to the different actions. More precisely, in the context of a state-action sequence $\mathcal{SA}$, a simple yet efficient measure for the relevance of an agent's sensor with a corresponding sensor symbol set $\mathbb{S}$ can be calculated as

$$rel_{\mathcal{SA}}(\mathbb{S}) := \frac{\sum_{s \in \mathbb{S}} \max_{a \in \mathbb{A}} P(s \wedge a) \max_{a \in \mathbb{A}} P(a \mid s)}{|\mathbb{S}|} \qquad (3.4)$$

where $P(s \wedge a)$ and $P(a \mid s)$ refer to the (conditional) relative frequencies of s and a occurring in the state-action pairs of $\mathcal{SA}$.

The intuition here is, that sensors with symbols that often occur with the same actions have a strong potential for being involved in rules that are able to cover larger parts of a state action sequence: The first factor of the sum ($\max_{a \in \mathbb{A}} P(s \wedge a)$) results in higher values for sensors with symbols that frequently occur together with a certain action in the data. The second factor of the sum ($\max_{a \in \mathbb{A}} P(a \mid s)$) strengthens sensors with symbols that might serve well to predict that action.

Example 3.8 (Potential Relevance of Sensors) An agent is equipped with three sensors with the corresponding sensor symbol sets $\mathbb{S}_x$, $\mathbb{S}_y$, and $\mathbb{S}_z$. Each sensor can provide two sensor values, i.e., $\mathbb{S}_x := \{x_1, x_2\}$, $\mathbb{S}_y := \{y_1, y_2\}$, and $\mathbb{S}_z := \{z_1, z_2\}$.

3. Knowledge Base Extraction

The agent is able to perform two different actions, i.e., its action symbol set is $\mathbb{A} := \{a1, a2\}$. The agent now performs four actions in its environment, resulting in the state-action sequence $\mathcal{SA} = \{\mathbf{p}_1, ..., \mathbf{p}_4\}$ shown in Table 3.1.

$\mathcal{SA}$	states			actions
$\mathbf{p}_1$	x_1	y_1	z_1	a_1
$\mathbf{p}_2$	x_2	y_1	z_1	a_1
$\mathbf{p}_3$	x_1	y_1	z_2	a_2
$\mathbf{p}_4$	x_2	y_2	z_2	a_2

Table 3.1 (Data for Potential Relevance)
The table shows the state-action sequence $\mathcal{SA}$ of an agent acting in its environment: For each state-action pair, the perceived sensor symbols of each of the three sensor are provided together with the corresponding actions.

Applying the potential relevance measure (3.4) to the three sensors in the context of the state-action sequence $\mathcal{SA}$ from Table 3.1, results in the following values:

$$rel_{\mathcal{SA}}(\mathbb{S}_x) = \frac{\frac{1}{4} \cdot \frac{1}{2} + \frac{1}{4} \cdot \frac{1}{2}}{2} = 0.125$$

$$rel_{\mathcal{SA}}(\mathbb{S}_y) = \frac{\frac{1}{2} \cdot \frac{2}{3} + \frac{1}{4} \cdot 1}{2} = 0.291\overline{6}$$

$$rel_{\mathcal{SA}}(\mathbb{S}_z) = \frac{\frac{1}{2} \cdot 1 + \frac{1}{2} \cdot 1}{2} = 0.5$$

Thus, the sensor's ordering regarding the potential relevance is:

$$rel_{\mathcal{SA}}(\mathbb{S}_x) < rel_{\mathcal{SA}}(\mathbb{S}_y) < rel_{\mathcal{SA}}(\mathbb{S}_z)$$

According to that, the most relevant sensor is the one with the sensor symbol set $\mathbb{S}_z$, whose sensor symbols $z_1, z_2 \in \mathbb{S}_z$ each explain in average 50% of the data. Since there are only two actions equally distributed over the four state-action pairs of the state-action sequence $\mathcal{SA}$, the most relevant sensor with the sensor symbol set $\mathbb{S}_z$ would already suffice here to completely explain the agent's actions. □

The proposed measure (3.4) integrates well with Algorithm 3.3, since it mostly relies on (conditional) relative frequencies. These can be cached and later reused by Algorithm 3.3, which can further increase the performance in the context of higher-dimensional data. (However, also other measures are imaginable here to estimate the relevance of an agent's sensors in advance.)

3.5 Advanced Knowledge Base Extraction

In the first of the two cases mentioned at the beginning of this section (where the number of the potentially relevant sensors is manually determined in advance), simply the $n' < n$ sensors with the highest potential relevance $rel_{\mathcal{SA}}$ will be taken into account, ignoring the $n - n'$ remaining ones.

In the second case (where a predetermined number of potential relevant sensors is not provided), an eligible number of relevant sensors is found automatically by performing a k-means clustering (see [61] for an overview). The clustering is performed with $k := 2$ and with initial centroids $c_1^{\text{init}} := \min_{\mathbb{S}_i \in \mathfrak{S}} \left(rel_{\mathcal{SA}}(\mathbb{S}_i) \right)$ and $c_2^{\text{init}} := \max_{\mathbb{S}_i \in \mathfrak{S}} \left(rel_{\mathcal{SA}}(\mathbb{S}_i) \right)$, where $\mathfrak{S} := \{\mathbb{S}_1, ..., \mathbb{S}_n\}$ is the set of all sensor symbol sets. Except for the uncommon case that all of the agent's n sensors have the exact same potential relevance according to (3.4), this will result in a low relevance cluster (around the final centroid c_1) and a high relevance cluster (around the final centroid c_2). After that, the sensors from the resulting cluster around c_2 will be taken into account, ignoring all $n - n'$ other sensors from the resulting cluster around c_1.

3.6 Summary

HKBs are a multi-abstraction level knowledge representation approach based on the idea of rules with exceptions (a common concept, which is also known in a similar way in default logic [55] and answer set programming (ASP) [19]). HKBs seem to be easy to read (also for non-computer scientists without expert knowledge in logic) and allow for fast reasoning.

Due to their readability, HKBs are an eligible approach for representing knowledge learned by agents. Exploiting the idea of rules with exceptions on multiple abstraction levels, agent behavior can be represented in a compact way (see Proposition 3.1).

Different algorithms have been developed that range from a basic adaption of preliminarily considered criteria (see Section 3.4.1 and Algorithm 3.2) over the incorporation of the well-known APRIORI algorithm (see Section 3.4.3) up to an advanced HKB extraction algorithm (Algorithm 3.3), which is much more efficient and shown to be complete (see Proposition 3.2). Moreover, in Section 3.5, efforts have been made to render these approaches applicable to numerical sensory data (Section 3.5.3) as well as to higher-dimensional data, i.e., agents having a large number of sensors (Section 3.5.4). (The advanced results have been implemented in the INTEKRATOR toolbox [38] for practical application, see Appendix A).

The approaches described in this chapter can be considered foundations for interesting applications in the context of agents in games, ranging from explaining learned knowledge up to advanced learning skills for agents, which will be presented in the upcoming chapters.

3.7 Bibliographic Remarks

Some of the work contained in Chapter 3 was previously published in papers with further co-authors besides the author's PhD supervisor Prof. Dr. Gabriele Kern-Isberner. For this reason, the author's contributions of the respective papers will be summarized here.

The study [41] is joint work together with Corinna Krüger and emerged from her bachelor's thesis [40]. The bachelor's thesis was co-supervised by the author together with Prof. Dr. Gabriele Kern-Isberner. The author contributed to the work by elaborating the proposal of the thesis topic, by providing ideas concerning the study design, by helping to perform the study as well as by writing and improving parts of the paper [41]. A larger part of this work has been provided by Corinna Krüger and the corresponding paper is referenced at several places here.

The knowledge base extraction algorithm in Section 3.5 (Algorithm 3.3) was published in a joint work [6] together with Lars Hadidi and Dr. Torsten Panholzer from Medical Informatics department of the Institute of Medical Biostatistics, Epidemiology and Informatics (IMBEI) at the University Medical Center of the Johannes Gutenberg University Mainz. In this work, behavioral rules were learned from multi-agent simulations for optimizing hospital processes. The rules were learned in the form of HKBs by using the implementation of Algorithm 3.3 in an earlier version of the INTEKRATOR toolbox [38] (see also Appendix A). It has been shown in [6], that the learned HKBs can improve the investigated hospital process (and variants of it), if the agents behavior is based on the learned HKBs. The development of the algorithm (Algorithm 3.3), its inclusion into the paper [6], the completeness considerations (Section 3.5.2) as well as the approaches for learning HKBs from numerical data (Section 3.5.3) and for handling higher-dimensional data (Section 3.5.4) were developed and elaborated by the author.[19]

The most important techniques presented here (especially those from Section 3.5) are implemented in the INTEKRATOR toolbox [38]. In a joint work [10] together with Dr. Torsten Panholzer, the INTEKRATOR toolbox has recently been proposed for automatically creating expert systems from data in the context of medical applications.

---

[19] Thanks to my supervisor Prof. Dr. Gabriele Kern-Isberner for proposing to further elaborate on the completeness aspect as well as to Chung Shing Rex Ha for a collaboration that helped pointing to the need for being able of handling numeric and higher-dimensional data.

The development, the implementation and the maintenance of the INTEKRATOR toolbox have also been done by the author of this work. (More details on the toolbox can also be found in Appendix A.)

4. Explaining and Analyzing Agent Behavior

Agent behavior, especially that of learning agents, can quickly become a black box: Even if the resulting behavior seems to be adequate, also in simple environments it can be hard to understand what an agent has learned (see Section 2.1.7 and Section 2.2). This, of course, does not primarily affect the operational reliability of an agent and there are a lot of agent success stories that make use of black box techniques like neural networks—especially in the context of games (e. g., [49], [60]). However, it is obvious that there is a need of understanding what an agent has learned and why it behaves in a certain way (e. g. when thinking of the agent's trustworthiness or when the agent is supposed to perform in an unknown environment after learning).

Simulations and other techniques may help to visualize an agent's current behavior (in case this is possible for the respective problem). But neither do these techniques really materialize what the agent has learned, nor do they provide any explanations why the agent behaves in a certain way for the provided percepts.

HKBs, in conjunction with the corresponding extraction algorithms presented in Section 3.4 and Section 3.5, are an eligible approach to overcome these kinds of issues, since they are able to materialize knowledge in a rule-based way, while at the same time offering a hierarchical structure. This allows for reading the knowledge from the general to the more specific, up to an adequate level of abstraction maximizing the comprehensibility in the context of the respective learning task. Although it is obvious that given a certain amount of complexity, even a hierarchical approach may reach its limits, it still allows for a much better interpretability than a "flat" collection of rules (as it is the case for many other knowledge representation paradigms). Furthermore, such a hierarchical representation seems to be in line with the generalization capabilities of the human thinking (cf. [27], pp. 210–211), while at the same time incorporating the basic principles of *defaults rules with exceptions* known from *default logic* [55] (see also Section 2.2). (A study on the comprehensibility of HKBs can be found in [41].)

In this chapter, two aspects of explaining and analyzing learned agent behavior will be considered in the context of different video games: At first, the behavior of human agents playing different video games will be materialized as HKBs from their playtraces and, by this means, it will be shown how HKBs can be used for explaining knowledge learned in the context of video games (Section 4.1). After that, based on these extracted HKBs, it will be described how the complexity of a learned HKB relates to the subjective strategic depth of a game and a measure for estimating the difficulty, that was subjectively sensed by human agents while playing, will be described (Section 4.2). Some of the results presented in this chapter (especially the ones from Section 4.2) emerged from a joint work [11] together with Dr. Vanessa Volz (formerly at TU Dortmund University, at the time of writing at Queen Mary University of London and modl.ai, Copenhagen). (See Section 1.4 and the bibliographic remarks in Section 4.4 for details.)

4.1 Knowledge Base Extraction in Games

This section considers different games from the *general video game artificial intelligence* (GVGAI) framework by Perez-Liebana et al. [52], to demonstrate and evaluate the extraction of HKBs for explaining and analyzing knowledge learned in the context of games.

The GVGAI framework is a widespread framework for *general video game playing*, where an agent has to play multiple different (a priori unknown) video games. It origins from the *AI in games community* and is also used for international research competitions on GVGAI [53]. The framework offers a variety of about hundred different games with five different levels each, which are easily accessible through a proper programming interface. Being open-source, both the framework and the games can be easily modified to adapt them for research and other purposes. This renders the GVGAI framework an eligible test environment for this chapter (and also for the upcoming Chapter 5).

In the following, several games of different complexity will be selected from the GVGAI framework and will be briefly described (Section 4.1.1). After that, the state-action space of the games will be modeled (Section 4.1.2). Finally, the resulting HKBs extracted from the human playtraces will be presented and the results will be discussed (Section 4.1.3).

4.1.1 Selected Games

For the extraction of HKBs that will be described in the following sections, two different levels of three games from the GVGAI framework will be selected (and will be partly slightly modified, where necessary). The games and their levels are selected according to an increasing complexity, which allows to study how this complexity is handled by the HKB extraction algorithm and reflected in the the resulting HKBs. The selected levels of the games are shown in Figure 4.1 and will be briefly explained in the following.

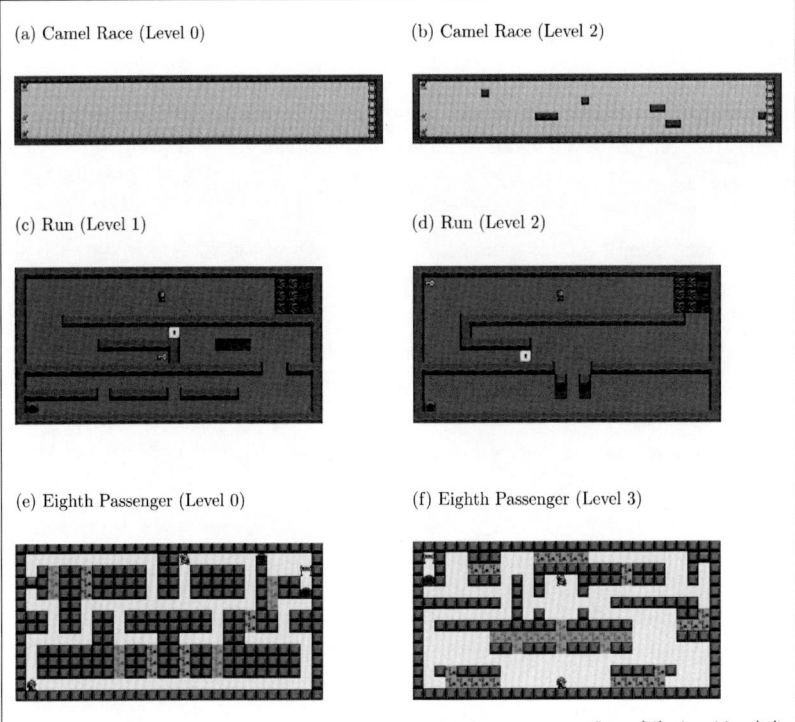

Figure 4.1 (GVGAI Games for HKB Extraction) (Source: [52], adapted from [11])
Three diverse games (two levels of each game) have been selected from the GVGAI framework [52] (and partly slightly modified) for materializing the knowledge contained in the respective playtraces of a human player as HKBs. The games start from a very simple one (*Camel Race*), over a more advanced one requiring basic planning skills (*Run*), up to a game where another agent is directly reacting to the player and thus a more strategic behavior is required (*Eighth Passenger*). The game mechanics of each game are described in detail in the text. (The same games will be considered later in Section 4.2 as well.)

Camel Race The game *Camel Race* is one of the simplest games of the GVGAI framework. The player controls the yellow camel in the middle and has to be the first reaching one of the goals on the right. Higher levels of the game include more complex architectures of the playground with more obstacles or invert the direction of the game. Although being simplistic, it can be a hard task for general video game playing agents, since state-of-the-art techniques like *monte carlo tree search* (MCTS) [21], that are widely-used in GVGAI, may fail, due to the goal being located far from the starting point (which would require a large tree depth).

Run In *Run*, the player controls a girl that must reach the door in the bottom left corner (see Figure 4.1 (c) and (d)), before the playground gets flooded by the steadily progressing water. A key must be collected to be able to open the yellow door, which incorporates some basic planning elements to the game. As an a priori intuition, this game seems to have a slightly increased complexity in comparison to Camel Race.

Eighth Passenger In this game, the player controls the elf (see Figure 4.1 (e) on the bottom left and (d) on the bottom in the middle) and has to reach the goal that is locked by two doors (in case of Level 0) or one door (in case of Level 1). The doors can be opened by pushing the button that is indicated by the teal stone in the upper left area (in case of Level 0) or in the upper right area (in case of Level 3). While trying to solve the task, the player has to avoid contact with the green orc that steadily moves toward the player's position. There are two kinds of tunnels: The blue ones can only be used by the player to hide from the orc, which renders the orc invisible at the same time, as long as the player is remaining in the tunnel. The red ones can only be traversed by the orc. Having multiple different objects to interact with and due to the orc directly reacting to the player's position, this game intuitively seems to be the most complex of the three games selected here.

4.1.2 Modeling the State-Action Spaces

To be able to apply an HKB extraction algorithm on playtraces resulting from the described games, the sensory inputs of the player agent as well as its possible actions will be defined here for each game, according to [11]:

The possible actions are identical for all of the three games and thus the corresponding action symbol set can be defined as

$$\mathbb{A} := \{\text{ACTION\_UP}, \text{ACTION\_DOWN}, \text{ACTION\_LEFT}, \\ \text{ACTION\_RIGHT}, \text{ACTION\_NIL}\} \quad (4.1)$$

where ACTION_UP, ACTION_DOWN, ACTION_LEFT, ACTION_RIGHT are denoting the actions according to their obvious meaning and ACTION_NIL is denoting that no action is performed in the respective time unit of the game.

The state spaces have to be modeled individually for each game, taking into account that a state must reflect all information that is relevant to the player. (Note that the subscripts of the sensor symbol sets used here, will later refer to the prefixes of the respective sensor symbols—except for the sets concerning the player's position whose subscripts have an additional prefix part to distinguish them among the different games. The additional part will later be omitted for the prefixes of the sensor symbols).

State Space of the Game Camel Race

For Camel Race, the modeling results in the four-dimensional state space

$$\mathbb{S}_{\text{CamelRace}} := \mathbb{S}_{\text{CAMEL\_PLAYER\_X}} \times \mathbb{S}_{\text{CAMEL\_PLAYER\_Y}} \\ \times \mathbb{S}_{\text{CAMEL\_PINK\_X}} \times \mathbb{S}_{\text{CAMEL\_GREEN\_X}} \quad (4.2)$$

where $\mathbb{S}_{\text{CAMEL\_PLAYER\_X}}$ and $\mathbb{S}_{\text{CAMEL\_PLAYER\_Y}}$ reflect the position of the player's camel and the remaining two dimensions reflect the positions of the pink and the green camel. Note that only the x-position of the pink and the green camel are considered here, since these camels only move in x-direction in this game.

The sizes of the respective sensor symbol sets (which are needed later for calculating the subjective strategic depth) are determined by the game mechanics as follows: $|\mathbb{S}_{\text{CAMEL\_PLAYER\_X}}| = 45$, $|\mathbb{S}_{\text{CAMEL\_PLAYER\_Y}}| = 7$ (both bounded by the surrounding walls), and $|\mathbb{S}_{\text{CAMEL\_PINK\_X}}| = |\mathbb{S}_{\text{CAMEL\_GREEN\_X}}| = 79$. Note that the sets of the pink and the green camel have a larger size since they move slower than the player's camel and therefore the game seems to create more fine-grained "intermediate" states for their movement. Also note that the green camel (at the bottom of the scenario) moves even slower than the pink one and therefore has even more fine-grained states—however, since both the pink and the green camel constantly move toward the goal, the green camel never reaches all of the theoretically possible states and thus, its state space has the same amount of 79 (more fine-grained) states.

State Space of the Game Run

For the game Run, the state space will also be considered four-dimensional as

$$\mathbb{S}_{\text{Run}} := \mathbb{S}_{\text{GIRL\_PLAYER\_X}} \times \mathbb{S}_{\text{GIRL\_PLAYER\_Y}} \times \mathbb{S}_{\text{WATER\_PROGRESS}} \times \mathbb{S}_{\text{KEY}}$$

where $\mathbb{S}_{\text{GIRL\_PLAYER\_X}}$ and $\mathbb{S}_{\text{GIRL\_PLAYER\_Y}}$ reflect the position of the player's avatar (the girl), $\mathbb{S}_{\text{WATER\_PROGRESS}}$ reflects the percentage of the water flooding the playground and $\mathbb{S}_{\text{KEY}}$ is a Boolean state dimension used to indicate whether or not the key has been collected.

4. Explaining and Analyzing Agent Behavior

The sizes of the respective sensor symbol sets are determined by the game mechanics as follows: $|S_{GIRL\_PLAYER\_X}| = 24$, $|S_{GIRL\_PLAYER\_Y}| = 11$ (both bounded by the surrounding walls), $|S_{WATER\_PROGRESS}| = 101$, (from 0% to 100% in 1% steps) and $|S_{KEY}| = 2$ (for having the key or not).

State Space of the Game Eighth Passenger

In case of the game Eighth Passenger, the state space is modeled with seven dimensions as

$$S_{EighthPassenger} := S_{ELF\_PLAYER\_X} \times S_{ELF\_PLAYER\_Y} \times S_{ORC\_X} \times S_{ORC\_Y} \\ \times S_{PREV\_ORC\_X} \times S_{PREV\_ORC\_Y} \times S_{DOOR}$$

where the $S_{ELF\_PLAYER\_X}$ and $S_{ELF\_PLAYER\_Y}$ dimensions reflect the position of the player's avatar (the elf), S_{ORC_X}, S_{ORC_Y}, $S_{PREV\_ORC\_X}$ and $S_{PREV\_ORC\_Y}$ reflect the position and the previous position of the orc (the latter to be able to encode the direction of the orc's current movement) and S_{DOOR} is a Boolean dimension used to indicate the state of the door(s) locking the goal (i.e., whether or not the door(s) is/are currently open).

The sizes of the respective sensor symbol sets determined by the game mechanics are: $|S_{ELF\_PLAYER\_X}| = 51$, $|S_{ELF\_PLAYER\_Y}| = 23$, $|S_{ORC\_X}| = |S_{PREV\_ORC\_X}| = 26$, and $|S_{ORC\_Y}| = |S_{PREV\_ORC\_Y}| = 12$ (all bounded by the surrounding walls). Note that the state sets of the orc are smaller than those of the player, since the player is able to move the elf between two cells of the "grid" whereas the orc can only move cell-wise.

4.1.3 Resulting HKBs

In this section, HKBs will be extracted from human playtraces of the games that have been considered in Section 4.1.1 and Section 4.1.2, to provide an impression of how the HKBs reflect the player's knowledge about the respective games.

For this purpose, playtraces will be considered *state-action sequences* (see Definition 2.6) of the states and actions resulting from the state-action spaces that were modeled individually for each of the three games in Section 4.1.2. Such playtraces were recorded from a human player learning to play the three games while playing the different levels multiple times in random order. The playtraces of the best iterations (i.e., the iterations that took the minimal time to complete the respective level) were selected to extract the HKBs.[20]

---

[20] The original data of the recorded playtraces stems from the study in [11] (see also Section 4.2).

4.1 Knowledge Base Extraction in Games

The following subsections now consider and discuss the resulting HKBs in detail (mainly) for one level of each of the three games.

Camel Race

Level 0 of the game Camel Race (see Figure 4.1 (a)) is rather simplistic and it is obvious that a human player will quickly understand that using only the action ACTION_RIGHT $\in \mathbb{A}$ immediately after the level has started until the goal on the right is reached will be the best strategy. Thus (maybe after a short initial learning phase), the resulting HKB will usually only contain one single abstraction level R_1 with the topmost rule $\top \to$ ACTION_RIGHT, i.e.,

$$\mathcal{KB}_{\text{CamelRace\_Level0}} = \{R_1\} \tag{4.3}$$

with $R_1 = \{\top \to \text{ACTION\_RIGHT}\}$.

However, Level 2 (see Figure 4.1 (b)) will already be more interesting, since the resulting HKB additionally reflects the exceptions stemming from the obstacles blocking the way to the goal. Figure 4.2 shows the HKB extracted from the human player's playtrace using Algorithm 3.2.

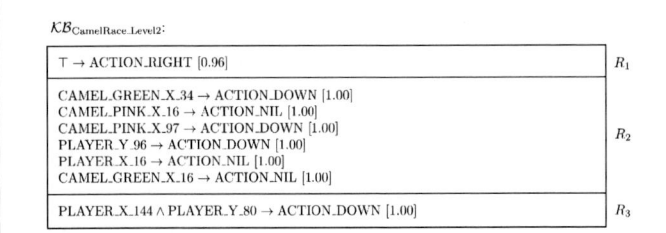

Figure 4.2 (Extracted HKB for Camel Race Level 2)
The HKB resulted from running Algorithm 3.2 on a playtrace by a human agent playing Level 2 of (a slightly modified version of) the game Camel Race from the GVGAI framework [52]. Besides the most general rule on level R_1 (stating that the player usually used ACTION_RIGHT), it comprises several exceptions on the levels R_2 and R_3 that are mostly provided by the obstacles blocking the direct way to the goal (cf. Figure 4.1 (b)).

As can be seen in Figure 4.2, the player usually uses ACTION_RIGHT. This behavior changes to avoid the obstacles that are blocking the directed way to the goal, which is reflected by the exception rules on level R_2 and R_3 (cf. Figure 4.1 (b)). Remarkably, not all of these exceptions are based on the coordinates of the player's avatar, but also on the position of the opponent camels: This is the case, since the extraction algorithm learned the HKB from the playtrace data only, without having any background knowledge. Thus, the algorithm can only statistically estimate, which dimension (i.e., which sensor) most probably explains an action best.

Furthermore, it can also be seen from the HKB shown in Figure 4.2, that in the beginning of the game, the player needed some response time after the game started: This is reflected by the rule PLAYER_X_16 → ACTION_NIL on level R_2, which indicates that the player did not immediately start, but remained at the starting position for a couple of time units. (The same can be observed for the rules with a starting position of one of the other camels as premise and ACTION_NIL as conclusion—for the reason provided in the previous paragraph.)

Run

The game Run seems to be slightly more complex than Camel Race, due to the more elaborate anatomy of the levels. Moreover, the planning aspect of getting the key to be able to open the door needs some more strategy to be involved. Figure 4.3 shows the HKB of a human playtrace for Level 2 of the game (cf. Figure 4.1 (d)).

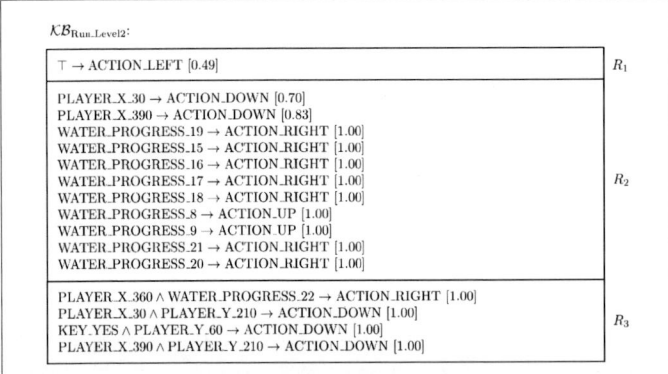

Figure 4.3 (Extracted HKB for Run Level 2)
The HKB resulting from running Algorithm 3.2 on a human playtrace of Level 2 of the game Run (see Figure 4.1 (d)). Some of the rules rely on the water progress here, since the algorithm does not involve any background knowledge about the meaning of sensor values and action. Thus it can only be determined statistically what explains an action best.

In the HKB shown in Figure 4.3, the rule on the topmost level R_1 indicates that the player mainly moved to the left. This makes sense in an intuitive way, since from the avatar's point of view, the goal is located on the left.

The remainder of the knowledge (getting the key, opening the door and navigating to the goal) is contained on the levels R_2 and R_3 of the HKB. The two rules PLAYER_X_30 → ACTION_DOWN and PLAYER_X_390 → ACTION_DOWN on level R_2 describe most of the player's downward movement on the left and in the center of the scenario (while the rest of the downward movement is covered by the additional exception rules on level R_3).

Note that, according to the remaining rules on level R_2 (and some of the rules on level R_3), the movement to the right (needed in the vertical center of the scenario) is mostly based on the water progress. Although this relation may be considered questionable, it is reasonable from the extraction algorithm's point of view: Since it has no information about the meaning of certain sensor values and actions, it only relies on the statistical search for a compact representation in the form of rules and exceptions. Thus, it uses the water progress in the same way as any other information. This leads to several exception rules reflecting the environment's dynamics that is induced by the progressing water (similar to the movement of the opponent camels in the game Camel Race). Later, in Chapter 5, an alternative way of representing the mechanics of a game using HKBs will be presented (Section 5.2).

Eighth Passenger

With multiple interactive objects like doors and buttons to open these doors, and with an opponent character being involved (the orc) that traces the player, this game intuitively seems to be much more complex than the two games that have been considered before.

Also unlike the two games considered before, the state-action space of Eighth Passenger comprises more dimensions: For Eighth Passenger the state-action space is eight-dimensional, whereas the state-action spaces of Camel Race and Run are both modeled with only five dimensions.

Figure 4.4 shows a corresponding HKBs of a human playtrace of Level 3 of the game (cf. Figure 4.1 (f)).

The HKB in Figure 4.4 shows that the player mainly moved to the left, as indicated by the rule on the topmost level R_1. Since the goal is located in the left of the avatar's starting position (see Figure 4.1 (f)), this intuitively makes sense.

4. Explaining and Analyzing Agent Behavior

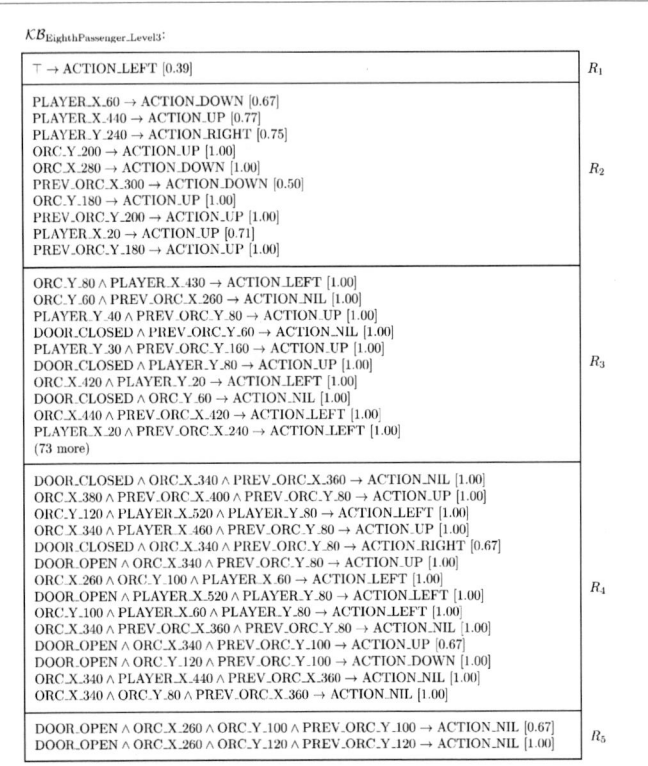

Figure 4.4 (Extracted HKB for Eighth Passenger Level 3)
The HKB resulting from running Algorithm 3.2 on a human playtrace of Level 3 of the game Eighth Passenger is much larger than the HKBs for the games Camel Race and Run. Nevertheless, also here, some details of the behavior can be seen immediately from the more general levels of the HKB: E. g., the rule on level R_1 implies that the player overall usually used the action ACTION_LEFT (the goal is located in the upper left corner), or the first three rules on level R_2 which describe the players movement in striking areas of the level. On level R_3, not all of the rules created by Algorithm 3.2 are listed here.

The level R_2 of the HKB contains the knowledge about some elementary behavior performed by the player: This comprises the navigation in the (mostly) fixed anatomy of the scenario (the first three rules listed on level R_2 of the HKB) as well as some kind of "flight behavior" to escape the orc (e. g., rule ORC_Y_200 → ACTION_UP, which can be interpreted as "if the orc is located in the bottom area of the scenario, the player tends to move upward").

On the more specific levels, the rules are already rather numerous and therefore, on level R_3, only a part of the rules created by Algorithm 3.2 are listed in Figure 4.4. However, also on these abstraction levels, some interesting relations can be seen, e.g., the second to last rule ORC_X_440 ∧ ORC_PREV_X_420 → ACTION_LEFT on level R_3 (which can be interpreted as "if the orc is in the right area of the scenario and moves to the left, then the player usually also moves to the left"), or the third to the last rule DOOR_OPEN ∧ ORC_Y_100 ∧ ORC_PREV_X_120 → ACTION_LEFT on level R_4 (which provides a similar statement for the vertical movement of the orc, if it is additionally known that the door was already opened).

Level R_5 finally covers some specific cases related to idle actions that involve already four of the seven sensors that were used for the modeling of the perceptions for the game (cf. Section 4.1.2).

Note that this game already shows that—even if the HKB can still be interpreted to some degree by reading it top-down—naturally, the interpretation becomes harder with an increasing amount of rules. (Chapter 5 (Section 5.2) will later show an alternative way of using HKBs.)

4.2 Subjective Strategic Depth

The previous section showed, how HKBs can be extracted from human playtraces of different games and how the extracted HKBs can be interpreted. As a first intuition, it could be seen that more complicated games seem to result in larger HKBs. This section will more deeply consider the relation of an HKB and the difficulty of a game, especially the difficulty that is subjectively sensed by a player—the so-called *subjective strategic depth*, which was introduced in [11].

For this purpose, following [11], a measure will be presented, that models the subjective strategic depth based on the size and the structural properties of an HKB (Section 4.2.1). After that, the evaluation of the presented measure will be described (Section 4.2.2) and, finally, the evaluation results will be provided (Section 4.2.3).

4.2.1 Subjective Strategic Depth Measure

This section describes a measure for the strategic depth that is subjectively sensed by human players when playing a game. The section follows the ideas first introduced in [11]. Such a measure does not only have to reflect the complexity of a game itself, but also individual subjective factors, like the current state of the player's learning process or its experience with (this kind of) games.

The main idea of the subjective strategic depth measure described here is, that the more exceptions are needed to describe the player's behavior for solving a game, the higher the subjective strategic depth should be. In other words: A problem that needs a lot of exceptions to be solved, usually appears more complicated than a problem that can be solved successfully with a few exceptions only (be it simply due to the size of the problem or due to its inherent complexity). Moreover, having less experience in solving a certain (kind of) problem, will more often lead to suboptimal solutions, usually resulting in more (unnecessary) exceptions.

Based on these assumptions, the size and the structure of an HKB (i.e., the number of exceptions and their depth) will be considered to reflect the subjective strategic depth, according to the following ideas:

- The size of an HKB $\mathcal{KB}$ potentially grows with the problem size (i.e., the number of sensors and actions being involved). Its maximum number of levels is $|\mathcal{KB}| = n + 1$ (with n being the number of sensors). The maximum number of rules on each level $R_j \in \mathcal{KB}$ depends on both the combinations of sensor values (according to the premise length $j - 1$ on that level) and the number of possible actions $|\mathbb{A}|$.

- More specific rules on lower abstraction levels potentially reflect more complex relations than more general rules on higher abstract levels, since they have longer premises with more sensor values being involved. Moreover, being more deeply rooted in the HKB, such rules have a higher potential to represent higher-order exceptions (i.e., exceptions of exceptions; cf. Definition 3.4).

With these ideas in mind, the subjective strategic depth measure can now be defined more formally, following [11]:

Definition 4.1 (Subjective Strategic Depth Measure) The measure for representing the subjective strategic depth sensed by a (human) player agent when playing a game is defined as a function

$$d_s(\mathcal{KB}, \mathfrak{S}) := \sum_{j=1}^{n+1} \binom{n+1}{j-1} b^{j-1} \frac{|R_j|}{\sum_{\substack{\mathbf{S} \subseteq \mathfrak{S} \\ |\mathbf{S}|=j-1}} \prod_{S \in \mathbf{S}} |S|} \tag{4.4}$$

where $\mathcal{KB}$ is an HKB representing the player's playtrace (i.e., its state-action sequence used to win the game), $\mathfrak{S} := \{S_1, ..., S_n\}$ is a set of all sensor symbol sets needed to describe a player's state, $n + 1 = |\mathfrak{S}| + 1$ is the maximum number of levels of $\mathcal{KB}$, b is a constant that determines the impact of exceptions on the overall strategic depth, and $R_j \in \mathcal{KB}$ is the j-th level of $\mathcal{KB}$.[21] □

The main idea of the function represented by Formula (4.4) is, to create a weighted sum over the ratios of the number of rules on each level $R_j \in \mathcal{KB}$ and the maximum number of possible rules on that level, according to the modeled state space (see the fraction at the end of Formula (4.4)). (Note that the maximum number of possible rules does not depend on the action space here—which makes sense, if only the best actions for the provided states are considered.)

The ratios in the sum are weighted by the binomial coefficients $\binom{n+1}{j-1}$ and the weights b^{j-1}, reflecting the impact of the rules according to their level in the HKB:

- The binomial coefficients balance the combinatorial growth of the possible number of rules on each level, which does not only depend on the number of sensor values of each sensor, but also on the number of possible *sensor combinations* of the sensors needed to describe a players state (see set $\mathfrak{S}$ in Definition 4.1). (The first level R_1 can be considered a special case here, since it always contains only one rule, according to Algorithm 3.2.)

- The weights b^{j-1} model the impact of (higher-order) exceptions on the overall strategic depth, i.e., it is assumed here, that the impact of exceptions grows exponentially with the depth of the level on which they are located in the HKB. (The constant b can be used to control the amount of growth on each level of the HKB; in the study presented in the following section it was considered to be 2, which reflected the strategic depth rather accurately there).

Note that the presented measure has no upper bound across different games, which reflects the fact that a game can be arbitrarily complex. However, the measure can be normalized by dividing it by $\sum_{j=1}^{n+1} \binom{n+1}{j-1} b^{j-1}$ (cf. [11]), in case one is interested in the "relative" strategic depth represented by a playtrace in relation to the maximum strategic depth possible, according to the game's sensor symbol sets and actions.[22]

---

[21] Note that Formula (4.4) corrects the corresponding formula of the original definition from [11], where the binomial coefficients were accidentally missing a "+1" in the upper part. Also note that the outer sum could start counting from 0 to n as well (for omitting the "−1" attached to the j in the formula)—however, to underline the intuition of summing over all levels of the HKB (starting from the first level R_1), this is provided as in the original definition from [11] in this case.

[22] In Section 5.1.2, this will be used to let an artificial agent estimate the potential complexity of a (partially) unknown environment while exploring it in the context of a learning process.

4. Explaining and Analyzing Agent Behavior

In the following example, the subjective strategic depth of two different levels will be calculated and compared.

Example 4.1 (Calculating and Comparing Strategic Depths) This example calculates and compares the subjective strategic depths of Level 2 of the game Camel Race (see Figure 4.1 (b)) and Level 2 of the game Run (see Figure 4.1 (d)), according to Definition 4.1. For this purpose, the corresponding HKBs $\mathcal{KB}_{\text{CamelRace\_Level2}}$ (see Figure 4.2) and $\mathcal{KB}_{\text{Run\_Level2}}$ (see Figure 4.3) will be considered, which were created from two human playtraces (of the same person), using Algorithm 3.2. The sizes of the respective sensor symbol sets are as described in Section 4.1.2.

For Level 2 of Camel Race, the subjective strategic depth d_s is calculated using the HKB $\mathcal{KB}_{\text{CamelRace\_Level2}}$ and the set of sensors $\mathfrak{S}_{\text{CamelRace}} := \{S_{\text{CAMEL\_PLAYER\_X}}, S_{\text{CAMEL\_PLAYER\_Y}}, S_{\text{CAMEL\_GREEN\_X}}, S_{\text{CAMEL\_PINK\_X}}\}$:

$$d_s(\mathcal{KB}_{\text{CamelRace\_Level2}}, \mathfrak{S}_{\text{CamelRace}}) = \sum_{j=1}^{5} \binom{5}{j-1} b^{j-1} \frac{|R_j|}{\sum_{\substack{\mathbf{S} \subseteq \mathfrak{S}_{\text{CamelRace}} \\ |\mathbf{S}|=j-1}} \prod_{S \in \mathbf{S}} |S|}$$

After expanding the outer sum by inserting the numbers of rules for each level (with the last two elements of the sum being 0, due to the corresponding levels R_4 and R_5 being empty), it is

$$d_s(\mathcal{KB}_{\text{CamelRace\_Level2}}, \mathfrak{S}_{\text{CamelRace}}) = \binom{5}{0} 2^0 \frac{1}{\sum_{\substack{\mathbf{S} \subseteq \mathfrak{S}_{\text{CamelRace}} \\ |\mathbf{S}|=0}} \prod_{S \in \mathbf{S}} |S|} + \binom{5}{1} 2^1 \frac{6}{\sum_{\substack{\mathbf{S} \subseteq \mathfrak{S}_{\text{CamelRace}} \\ |\mathbf{S}|=1}} \prod_{S \in \mathbf{S}} |S|} + \binom{5}{2} 2^2 \frac{1}{\sum_{\substack{\mathbf{S} \subseteq \mathfrak{S}_{\text{CamelRace}} \\ |\mathbf{S}|=2}} \prod_{S \in \mathbf{S}} |S|}$$

Now, the maximum numbers of rules for each level according to the state space will be inserted (where the first summand will be 1, due to the product in the denominator being the empty product), resulting in:

$$d_s(\mathcal{KB}_{\text{CamelRace\_Level2}}, \mathfrak{S}_{\text{CamelRace}}) =$$
$$1 + \binom{5}{1} 2^1 \frac{6}{45 + 7 + 2 \cdot 79} + \binom{5}{2} 2^2 \frac{1}{45 \cdot 7 + 2 \cdot (45 \cdot 79) + 2 \cdot (7 \cdot 79) + 79 \cdot 79}$$

$$= 1 + \binom{5}{1} 2^1 \frac{6}{210} + \binom{5}{2} 2^2 \frac{1}{14772}$$

$$\approx 1.29$$

The subjective strategic depth of Level 2 of the game Run can be calculated in the same way, resulting in:

$$d_s(\mathcal{KB}_{\text{Run\_Level2}}, \mathfrak{S}_{\text{Run}}) \approx 1.84$$

With $d_s(\mathcal{KB}_{\text{Run\_Level2}}, \mathfrak{S}_{\text{Run}}) \approx 1.84 > 1.29 \approx d_s(\mathcal{KB}_{\text{CamelRace\_Level2}}, \mathfrak{S}_{\text{CamelRace}})$, the strategic depth sensed by the human player that played both levels will be estimated to be $\approx 43\%$ higher when playing the game of Run (which involves basic planning capabilities—in contrast to the rather simplistic game of Camel Race, where only obstacles have to be avoided with a purely reactive behavior). □

Having now introduced the main ideas of measuring the strategic depth sensed by a human player based on rules and exceptions in the form of HKBs, the following sections will concern the evaluation of the measure.

4.2.2 Evaluation

To evaluate the strategic depth measure from Definition 4.1, a survey was designed, where human players had to play the six levels shown in Figure 4.1 in random order. For each individual level, the corresponding playtraces were stored and the players where asked for their subjectively sensed strategic depth. The stored playtraces were used later for extracting HKBs (as described in Section 4.2.1) and based on these extracted HKBs, the respective strategic depth was calculated, according to Definition 4.1. The calculated strategic depths were then evaluated against the sensed strategic depths provided by the players. In the following, the individual components of the survey will be described more detailed.

Survey Software

A special survey software was developed, based on the GVGAI framework [52], for collecting the data from players. This software allowed the players to play the six levels from Figure 4.1 in random order (to avoid biases due to learning effects of the players).

After starting, the survey software first displayed a general description text to the player (including legal/anonymization hints). Moreover, before each level, an additional introductory text was displayed, briefly describing the upcoming game.

The software recorded the playtraces of a player individually for each level by only keeping the best playtrace of each level won by the player. Playtraces in which the player lost the game were not stored for reasons of comparability: Such playtraces might be rather short (independently from the specific game) and the complexity of the game's task(s) might not be well reflected by the playtrace, since not being performed successfully. The recorded playtraces were later processed to extract HKBs, using Algorithm 3.2.

At the end of each level, a slider was displayed to the player and the player was asked to enter the subjectively sensed strategic depth using the slider. The slider showed a range of $[0, 10]$ annotated in whole numbers and had a granularity of 0.1, resulting in a near-continuous feel.

Participants

For running the survey, eight voluntary players were acquired as participants with an appropriate affinity for games (one psychologist, one industrial engineer and six computer scientists, see [11]). This ensured that the players were aware of the meaning of the term "strategic depth" in the context of games.

Note that the number of acquired players might appear to be rather low. However, since each of the players played six levels and (besides the playtraces) additionally provided the subjectively sensed strategic depth for each level, in the end, there were about $(8 \cdot 6) \cdot 2 = 96$ data points resulting from the survey (minus some few missing values, that will be considered more detailed in the next section).

Data Processing

The raw data that resulted from the survey can be divided for each player p into two sets, which will be referred to in following as $\mathbb{D}_p$ and $\mathbb{D}_p^{\text{HKB}}$.

The set $\mathbb{D}_p$ contains the subjectively sensed strategic depth values that were provided directly by a player p for each level (using the slider).

The set $\mathbb{D}_p^{\text{HKB}}$ contains the strategic depth values that were calculated from the recorded playtraces for each level successfully played by a player p: For this purpose, an HKB was extracted at first from each recorded playtrace using Algorithm 3.2. These HKBs were then used to calculate the strategic depth values, according to Definition 4.1.

For reasons of comparability, the raw values contained in $\mathbb{D}_p$ (directly provided by a player) and those contained in $\mathbb{D}_p^{\text{HKB}}$ (calculated from the extracted HKBs) were normalized to a range of $[0, 1]$. This was done by calculating for each $v_{\text{raw}} \in \mathbb{D}_p$ and each $v_{\text{raw}}^{\text{HKB}} \in \mathbb{D}_p^{\text{HKB}}$ the corresponding normalized values

$$v := \frac{v_{\text{raw}} - \min(\mathbb{D}_p)}{\max(\mathbb{D}_p) - \min(\mathbb{D}_p)}$$

and

$$v^{\text{HKB}} := \frac{v_{\text{raw}}^{\text{HKB}} - \min(\mathbb{D}_p^{\text{HKB}})}{\max(\mathbb{D}_p^{\text{HKB}}) - \min(\mathbb{D}_p^{\text{HKB}})} \tag{4.5}$$

respectively (see [11]).

A problem of this kind of normalization is related to the missing values: In rare cases, some of the participating players did not play each level successfully, which resulted in some of the raw data sets $\mathbb{D}_p^{\text{HKB}}$ being incomplete. Applying the normalization scheme according to Formula (4.5) in these cases could lead to a distortion of the resulting scales. For this reason, the missing values of a level were imputed by the average value of the corresponding levels of all other players, before the normalization was performed.

The imputation was done only in the context of the normalization and the imputed values were not considered further in the evaluation process, to avoid any further influence on the results. Moreover, with an overall missing value rate of $\approx 4.17\%$ (see [11]), the effect of the imputation on the results should be considered small here.

4.2.3 Results

This section summarizes the evaluation results of the subjective strategic depth measure that was presented in Section 4.2.1.

Following [11], the approach of calculating the subjective strategic depth based on HKBs that are extracted from human playtraces, will be evaluated against the subjective strategic depth sensed by human players. This evaluation will be done in the context of the games from Figure 4.1.

More concretely, to quantify the accuracy of the subjective strategic depth measure, for each level, averaged over all players, the normalized calculated strategic depth will be compared to the normalized strategic depth that was sensed by the players. The results of this comparison are visualized in a bar plot that is shown in Figure 4.5.

As can be seen in Figure 4.5, the subjective strategic depth that was sensed by the players is well reflected by the measure from Definition 4.1: The measure is especially able to reflect the different proportions of the subjective strategic depth for the different levels.

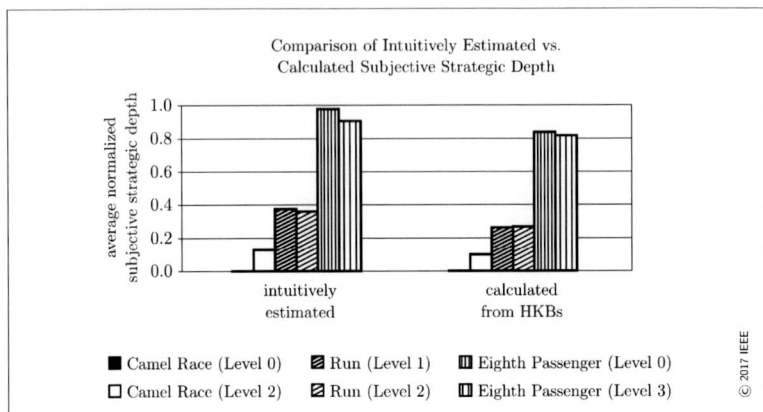

Figure 4.5 (Evaluation of the Strategic Depth Measure) (Source: adapted from [11])
The intuitively estimated strategic depth (left plot), that was directly provided by the players after each level using a slider, is compared against the calculated strategic depth (right plot), that was determined by applying the subjective strategic depth measure from Definition 4.1 to the HKBs extracted from the corresponding playtraces. The levels correspond to those provided in Figure 4.1. The subjective strategic depth values have been normalized for both plots to be in a range of $[0, 1]$ and the values for each level have been averaged over all players. It can be seen that the subjective strategic depth measure models the strategic depth sensed by the players well (with a slight tendency for underestimation).

A minor issue (that was already mentioned in [11]) is, that the approach seems to slightly underestimate the player's intuitions. According to [11], a possible solution to that might be to adapt the constant b in Formula (4.4).

More detailed, according to the results of the survey, the average deviation of the measure from the strategic depth sensed by the players is $\approx 7.71 \cdot 10^{-2}$ and the average *relative* deviation to the strategic depth sensed by the players is $\approx 1.71 \cdot 10^{-1}$ (i.e., $\approx 17.1\%$). Since the different proportions among the levels are well reflected, most of the deviation amount seems to stem from the overall underestimation of the measure. By introducing a proportionality factor of ≈ 1.27 (estimated from the ratios of the calculated strategic depth values and the strategic depth values $\neq 0$ provided by the players), the deviation is reduced to $\approx 4.70 \cdot 10^{-2}$ and the average relative deviation is reduced to $\approx 7.06 \cdot 10^{-2}$ (i.e., $\approx 7.1\%$).

It seems that the number of exceptions and their nesting depth needed to describe a player's behavior (as provided by the HKBs), can be considered an eligible approach to model the strategic depth that is subjectively sensed by a human player. This conforms to the intuition that situations comprising more exceptions (like routes with multiple branches) are usually considered more complicated than those that can be described with a small set of simple rules. In the described study, the subjective strategic depth measure was able to reflect the differences among the levels of diverse complexity similar to how humans were sensing it. (Later, in Chapter 5, it will also be shown how artificial agents can benefit from this approach.)

4.3 Summary

Due to the readability properties and the compact hierarchical organization of the knowledge contained in an HKB, a major application of HKBs is the materialization of learned knowledge.

Besides having shown application for that in the context of video games from the GVGAI competition [65] in Section 4.1, this chapter provided a further application that builds on the concept of HKBs:

By exploiting the hierarchical organization of knowledge in the form of rules with exceptions, a measure for strategic depth has been presented in Section 4.2, which resulted from a joint work with Dr. Vanessa Volz (see Section 1.4 and the bibliographic remarks in Section 4.2 for details). This measure allows to estimate the subjectively experienced strategic depth when playing video games. It provided accurate results for human players when being evaluated against their subjective intuition on the strategic depth of different games in the study performed in [11].

The concepts of HKBs in games in conjunction with the described measure for strategic depth resulted later in an exhibit, which traveled around several German and Austrian cities in 2019 and is still shown at the *Deutsches Museum Bonn* (German Museum in Bonn) [24] at time of writing in the context of an exhibition on AI [48] (see bibliographic remarks in Section 4.4 for details).

In the upcoming Chapter 5, the measure for strategic depth will also be used in an artificial agent model that allows agents to estimate the complexity of their environment from observations and thereby allows them to decide on their own, when to use rougher heuristics.

4.4 Bibliographic Remarks

Some of the contents of this chapter (especially those from Section 4.2) have their origins in a joint work [11] together with the author's former colleague Dr. Vanessa Volz (formerly at TU Dortmund University, at time of writing at Queen Mary University of London and modl.ai, Copenhagen). This work was originally dedicated to finding a model for (subjective) strategic depth, but also helped later to further stimulate the research on HKBs, especially for using them in the context of video games (as will be shown in Chapter 5). Moreover, it opened doors to the *AI in games* research community, resulting in fruitful further works in this field.

In [11], the author's part mostly concerned the games selection, the modeling of the state-action spaces for the HKBs in the context of the games and the development of the strategic depth measure based on HKBs. Dr. Vanessa Volz contributed her knowledge in the field of *AI in games* by overtaking the part of embedding the work in the context of related works like [20, 46, 67] and provided some analysis and relevant conclusions thereof.

Section 4.1 provided some deeper insights into the extraction of HKBs from playtraces of the GVGAI games as it is the case in [11]. By shifting the focus more toward the modeling of HKBs in the context of games, this section also serves as a preliminary work for the upcoming Chapter 5. Besides the correction of the formula of the strategic depth measure being provided in Section 4.2, the analysis of the results provided in Section 4.2.3 also introduced some new aspects about the relative deviation of the measure and the proportionality factor.

Some additional results from [11] were not further considered here, as they are more closely related to Dr. Vanessa Volz's work (e. g., regarding automatic game balancing aspects). This concerns especially the comparison of the subjective strategic depth measure to the strategic depth calculated from (nearly) *perfect playtraces*, which turned out to be much less accurate for predicting the strategic depth sensed by the players, according to [11].

Finally, parts of the work (especially from Section 4.2.1) have been used as foundation for creating an interactive exhibit, that was developed for the Z Quadrat GmbH in Mainz, Germany. The exhibit allows users to play different levels of a game (similar to the one from Figure 3.2). After each level, the knowledge used to solve the level is provided (in an HKB-like manner) together with an estimation based thereon which indicates how difficult the level was for the current user. By this means, it can be used to teach users how knowledge can be represented compactly in the form of rules with exceptions and allows the users to validate the provided strategic depth estimations against their own subjective intuitions for each level. The exhibit was accepted for the German exhibition ship *MS Wissenschaft* [50] and traveled to several cities of Germany and Austria in 2019. It was then selected for the *ScienceStation* traveling exhibition [59] (another project of the German scientific communication organization *Wissenschaft im Dialog*, WiD) and was shown at several train stations in Germany in 2019. Furthermore, it was selected by the *Deutsches Museum Bonn* (German Museum in Bonn) [24] for an exhibition on AI [48].[23]

---

[23] The exhibition was originally planned for 2020 but seemed to be delayed due to the COVID-19 pandemic; it (re)opened at May 29th, 2021 (according to [48]).

5. Enhancing Learning Agents

In the previous chapter, the approach of extracting exception-tolerant hierarchical knowledge bases (HKBs) from playtraces of different games has been used to materialize the knowledge needed by a (human) player for solving a game. Moreover, this knowledge was also used for determining a score that reflects the strategic depth that was subjectively sensed by the player agent (i.e., how "difficult" the game appeared to the agent).

In this chapter, several of these ideas are now used for enhancing the skills of learning agents. This is mainly realized by incorporating the ability of extracting knowledge bases into an artificial agent model.

More detailed, different approaches of incorporating the extraction of HKBs into the learning process of an agent will be considered: In Section 5.1, a classical reinforcement learning process [62, 68] will be accelerated by equipping the learning agent with the ability of extracting HKBs and by exploiting this knowledge during the learning process (Section 5.1.1). This approach will then be extended by also providing the agent with the ability of estimating the difficulty of the unknown environment in which it is located (Section 5.1.2). After that, the approach of extracting knowledge bases from a playtrace will be extended for learning the mechanics of an a priori unknown game (i.e., the *forward model*), that can later be exploited by state-of-the-art techniques used, e.g, for AI in games, like *monte carlo tree search* (MCTS) [21] (Section 5.2).

5.1 Accelerating an Agent's Learning Process by Knowledge Base Extraction

This section incorporates ideas from knowledge base extraction into a classical reinforcement learning agent, that is based on approaches as in [62, 68]. During the reinforcement learning process, the agent will be able to extract a knowledge base in the form of an HKB from the knowledge that was learned so far through the underlying reinforcement learning approach. The approaches that will be presented here do not rely on a specific underlying learning paradigm.

At first, it will be investigated at which point during the learning process the agent benefits the most from extracting an HKB and exploiting the contained knowledge (Section 5.1.1). After that, the approach will be completed to an agent model that is able to decide on its own, when to rely decisions on an HKB that was extracted from the knowledge learned so far by the underlying reinforcement learning approach (Section 5.2.2).

The latter will be based on the results from Section 4.2, with the idea in mind that the agent should rely its decision on an extracted HKB when the strategic depth is underneath a certain threshold (since in this case, the unknown environment appears to be simple enough to follow the rougher heuristics of the HKB instead of the learned knowledge from which it was extracted).

Finally, the HKB-based integration of a priori knowledge in the context of the agent model from Section 5.1.2 will be considered (Section 5.1.3).

5.1.1 Extracting and Exploiting HKBs during Learning

This section makes first attempts to incorporate the extraction of HKBs (as presented in Chapter 3) into a classical reinforcement learning agent [62]—i.e., a Q-learning agent [68] (see Section 2.1.7). By following [7], it will be especially investigated here whether such learning agents can benefit from extracting and exploiting HKBs. This leads to the interesting question, at which point during a learning process, the agent's benefit will be maximized?

On the one hand, if the extraction will be done too early, the knowledge learned by the Q-learning approach could still be of poor quality and thus an HKB extracted from the learning algorithm's Q-matrix might result in bad or even wrong rules and exceptions. On the other hand, if done too late, the Q-learning algorithm might have solved the problem already, rendering the extraction and exploitation of an HKB superfluous.

Basic Ideas

In psychology, *implicit* and *explicit* knowledge can be distinguished (see [27], p. 65): While implicit knowledge allows for performing a learned task, explicit knowledge also allows for materializing the knowledge about the learned task, e.g., by having an explicit model in mind that explains how to come to a solution. Such knowledge can be easily verbalized and communicated to others. In [27], p. 65, Dörner underpins this with the following example (1992, Rowohlt Taschenbuch, translated from German):

"A good example of implicit knowledge is the knowledge of a music lover, which allows him to to say: «I don't know this, but it's Mozart», without being able to tell from what exactly he recognized that it is Mozart."

Although the music lover in the provided example learned to classify the music correctly, he is not aware of the features and their respective properties from which the correct classification can be inferred.[24]

According to the ideas provided in [7], when a human is being confronted with a new unknown task to be solved (such as an a priori unknown environment in the case of an artificial agent), a learning process usually starts with some early attempts and progresses until the task is learned. At some point during the learning process, the human learner might not only be able to perform the task to be learned, but also might start to create a (simplified) explicit model of it, that comprises the knowledge about how the task can be solved in an explicit form.

In the context of artificial learning agents, *sub-symbolic* and *symbolic* approaches can be distinguished in a similar way: Sub-symbolic approaches like neural networks, that are used, e.g., as function approximators in reinforcement learning (see subsection Neural Networks as Function Approximators of Section 2.1.7), seem to have a more implicit character, as they often provide good results after learning, but are not really able to explain what has been learned. The knowledge is implicit in the sense that it is hidden in the numerous learned weights of the network. In contrast, HKBs can serve as comprehensible explicit models of learned tasks (see [41] for a study on the comprehensibility of HKBs) and, at the same time, seem to be able to reflect to some degree how humans create models, as indicated by the results of Chapter 4 in the context of games (especially those from Section 4.2).

In the following, it will be investigated, whether a reinforcement learning process benefits from explicit models in the form of HKBs that are extracted and exploited by an agent at some point during the learning process. Moreover, it will be investigated, at which point during a learning process the benefit will be maximized. This will be done in the context of two reinforcement learning scenarios that can be found similarly in reinforcement learning literature (e.g., [62]). For the latter, it will also be necessary to define, when a learning process can be considered *completed*.

Scenarios of the Experiments

To investigate whether (and if so when) during a learning process an agent can benefit from explicit knowledge, two scenarios will be considered here. In both scenarios,

---

[24] Note that in [27], Dörner also considers the inverse case, where explicit knowledge is available to a person as "theoretical" knowledge, without the person being able to apply it.

an agent is located in a two-dimensional grid world environment and has to get from a starting point to a destination. (Similar scenarios can be found, e.g., in [62] and have also been considered earlier, in Chapter 2 and Chapter 3 of this work).

Figure 5.1 shows the two grid world scenarios that are relevant for the upcoming experiments. The scenario that is represented by Figure 5.1 (b) corresponds to that of Figure 2.5 from Section 2.1.7 and is shown here again for reasons of comparability of the two scenarios considered here.

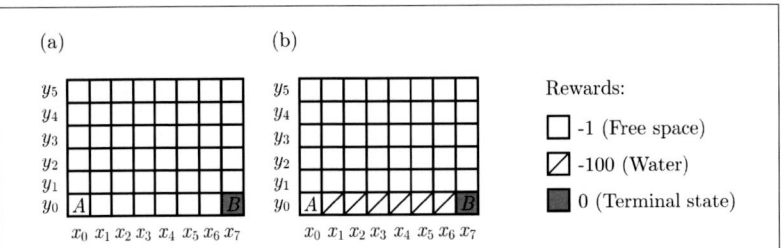

Figure 5.1 (Grid Worlds for Learning with Explicit Knowledge) (Source: a. f. [7])
In these two grid worlds scenarios, an agent has to navigate from the starting point A to the destination B. Scenario (b) corresponds to the scenario from Figure 2.5 and Scenario (a) represents a simplified version of Scenario (b). Scenario (a) can be solved by simply moving to east, whereas in Scenario (b), the agent has to navigate around the "river" in the south of the scenario. However, since both scenarios are a priori unknown to the agent, learning algorithms will need numerous iterations to explore the environment, until one of these solutions will be found.

The state-action space of the two scenarios shown in Figure 5.1 is the same as that of the scenario from Figure 2.5: The agent is equipped with two sensors for determining its x and y positions in the environment, resulting in the sensor symbol sets $\mathbb{S}_x := \{x_0, ..., x_7\}$ and $\mathbb{S}_y := \{y_0, ..., y_5\}$; the action symbol set is $\mathbb{A} := \{\text{North, South, East, West}\}$ (see also Example 2.4).

Obviously, the optimal behavior for moving from the starting point to the destination in case of Scenario (a) of Figure 5.1 is simply to move to east, resulting in the state-action sequence:

$$\mathcal{SA}_1 = \{(x_0 \wedge y_0, \text{East}), ..., (x_6 \wedge y_0, \text{East})\} \tag{5.1}$$

The optimal behavior of Scenario (b) is slightly more complex, since the agent has to learn to navigate around the highly negative rewarded area of water in the south of the scenario (as indicated by the arrows in Figure 2.5 (c)). This results in the state-action sequence:

$$\mathcal{SA}_2 = \{(x_0 \wedge y_0, \text{North}), (x_0 \wedge y_1, \text{East}), ..., (x_6 \wedge y_1, \text{East}), (x_7 \wedge y_1, \text{South})\} \tag{5.2}$$

However, since in the experiments, the environments of both scenarios are a priori unknown to the agent (with no background knowledge being involved), the reinforcement learning algorithm has to explore larger parts of the environments until it converges to the optimal policies. This requires numerous runs by the agent from the starting point A to the destination B (see Figure 2.5 (a)–(c) for getting an intuition of the improvement of the policies during the learning process). The number of such iterations until the reinforcement learning process can be considered completed will be discussed in detail in the following subsection.

Learning Process

Following [7], a classical reinforcement learning algorithm (Q-learning [68, 62]) will be used for learning an agent's multi-dimensional weight matrix Q, by starting from a zero matrix and updating their weights successively.

For this purpose, multiple runs will be performed for every scenario of Figure 5.1. In every run, the agent starts from the starting state (point A) and navigates through the environment, until it reaches the terminal state (point B). During a run, after every action, the agent is rewarded with the reward value of the subsequent state and the corresponding weight of the Q-matrix is updated according to Formula (2.2), as described in the foundations chapter (Chapter 2, see "Q-Learning" subsection of Section 2.1.7).

For the experiments, the following parameters will be used:

- The *learning rate* (determining how much of the new information will be incorporated into the old knowledge with every weight update) will be set to $\alpha := 0.1$.

- The *discount factor* (determining the degree to which the knowledge about future states is considered) will be set to $\gamma := 0.9$.

- An *exploration rate* of $\epsilon := 0.1$ will be used (determining that in 10% percent of the cases, the agent will perform a random action, even if this is not the best action according to what was already learned).

Note that the choice of the parameters should not have a large impact on the experiments, since influencing the learning speed through these parameters would also influence the quality of the extracted HKBs at a certain point during the learning process in a similar way. The same argument holds for using alternative or more advanced reinforcement learning algorithms (like SARSA [62] or modern approaches like Q-learning combined with deep convolutional neural networks, as in [49]).

To investigate at which point during the learning process of the Q-learning algorithm, the agent benefits most from extracting an HKB and relying its decisions on the HKB rather than on the Q-matrix, it must be defined at first, when a learning process can be considered *completed*. At a first glance, this might sound trivial, since an obvious answer could be to determine the end of a learning process by the first run, after which the agent found the optimal path to the terminal state. However, this is problematic, since the learning process also relies on random decisions (to explore the a priori unknown environment). Thus, the agent might only apparently behave according to the optimal policy, in case random decisions are involved in the behavior.

According to [7], a more elaborated idea will be to consider the learning process of a scenario as completed, if the policy for the optimal path from the starting point to the destination was found and is not changing anymore.[25] Since *exploration* (i. e., performing random sub-optimal actions instead of following the so far learned maximum weights of the Q-matrix) is an important prerequisite for changing a learned policy, the learning process will be considered completed, if the probability that the learned policy will change is smaller than a certain threshold. This is the case, if the following inequation holds for a minimal k (see [7]):

$$(1 - (1 - \epsilon\phi)^l)^k \leq \beta \tag{5.3}$$

where ϵ is the exploration rate (i. e., the probability for performing a random action), $\phi := 1 - \frac{1}{|A|} = 0.75$ is the conditional probability that a sub-optimal action is performed given that a random action is performed, l is the length of the state-action sequence from the starting point to the destination according to the optimal policy, k is the number of (subsequent) runs and β is the threshold for the probability that exploration was involved in producing the optimal state-action sequence from the starting point to the destination. The inner term $(1 - \epsilon\phi)^l$ of the inequation's left side reflects the probability that the agent randomly performed the optimal path through the environment; the entire left side of the inequation $(1 - (1 - \epsilon\phi)^l)^k$ reflects the probability, that this occurs in k (subsequent) runs.

For the upcoming experiments, $\beta := 0.01$ will be used, and by solving (5.3), the respective values of a minimal k can be determined for both scenarios of Figure 5.1. By having determined k for each of the scenarios, the average number of runs $\bar{r}$ that are needed to consider the learning process completed can now be determined by repeatedly running the learning process for each scenario until the agent shows the

---

[25] In [7], the policy is called *stable* in this case.

optimal path in k subsequent runs. The results will then be averaged over 200 repetitions for each scenario. Table 5.1 summarizes the resulting values of the variables considered here for each of the two test scenarios from Figure 5.1.

	opt. state-action sequence length l	subsequent opt. policy runs k	avg. number of runs $\bar{r}$
Scenario (a)	7	6	≈ 196
Scenario (b)	9	7	≈ 219

Table 5.1 (Parameters for Learning Agent Experiments) (Source: adapted from [7])
The number of subsequent optimal runs k that are needed to consider the learning process completed in the scenarios from Figure 5.1 are determined from the lengths l of the optimal state-action sequences using inequation (5.3). The average number of runs is then determined by running each scenario until k subsequent optimal runs were performed (averaged over 200 runs).

Results

Having described now when the learning process of the Q-learning agent can be considered completed in either of the two scenarios from Figure 5.1, this subsection will present the results. Still following [7], it will be presented, whether the Q-learning agent benefits from relying its decisions on explicit knowledge and, if so, at which point during the learning process the Q-learning agent can benefit most from the explicit knowledge.

For this purpose, during the Q-learning process, HKBs will be extracted after completing a run, using Algorithm 3.2:

At the beginning of the learning process, after only a couple of runs have been performed, many of the weights contained in the agent's Q-matrix are still zero (since the learning process starts from a zero matrix) or the weights represent wrong or incomplete knowledge (e. g., in case not all actions have already been tried out in a state). Thus, at the beginning of the learning process, it can be expected, that the extracted HKBs will be of rather poor quality. As the learning process progresses, the agent behavior slowly converges to the optimal policy and the extracted HKBs will become better over time.

At the end of the learning process (i. e., after ≈ 196 or ≈ 219 runs, respectively; see Table 5.1), the resulting HKBs will look as provided in Figure 5.2.

5. Enhancing Learning Agents

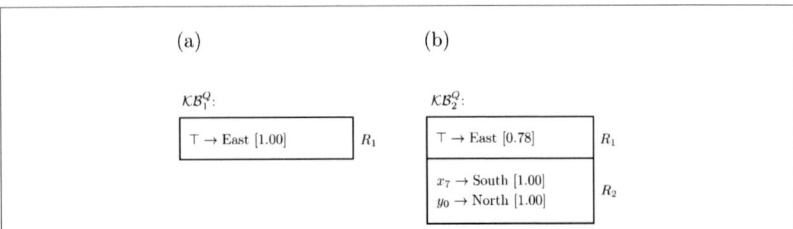

Figure 5.2 (Extracted HKBs after Completed Learning Process) (Source: a. f. [7])
The HKBs shown here represent the knowledge of the optimal state-action sequences (5.1) and (5.2) from the start to the destination in Scenario (a) and Scenario (b). The HKB $\mathcal{KB}_1^Q$ states that the agent should always move to east. $\mathcal{KB}_2^Q$ states that the agent should usually move to east, except when y_0 is perceived, then the agent should move to north or, when x_7 is perceived, then the agent should move to south (cf. Figure 5.1).

If it will be beneficial to incorporate extracted knowledge in the learning process (by relying the agent's decisions on the extracted HKBs rather than on the Q-matrix), there must be a point during the learning process, where the benefit is maximized: When extracted too early, the HKB can be of poor quality, leading to no benefit. When done too late, there might be also no benefit, since the optimal path is found by the Q-learning algorithm itself. Figure 5.3 shows the results by considering the reward of the agent when navigating through the scenarios.

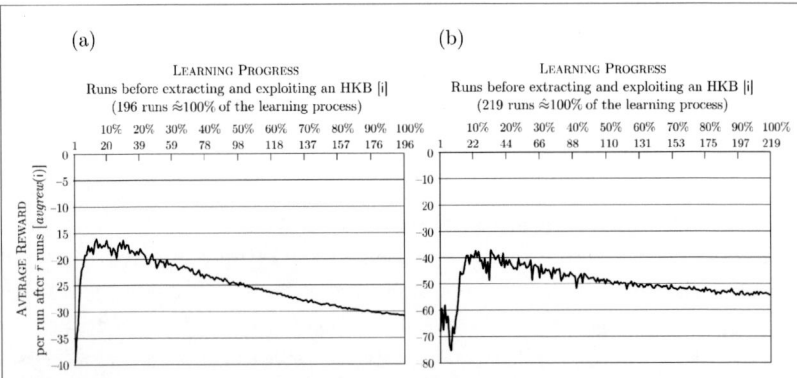

Figure 5.3 (Results for Incorporating HKBs during Learning) (Source: adapted from [7])
The plots show the average reward of the agent in Scenario (a) and Scenario (b) from Figure 5.1, when relying its (non-exploration) decisions on the extracted HKBs at some point during the learning process. It can be seen that in both scenarios, the benefit is maximized already very early, after approximately 10% to 15% of the learning process. The end of the plots denotes the performance when no HKBs are involved.

5.1 Accelerating an Agent's Learning Process by Knowledge Base Extraction

In Figure 5.3, the x-axis represents the number of runs, after which an HKB has been extracted and exploited by relying the agent's decisions on the HKB rather then on the Q-matrix. The y-axis represents the average reward collected by the agent during the simulation. The plot for Scenario (b) shows an overall larger negative reward, since this scenario has a highly negative rewarded area in the south (see Figure 5.1 (b)). This is also correspondingly reflected by the scale of the y-axis for this scenario.

The results presented in Figure 5.3 show clearly that

(1) the agent benefits from relying its decisions on the extracted HKBs (since the reward is maximized when incorporating HKBs in the learning process) and

(2) the benefit is maximized, if the HKBs are extracted and exploited very early in the learning process (after $\approx$ 10%–15% of the learning process).

This is because the HKBs allow to fall back to more general rules, in case the currently perceived sensor values do not satisfy the more specific rules—in contrast to the Q-matrix, where such default-like fall back mechanisms do not exist: Either the agent already learned about the quality of a certain action performed in a specific state (and subsequent states) by means of exploration, or there will be no information available on whether or not it is beneficial to perform the action in this state.

Furthermore, it can be seen in Figure 5.3 that the plot for Scenario (b) shows much more fluctuations (especially in the beginning) than the one from Scenario (a). This effect can be explained by Scenario (b) being more complex than Scenario (a) (the agent has to learn to navigate around the "river" in the south of the scenario here; see Figure 5.1 (b)). Thus, relying the decisions on an HKB requires the HKB to already contain some of the important rules that let the agent navigate around the "river"—otherwise this can result in large negative rewards. In an early phase of the learning process, this in turn depends on the agent's exploration, i.e., which random experiences have been made by the agent so far. In a more complex scenario, this can more easily lead to wrong decisions (especially in the beginning of the learning process) than in a scenario that follows simpler rules with less exceptions being involved. Note that the total negative reward is limited here for each of the scenarios, in case the agent gets stuck in a run due to wrongly learned rules (which could otherwise lead to infinitely high negative rewards).

Since both scenarios have a simple and clear structure, they can be solved more easily by extracting and exploiting explicit knowledge in the form of HKBs, which may serve as a rougher heuristic. Such clear structures seem to appear quite often in practice—especially in those environments that are designed by (and for) humans: Such environments are usually also created following simple rules, such as streets, that are usually build straight (where possible), or games, whose game mechanics are designed as simple as possible to realize the intended game play.

In the following section, this will be underpinned by applying the presented approach to further scenarios, including a game from the GVGAI competition [52]. The approach will also be further developed to an agent model that incorporates both implicit and explicit knowledge in the form of HKBs: This agent model will also be able to decide on its own, when to exploit an extracted HKB during a learning process, depending on the estimated complexity of the (unknown) environment (based on the measure from Section 4.2.1).

5.1.2 A Combined HKB/Reinforcement Learning Agent Model

This section presents an agent model according to [9], that extends a reinforcement learning [62] agent by the capability of extracting and exploiting HKBs during a continuously progressing learning process.

While the previous experiments from Section 5.1.1 focused on finding out at which point during the learning process a learning agent can benefit most from extracting and exploiting an HKB, here, an agent model will be presented that is able to decide on its own, when to rely the decisions on an HKB rather than on the underlying learning approach. For this purpose, the agent will be equipped with the ability of estimating the complexity of an (unknown) environment during the learning process, by using a normalized version of the strategic depth measure from Section 4.2.1.

More concretely, the agent model presented here will provide the following features:

- It will be able to extract rule-based symbolic knowledge during a reinforcement learning process (e.g., Q-learning [62, 68]; see also the subsection "Q-Learning" of Section 2.1.7).

- An agent of that model can estimate the strategic depth of its environment in dependence of its learning progress and, based on that, it can decide on its own, when to rely its decisions on an extracted HKB. (The idea here is that the less complex an environment is, the earlier the agent can rely its decisions on an extracted HKB, since a rougher HKB will suffice to adequately lead the agent through the environment.)

- The underlying learning approach can in principle be modularly exchanged by learning approaches other than Q-learning (e.g, SARSA [62] or a more modern Q-learning approach with a neural network as function approximator; see the corresponding subsection of Section 2.1.7).

Following [9], the model will be evaluated in the context of different scenarios (including a game from the GVGAI framework [52]) to show the benefit of the hybrid approach over classical Q-learning and an HKB-only approach.

Normalized Subjective Strategic Depth Measure

As already briefly mentioned in Section 4.2.1, the measure for subjective strategic depth provided by Definition 4.1 has no upper bound, since games can in principle be arbitrarily complex. However, when equipping a learning agent with the capability of estimating the strategic depth of its (a priori unknown) environment, the measure should be normalized to be in range [0;1], since the number of agent sensors can be assumed to be fixed, which limits the number of levels of an HKB—which in turn limits the maximum subjective strategic depth possible, according to Formula (4.4).

According to [9], such a normalized version of the subjective strategic depth measure will be extremely useful here, since it will allow an agent to estimate the subjective strategic depth of an a priori unknown environment in relation to the maximum subjective strategic depth possible with the agent's sensor symbol sets $\mathbb{S}_1, ..., \mathbb{S}_n$. The normalized version of the subjective strategic depth measure is defined as follows (cf. [9]):

Definition 5.1 (Normalized Subjective Strategic Depth) The normalized subjective strategic depth perceived by an agent is defined as a function

$$\bar{d}_s(\mathcal{KB}, \mathfrak{S}) := \frac{d_s(\mathcal{KB}, \mathfrak{S})}{\sum_{j=1}^{n+1} \binom{n+1}{j-1} b^{j-1}} \quad (5.4)$$

where $\mathcal{KB}$ is an HKB representing the agent's (so far learned) state-action sequence through its environment, $\mathfrak{S} := \{\mathbb{S}_1, ..., \mathbb{S}_n\}$ is a set of all sensor symbol sets needed to describe a state of the agent, $d_s(\mathcal{KB}, \mathfrak{S})$ is the non-normalized subjective strategic depth measure (as provided by Definition 4.1), $n + 1 = |\mathfrak{S}| + 1$ is the maximum number of levels of $\mathcal{KB}$ and b is the same constant as used in $d_s(\mathcal{KB}, \mathfrak{S})$ (see (4.4)).[26] □

Definition 5.1 provides the possibility of estimating the subjective strategic depth based on a state-action sequence, that was learned so far by an agent's underlying reinforcement learning approach (i. e., how difficult the problem appears to the agent

---

[26] Note that Formula (5.4) slightly differs from the original definition provided in [9], since it is adapted here to be consistent with Formula (4.4). The latter corrects its original definition from [11], where a "+1" was accidentally missing in the upper part of the binomial coefficients (see also Footnote 21 on page 115).

according to its current learning progress). Since the measure is normalized to the range of [0, 1], it provides a reference point for this estimation.

At first, as a proof-of-concept, it will be evaluated now, how the subjective strategic depth evolves during an agent's reinforcement learning process. This will be done by considering the hypothesis, that the subjective strategic depth should overall decrease during a learning process as the agent learns more about the environment. In the end, it should converge to the "real" strategic depth value of a scenario: Since the agent learns more and more about its environment, the agent's behavior (based on which the strategic depth is calculated) becomes more and more accurate and thereby approaches the optimal behavior for the environment.

For this purpose, four grid world scenarios of different complexity will be considered: Three of which have been considered already earlier in this work (e.g., in Figure 2.5, Figure 3.1 and Figure 5.1); the fourth scenario stems from [11].

Also here, in each of the four scenarios, the agent is equipped with two sensors to perceive its x and its y position in the grid world environments. Furthermore, the agent can choose actions from the action symbol set $\mathbb{A} := \{\text{North}, \text{South}, \text{East}, \text{West}\}$ to get from the starting point A to the destination B in the a priori unknown environment. A classical Q-learning [62, 68] approach will be used, with the same parameters as described in Section 5.1.1 (in subsection "Learning Process"):

- learning rate $\alpha := 0.1$
- discount factor $\gamma := 0.9$
- exploration rate $\epsilon := 0.1$

To extract the HKBs, based on which the normalized subjective strategic depth will be calculated, Algorithm 3.2 will be used. The extraction is done at the end of each run, after the terminal state is reached by the agent. Each scenario is run for 250 runs and the results are averaged over 30 repetitions for each scenario.

Figure 5.4 shows the results for measuring the normalized subjective strategic depth of the Q-learning agent in the different scenarios, while learning about the a priori unknown environment.

5.1 Accelerating an Agent's Learning Process by Knowledge Base Extraction

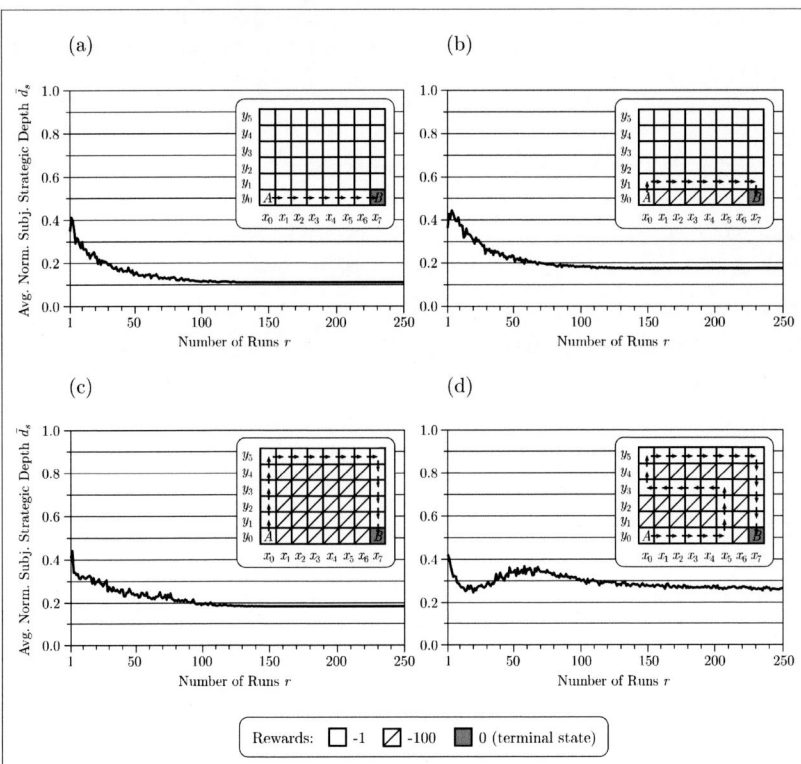

Figure 5.4 (Subjective Strategic Depth during Learning) (Source: adapted from [9])
The normalized subjective strategic depth of a reinforcement learning agent that uses Q-learning [62, 68] to learn about its environment is measured after every run in the respective grid world scenarios (averaged over 30 repetitions). The environments of the scenarios have an increasing complexity from (a) to (d). It can be seen, that in all of the four plots, the normalized subjective strategic depth decreases as the agent's learning process progresses. In plot (d), the normalized subjective strategic depth decreases less monotonically (see the text for explanation). At the end of each plot, the strategic depth converges.

Following [9], the following two effects can be observed from Figure 5.4:

- The normalized subjective strategic depth overall decreases as the agent's learning process progresses: During the agent's learning process, its knowledge about the respective environment increases, and therefore, the corresponding scenario appears successively simpler to the agent.

- The measured normalized subjective strategic depth in a scenario converges to the "real" normalized strategic depth of that scenario. (Note that here, "real" means the strategic depth calculated from a (nearly) perfect movement of the agent, assuming that the Q-learning algorithm learns the optimal policy in the end.)

In case of the fourth scenario (see Figure 5.4 (d)), the normalized subjective strategic depth decreases less monotonically, since the scenario has straight local path structures that seem to quickly lead to simple rules. However, the straight local paths form a more complex structure from a global point of view, which has to be adopted by the Q-learning algorithm, and consequently by the extracted HKB (cf. [9]).

The results of Figure 5.4 seem to confirm the hypothesis from the beginning of this subsection: The subjective strategic depth of the agent decreases during its learning process, as the agent's knowledge about the environment increases. In the end, it converges to a strategic depth that is calculated from an HKB representing the knowledge of a (nearly) optimal agent behavior in the respective scenario.

Hybrid Agent Model

By knowing from Section 4.2 that the subjective strategic depth measure relates to what humans sense when playing games, and by having shown in the previous subsection that the measure can also be applied in the context of learning agents, this subsection now describes an agent model, that incorporates the measure together with both reinforcement learning and reasoning based on extracted HKBs. This will be realized, by using the subjective strategic depth measure to decide when to rely the agent's decisions directly on the reinforcement learning process and when to rely them on an extracted HKB.

The intuition is as follows here: If at a certain point, the agent realizes (based on the subjective strategic depth) that its environment seems to be sufficiently simple, the decision-making will be switched to extracted HKBs. By this, the rules of an extracted HKB can be exploited as a rougher heuristics through the environment. This apparently applies better to environments that are based on straight and simple rules, which renders the subjective strategic depth measure an eligible criterion here. Especially human-designed environments (like games, street networks, buildings, etc.), are usually created with a simple and functional design in mind where possible (as already discussed at the end of the Results subsection of Section 5.1.1).

Note that, during a learning process, both the agent's so far learned knowledge about the environment, as well as the strategic depth of the environment itself, must be taken into account here: In an early phase of the learning process, a simple environment may appear more complex than it is to the agent, as well as complex environment may appear simple, in case the agent spend enough learning time in it. As

5.1 Accelerating an Agent's Learning Process by Knowledge Base Extraction

the subjective strategic depth measure overall decreases during the learning process (which reflects the agent's knowledge gain) and converges in the end (which reflects the "intrinsic" strategic depth of the environment; see Figure 5.4), both aspects seem to be adequately reflected by the subjective strategic depth measure.

According to [9], the agent model comprises two major parts:

- An *initialization part*, that is executed every time before a new run starts.
- The *agent cycle*, which is executed in every time step.

Figure 5.5 visualizes the agent model.

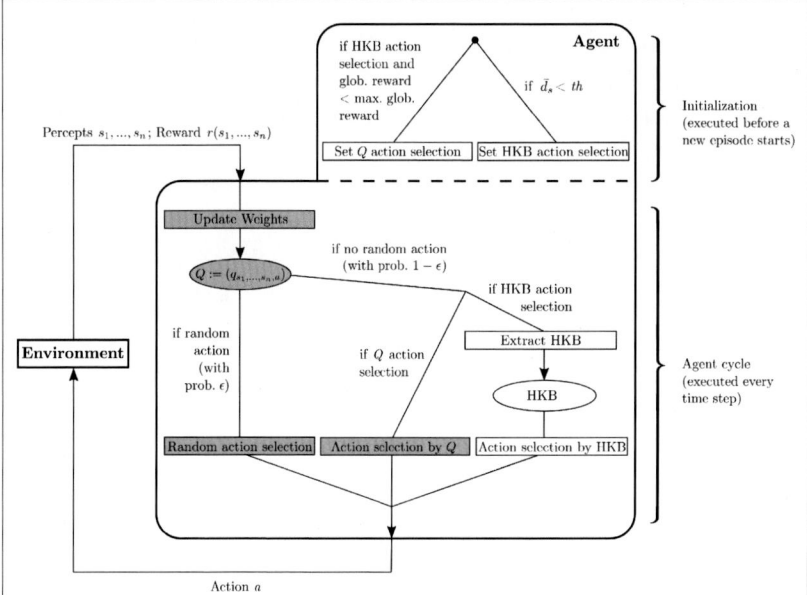

Figure 5.5 (Hybrid Reinforcement Learning/HKB Agent Model) (Source: a. f. [9])
The agent model comprises two major parts: The upper part concerns the *initialization*, which is executed every time before a new run starts; the lower part represents the *agent cycle*, which is executed in every time step. Components belonging to the reinforcement learning approach are shaded gray, whereas the HKB heuristics extensions are represented in white.

In the initialization part, at the beginning of a run, it is decided for the upcoming run whether the agent will rely its decisions on the weights learned so far by the used reinforcement learning approach (represented by the Q-matrix), or on the HKB $\mathcal{KB}$ extracted thereof. The decision is based on a threshold th of the agent's current

139

normalized subjective strategic depth $\bar{d}_s(\mathcal{KB}, \mathfrak{S})$, that is calculated from the current extracted $\mathcal{KB}$. Depending on the outcome of the initialization, in the agent cycle, the agent either performs a random action (for exploring the environment), or decides to choose an action based on the learned weights (represented by Q) or the extracted HKB $\mathcal{KB}$.

Note that the Q-learning approach (gray components in Figure 5.5), can be replaced in a modular way by any other reinforcement learning approach. This will neither require to change the overall architecture nor to adapt the HKB extraction. In general, it can be assumed here, that the earlier the used reinforcement learning approach converges to the optimal policy, the earlier the knowledge of the extracted HKB will be of sufficient quality and serve as eligible heuristics.

Following [9], the described agent model from Figure 5.5 will now be evaluated in the upcoming two subsections: At first, the model will be evaluated in the context of four grid world scenarios. After that, an additional evaluation in two slightly modified levels of the game *Camel Race* from the GVGAI framework [52] (see Figure 4.1 (a) and (b)) will be provided.

Evaluation in Grid Worlds

This subsection evaluates the agent model described in the previous section by closely following [9]: An agent instance of the agent model from Figure 5.5 will be run for 50 runs in each of the four grid world scenarios from Figure 5.4. This experiment will be repeated 200 times for each scenario and the percentage will be measured, in how many of the repetitions the optimal path was found during the 50 runs. The state-action space of the agent is the same as described earlier for the scenarios of Figure 5.4. As reinforcement learning approach, Q-learning [62, 68] will be used again, with the same parameters as described at the beginning of Section 5.1.2 in the subsection "Normalized Subjective Strategic Depth Measure" (i. e., learning rate $\alpha := 0.1$, discount factor $\gamma := 0.9$ and exploration rate $\epsilon := 0.1$).

To determine when to exploit an extracted HKB as eligible heuristics, a threshold of $th := 0.2$ will be chosen for the the normalized subjective strategic depth $\bar{d}_s$. According to the results from Figure 5.4 (and still following [9]), this means that the agent will *in average* try to exploit an extracted HKB after:

- ≈25 runs, in case of Scenario (a)
- ≈75 runs, in case of Scenario (b)
- ≈100 runs, in case of Scenario (c)

(see the crossings of the 0.2 bound in Figure 5.4).

5.1 Accelerating an Agent's Learning Process by Knowledge Base Extraction

According to [9], for Scenario (b) and Scenario (c), this may appear confusing at a first glance, since a total number of only 50 runs will be performed: Note that Figure 5.4 shows the *average* development of the measure $\bar{d}_s$ and thus, it can be expected that there will be single runs during the experiments, where $\bar{d}_s$ falls below the threshold $th := 0.2$ before the 50th run in these scenarios (even if in average this usually happens later).

In case of Scenario (d), the agent will usually never exploit any heuristics, since the normalized subjective strategic depth does in average not decrease below $th := 0.2$. (However, also here it may in principle occur that it does in single runs.) This can be interpreted as follows, according to [9]: Scenario (d) comprises too many exceptions, such that an exploitation of heuristics does not make sense from the agent's point of view. The sensitivity to this "point of view" is finally what is controlled by the parameter th. Higher values render the agent more "heuristics-affine", whereas lower values render the agent more "conservative" in the sense that it will need stronger evidence that it might be beneficial to exploit the extracted HKB as a heuristics. Note that Scenario (d) is of course a very simple environment from an absolute point of view. However, the agent measures the subjective strategic depth in a normalized way, i.e., in relation to the maximum subjective strategic depth possible with the agent's number of sensors and the resulting state space (see the denominator of Formula (5.4)).

Table 5.2 now provides the results of the comparison of the described agent model against a plain Q-learning agent with the same parameters for the learning components (gray components in Figure 5.5).

	plain Q-learning	with HKBs ($th := 0.2$)	HKBs only
Scenario (a)	3.5%	66.5%	43.0%
Scenario (b)	4.5%	20.0%	10.0%
Scenario (c)	0.0%	10.5%	0.03%
Scenario (d)	0.0%	0.0%	0.0%

Table 5.2 (Plain Q-Learning vs HKB Approach) (Source: a. f. [9])
A plain Q-learning [62, 68] agent is compared to the agent model from Figure 5.5 in the context of the four grid world scenarios shown in Figure 5.4: The results are provided for a threshold of $th := 0.2$ and for an HKBs-only approach (see footnote on page 142), where the weights of the Q-matrix are never considered directly for action selection. The agent model clearly outperforms plain Q-learning in scenarios (a)–(c).

The results shown in Table 5.2 comprise a plain Q-learning agent, an agent using extracted HKBs as heuristics (see Figure 5.5) and, for reasons of comparison, an HKBs-only version of the latter.[27] The HKBs-only version always relies its decisions on the HKB-heuristics and never considers the Q-matrix directly for any action selection (i.e., in the initialization phase in Figure 5.5, the branch for "Set HKB action selection" is always selected).

The results show that the plain Q-learning agent rarely manages to reach the target point B within 50 runs in Scenario (a) and Scenario (b) (only in about 3.5% and 4.5% of the cases, respectively). As for Scenario (c) and Scenario (d), plain Q-learning was never able to reach the target point within 50 runs. This is a typical agent behavior in the context of reinforcement learning approaches, since the a priori unknown environment needs to be explored without the possibility of distinguishing between simpler or more complex environments.

The heuristics approach based on HKBs clearly outperforms the results of the plain Q-learning approach: Using a threshold of $th := 0.2$, the agent reaches in more than two-thirds of the cases the target point B within 50 runs in case of Scenario (a). This performance gain naturally decreases, as the scenarios become more complex, since it will take longer until the extracted HKBs are of sufficient quality to be exploited. However, even in Scenario (b) and Scenario (c), the agent reaches the target in about 20% and 10.5% of the cases (whereas the plain Q-learning agent reaches the target only in about 4.5% and 0% of the cases in the respective scenarios). (Only in Scenario (d), none of the approaches were able to reach the target within 50 runs. Note that, according to Figure 5.4 (d), $\bar{d}_s$ will rarely fall below the threshold th here and thus the extracted HKBs can rarely be exploited in this scenario.)

In case of the heuristics-only approach, the results are worse (but still better than the plain Q-learning approach in the considered scenarios): According to [9], this seems to be the case, since the agent starts too early to rely its action selection on the HKBs (which may contain a lot of wrong rules in the beginning of the learning process). This can counteract the adequate exploration of the environment, which underpins the usefulness of applying an adaptive decision criterion when to exploit the extracted HKBs, as provided by the measure $\bar{d}_s$.

Evaluation in a GVGAI Game

After having evaluated the proposed agent model from Figure 5.5 in different grid world scenarios of increasing complexity, this subsection will now additionally evaluate the agent model in the context of more dynamic scenarios, following [9]. For this

---

[27] Thanks to an anonymous reviewer of the original paper [9] for proposing the idea of evaluating also against a version of the agent model that relies its decisions only on the HKB heuristics.

purpose, the two (slightly modified) levels of the game *Camel Race* from the GVGAI framework [52], that were shown already in Figure 4.1 (a) and (b), will be considered as environments here.

As described already earlier in Chapter 4 (see Section 4.1.1), in the selected (and slightly modified) levels of the game Camel Race, the agent controls the yellow camel in the middle and has to be the first reaching the goals on the right (see Figure 4.1). The state-action space of the agent for the game Camel Race will be the same as described earlier in Section 4.1.2: The action space will be defined as in Formula (4.1) and state space will be the same as provided by Formula (4.2). As reward, in the upcoming experiments, the agent will perceive the *current distance in x-direction to the fastest opponent camel*.

Even if the game of Camel Race seems to be quite simple, it comprises interesting aspects regarding its dynamics, according to [9]: Due to the time-dependent movement of the opponent camels in the environment, the agent oftentimes perceives new and previously unseen states. Thus, larger parts of the state-action space have to be explored by the agent to learn the respective weights of the Q-matrix, although the game could be won quite easily, e.g., by just moving to the right, in case of the first level. This renders the game Camel Race an eligible test environment for the upcoming experiments.

Similar to the evaluation in the context of the grid world scenarios and still following [9], 100 runs will be performed for each of the two levels and it will be measured, in how many percent of the cases, the agent is able to reach the goal within 30 repetitions of the respective experiment. Also here, plain Q-learning is compared against the agent model from Figure 5.5 with the extracted HKBs being exploited in dependence of the measure $\bar{d}_s$ and against the HKBs-only approach (where the agent always exploits the extracted HKBs as heuristics). The parameters of the agent model are the same as for the experiments in the context of the grid worlds (i.e., learning rate $\alpha := 0.1$, discount factor $\gamma := 0.9$, exploration rate $\epsilon := 0.1$ and the threshold for the $\bar{d}_s$ measure is set to the value $th := 0.2$).

Table 5.3 shows the results for the two levels of the game Camel Race shown in Figure 4.1 (a) and (b).

	plain Q-learning	with HKBs ($th := 0.2$)	HKBs only
Scenario (a)	0.0%	63.3%	66.0%
Scenario (b)	0.0%	53.3%	60.0%

Table 5.3 (Q-Learning vs HKB Approach in a Game) (Source: a. f. [9])
The plain Q-learning agent and the agent model from Figure 5.5 with the same parameters as in Table 5.2 are compared here in the context of two levels of the game Camel Race from the GVGAI framework [52]. The table shows the percentage of 30 repetitions in which the agent was able to reach the goal within 100 runs. The agent model involving HKBs clearly outperforms plain Q-learning by reaching the goal in more than 50% percent of the cases in both levels.

As can be seen in Table 5.3, the agent using plain Q-learning is not able to reach the goal within 100 runs in any of the 30 repetitions. By using the agent model from Figure 5.5 with a threshold of $th := 0.2$, the agent model clearly outperforms plain Q-learning by reaching the goal in more than 50% of the cases in both levels. In contrast to the grid worlds, the HKBs-only approach performs even better here: According to [9], this seems to be the case, since the considered levels allow for rougher heuristics than most of the grid worlds: Although the game comprises—in contrast to the grid worlds—dynamics and can be considered more complex in this sense, the goal can be reached much easier than in the grid world scenarios, since it is not located in a single corner of the environment. Instead, the game can be won by just reaching the right side of the screen, which can be achieved already with a poor HKB as heuristics.

The results presented in this section show that the agent model clearly outperforms plain Q-learning in the context of the presented experiments. These results are accompanied by an online (video) appendix (Appendix B), where the two approaches are compared visually.

5.1.3 Integrating A Priori Knowledge through HKBs

This section finally provides some intuitions on how HKBs can be used to integrate a priori knowledge in a reinforcement learning process. For this purpose, it will be referred again to the agent model described in Section 5.1.2 (see also Figure 5.5).

Basic Integration Approach

To integrate heuristics as a priori knowledge, an agent instance of the agent model from Figure 5.5 can simply start with a predefined HKB that represents the a priori known heuristics. Furthermore, it must be ensured that the agent starts with HKB action selection in this case, to rely its decisions on the provided a priori knowledge in the first run (see the right side of the initialization phase in Figure 5.5).

When combining symbolic a priori knowledge with a reinforcement learning approach, an interesting question is, how the a priori knowledge can be properly reflected in the weights of the underlying learning approach. This is not a trivial question since the reward distribution of the environment could (at least partly) be unknown to the knowledge engineer who is defining the a priori knowledge. As a consequence, the provided a priori knowledge can even contradict the rewards returned by the environment, e.g., in case it is exploited as heuristics and contributes well to reach a long-term goal, but leads to locally bad rewards in some situations. Furthermore, the used learning approach could not allow for the direct manipulation of the weights, e.g., in case a neural network is used as function approximator for approximating the Q-matrix (as it is usually the case in modern deep reinforcement learning approaches, e.g., [49]).

The presented agent model from Section 5.1.2 avoids these problems by not explicitly manipulating the weights of the Q-matrix to incorporate the knowledge: Performing actions based on an HKB simply leads to normal updates of the weights, as needed by the underlying learning approach (see Figure 5.5). By this, the update mechanism is not influenced numerically by the provided a priori knowledge, besides the rewards perceived through the environment when performing actions according to the HKB. Thus, the rewards perceived from the environment as a consequence of decisions derived from the a priori knowledge are incorporated the same way by the learning approach as without any knowledge being involved. This basically leads to the following three cases:

(1) *The heuristics described by the a priori knowledge fit well to both the long-term goal of the agent and local rewards*:
For those states that are visited by the agent in the first runs, the provided a priori knowledge will be properly reflected in the corresponding weights of the underlying learning approach.

(2) *The heuristics described by the a priori knowledge are good in the sense of a long-term goal but contradict local rewards*:
In this case, the agent learns about the environment according to the underlying learning approach until a policy derived from the weights outperforms the

policy derived from the heuristics. If this is the case, the new (refined) heuristics are extracted from the best policy found and the heuristics and the learning approach are consistent again.

(3) *The provided a priori knowledge is bad (or even wrong)*:
In this case, performing actions according to this knowledge will usually lead to bad local rewards in the visited states of the first run(s) (and will not get significantly better over multiple iterations, in case the provided heuristics even contradict the long-term goal). Thus, the agent will avoid these states in upcoming runs which will successively lead to a better overall performance and can finally result in finding other, better heuristics (cf. Figure 5.6).

Advanced Integration

As a further extension, one could also be interested in incorporating the provided a priori knowledge into a larger portion of the weights than only those concerned by *one single state-action trace* of the first run in which the a priori knowledge was exploited (as described in the previous section).

Here, an intuitive idea is to additionally exploit the provided a priori knowledge in *all states* in which no meaningful decision could be made by the learning approach— i.e., in all new, previously unseen states and in all those states in which the weights of all possible actions are equal. This triggers the update mechanism of the underlying reinforcement learning approach with the reward returned by the environment for those actions selected according to the a priori knowledge. Depending on how well the heuristics resulting from the a priori knowledge comply with the reward distribution of the environment, these updates are then a (more or less) adequate initialization of the corresponding weights of the learning approach. This reflects the a priori knowledge in the reinforcement learning approach as far as it is compatible with the reward distribution of the environment. Furthermore, as the number of unknown states usually decreases during the learning process, the provided a priori knowledge gets less influence on the overall behavior of the agent, whereas the refined knowledge representing the heuristics found by the agent itself gets more influence over time.

Nevertheless, since this extension requires access to the information whether or not a state is visited for the first time, it could possibly not be combined with all subsymbolic learning approaches.

Figure 5.6 shows the evolution of a priori knowledge provided as HKB during a learning process of an agent based on the agent model from Figure 5.5. The agent is run in the context of the third level of the game Camel Race (see Figure 4.1 (b)) with the same state-action space and reward as in the last subsection of Section 5.1.2 (see also (4.1) and (4.2) in Section 4.1.2).

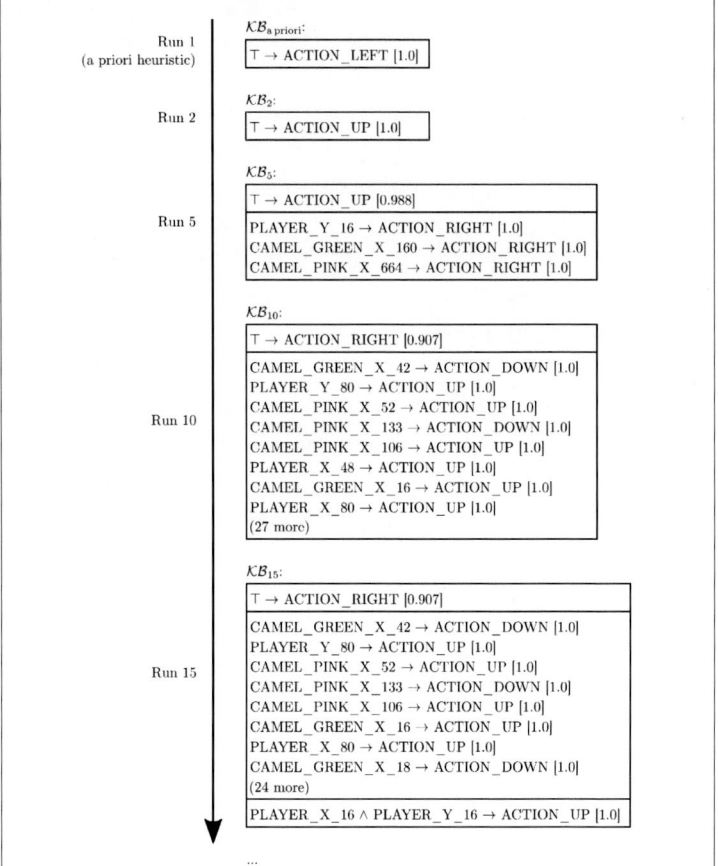

Figure 5.6 (Knowledge Evolution during Learning Process)
An agent based on the agent model from Figure 5.5 is considered here in a slightly modified version of the game Camel Race from the GVGAI framework (see Figure 4.1 (b)): To demonstrate how the knowledge evolves, the agent is intentionally provided with contra-intuitive a priori knowledge consisting of the heuristic to move to the left. The advanced integration approach described in the corresponding subsection of Section 5.1.3 is used here. The figure shows the evolution of the HKB over the first 15 runs. It can be seen that the a priori knowledge develops quickly toward the correct heuristic to move to the right, which is then successively refined.

To demonstrate the development of the knowledge during the learning process, in Figure 5.6, the agent starts with an HKB as a priori knowledge that represents the contra-intuitive heuristic to move to the left (cf. Figure 4.1 (b)). After a few runs, the HKB already starts evolving toward the intuitive knowledge of moving to the right: At first, the top level rule changes to $\top \to$ ACTION_UP and the intuitive knowledge of moving to the right is contained in the form of exceptions on the more specific levels of the HKB (see Run 5 in Figure 5.6). Several runs later, the movement to the right is learned as a general rule, which is then successively refined with exceptions (and exceptions of exceptions) in the following (see Run 10 and Run 15 in Figure 5.6).

5.2 Forward Model Learning

In the previous section (Section 5.1), it has been shown how the learning process of an agent based on a reinforcement learning approach can be accelerated to solve a single task (e.g., a level of a game). The idea there was to learn an (optimal) behavior or policy in the respective environment. This complies with other successful approaches in reinforcement learning from the recent years—especially in the context of games (e.g., [49]).

However, these kinds of approaches have a drawback in generality, when it comes to problems like *general video game playing* [52, 53], where the task is not to learn to play a single (level of a) game, but to learn to play multiple different a priori unknown games. The GVGAI competition [65] aims at stimulating research in this field and results might also be interesting for the development of more general AI approaches in other areas.

Regarding the task of general video game playing, the GVGAI competition can be mainly divided into two tracks:

- a planning track, and
- a learning track.

In the former, an agent is provided with a *forward model* of the game, i.e., the agent knows the game mechanics in advance and can thereby perform *forward simulations* of a game to find good decisions and/or plans to win the game. Algorithms like *monte carlo tree search* (MCTS) [21] and their derivatives are a popular choice here.

In the latter, no forward model is a priori provided to the agent. Depending on the rules of the competition's current round, an agent is, e.g., trained on three levels of an a priori unknown game and is then evaluated on two other levels of the same game. As a consequence, it is not sufficient to optimize a certain level using a common learning algorithm—instead, the agent must learn how to play the game, i.e., both the game mechanics and the strategy how to master it.

According to these requirements, this section follows a different approach than the the approaches presented in Section 5.1: Instead of learning and representing an (optimal) behavior or policy of an agent, here, a forward model of the game will be learned and represented as an HKB. Such an HKB describes the mechanics of the game (i.e., "how things work") and can be used by the agent to perform forward simulations of the game for estimating the best next action, by using eligible algorithms known from the planning track (like MCTS [21]).[28]

5.2.1 Learning Forward Models of Games

This section addresses the issue of learning forward models in the context of a priori unknown games from the GVGAI framework [52]. To be able to learn forward models of such games, the same basic agent model as described in Section 2.1 will be considered as a foundation. In contrast to former approaches that were presented earlier here, this means that the agent is equipped with n sensors, where each sensor provides values of one dimension from a *general* state space. Since the game to be played is not known in advance, the corresponding sensor symbol sets $\mathbb{S}_1, ..., \mathbb{S}_n$ comprise rather abstract symbols, such as *types of objects* near the agent's avatar (distinguished by numeric identifiers) as well as symbols about the avatar's *position* or the game's *score*. No concrete game-specific information are provided here. The agent's action symbol set is defined similarly as in Section 4.1.2 (see Formula 4.1), with an additional generic action ACTION_USE, which is usually used (depending on the game) for non-navigation actions:[29]

$$\mathbb{A}^+ := \{\text{ACTION\_UP}, \text{ACTION\_DOWN}, \text{ACTION\_LEFT},$$
$$\text{ACTION\_RIGHT}, \text{ACTION\_USE}, \text{ACTION\_NIL}\} \quad (5.5)$$

---

[28] This approach was first proposed in a joint work by Jun.-Prof. Dr.-Ing. Alexander Dockhorn (from Leibniz University Hannover) and the author. The approach was also mentioned in the book on GVGAI [53]—see bibliographic remarks in Section 5.4 for details.

[29] Note that, in the GVGAI framework [52], another action ACTION_ESCAPE exists, which allows an agent to immediately exit a level in the training phase. Since this is not directly relevant for the learning problem of playing different games, it is not explicitly considered here.

HKBs as Forward Models

Learning a forward model in the form of an HKB is different from learning an HKB that represents a behavior or a policy (as described in Section 5.1): An HKB representing a behavior or a policy maps a perceived state to an action, whereas an HKB representing a forward model maps a perceived state and an action (a *state-action conjunction*) to an information describing certain changes of a resulting subsequent state. For this purpose, the definition of a rule, as provided in Section 3.1.2 (cf. Definition 3.2), has to be adapted here, following [5, 26]:

Definition 5.2 (Forward Model Complete/Generalized Rule) *Forward model complete rules* and *forward model generalized rules* are of the form $p \wedge a \to p'\ [w]$, (i.e., "if p and a are known, then p' can be concluded"), where p is either a *complete state* (in case of a *forward model complete rule*) or a *partial state* (in case of a *forward model generalized rule*), $a \in \mathbb{A}$ represents an action of the agent's action symbol set $\mathbb{A}$, p' represents (a part of) the changes leading to the subsequent state (resulting from action a being performed in state p) and $w \in \mathbb{R}$ is the rule's weight (indicating the "strength" of the rule).[30] □

Note that the related definitions 3.3–3.5 from Section 3.1.2 can be considered compatible to Definition 5.2 by simply adapting the rules' premises and conclusions accordingly there.

To learn an HKB as forward model from observations using the extraction algorithms described in Section 3.4 and Section 3.5, an additional filter step will be performed at the end of the extraction algorithms for removing all rules $\rho \in R_{j>1}$ whose premises do not contain an action and therefore do not comply with Definition 5.2.

Meta-HKB

According to [5, 26], in the context of diverse games, several different aspects of the game mechanics can be of importance. To properly reflect these different aspects, one separate HKB for one aspect of the game mechanics will be considered here. These HKBs then form a *meta-HKB* representing the forward model. Following [5], the selected aspects of the game mechanics that are covered by the different HKBs are:

- *Movement* ($\mathcal{KB}_{\text{move}}$): The HKB $\mathcal{KB}_{\text{move}}$ represents the knowledge about the possible movement of the agent's avatar depending on the *relative* position of surrounding other objects in a game (like obstacles, etc.).[31]

---

[30] In [5, 26], *forward model rules* are simply called *modified rules*.

- *Scoring* ($\mathcal{KB}_{\text{score}}$): This HKB represents knowledge about relative score changes depending on the interaction with other objects in a game (like objects that can be collected for benefit).

- *Winning/Losing* ($\mathcal{KB}_{\text{win}}$): $\mathcal{KB}_{\text{win}}$ represents knowledge about winning or losing a game when interacting with certain objects (e. g., an exit or a checkered flag).

Each of the three HKBs for the different aspects of a game's mechanics will be created by merging several smaller HKBs, to accelerate the extraction process. This will be described in detail in the following subsection.

Accelerating HKB Creation by Merging Smaller HKBs

In the context of games—and especially in the context of the GVGAI competition—performance plays an important role. For this purpose, instead of learning one HKB as a complete forward model for one aspect of a game's mechanics, for each HKB of the meta-HKB described in the previous subsection, multiple smaller HKBs will be learned here, as proposed in [5, 26]. Each of the smaller HKBs covers only a part of the agent's state-action space. This reduces the number of dimensions that need to be considered by the extraction algorithm, which helps increasing the extraction performance. The resulting smaller HKBs are then *merged* to create the complete HKB that represents the respective aspect of a game's mechanics.

The merging of the smaller HKBs to create the complete HKB that represents one aspect of the game's mechanics can be done efficiently by iterating over the levels of the smaller HKBs and merging the single levels. In case a rule with the same premise and conclusion exists in multiple smaller HKBs, the one with the lower weight will be adopted.

The following example demonstrates the creation of the HKB $\mathcal{KB}_{\text{score}}$, which describes the knowledge about the score changes of the game to be learned (i. e., which actions result in which score changes considering the orientation of the agent's avatar and the types of objects currently surrounding it). The creation process is very similar for the other two HKBs of the meta-HKB ($\mathcal{KB}_{\text{move}}$ and $\mathcal{KB}_{\text{win}}$), as described in the previous subsection. (The example can be found similarly in [5] and [26].)

---

[31] Note that knowledge about the movement depending on the *absolute* position of game objects are not considered here, since, according to the ideas of general video game playing, the agent might be trained in levels that are different from the ones used for evaluation. Thus, the levels' anatomy (like bounding walls or obstacles) may change, even in case of static objects.

5. Enhancing Learning Agents

Example 5.1 (Merging of Smaller HKBs for Scoring) To create the HKB $\mathcal{KB}_{\text{score}}$ that describes the knowledge about the game's scoring mechanism, according to [5, 26], one possibility would be to apply the knowledge base extraction algorithm from Section 3.4.2 (Algorithm 3.2) to a seven-dimensional input matrix

$$Q_{\text{score}} := (q_{s_{\text{above}}, s_{\text{below}}, s_{\text{left}}, s_{\text{right}}, s_{\text{orient}}, a, s_{\text{score}}}) \tag{5.6}$$

with $s_{\text{above}}, s_{\text{below}}, s_{\text{left}}, s_{\text{right}} \in \mathbb{S}_{\text{obj}}$, $s_{\text{orient}} \in \mathbb{S}_{\text{orient}}$, $a \in \mathbb{A}$ and $s_{\text{score}} \in \mathbb{S}_{\text{score}}$. The set $\mathbb{S}_{\text{obj}}$ is a set of object type symbols identifying the different object types in a game, $\mathbb{S}_{\text{orient}}$ is a set of symbols representing the different possible orientations of the agent's avatar, set $\mathbb{A}$ contains the agent's action symbols (see Formula (5.5)) and $\mathbb{S}_{\text{score}}$ is a set of symbols describing the score changes of a game. Every element of Q_{score} represents the relative frequency of a score change, when performing a certain action in a given state (i.e., the agent avatar's orientation and the types of objects above, below, to the left and to the right of the agent's avatar).

However, instead of creating the complete HKB $\mathcal{KB}_{\text{score}}$ directly from the seven-dimensional matrix Q_{score}, four smaller HKBs $\mathcal{KB}_{\text{score}}^{\text{above}}$, $\mathcal{KB}_{\text{score}}^{\text{below}}$, $\mathcal{KB}_{\text{score}}^{\text{left}}$ and $\mathcal{KB}_{\text{score}}^{\text{right}}$ can be created. Each of these smaller HKBs will consider (besides the agent's actions and the orientation of the avatar) only the type of the corresponding object above, below, to the left or to the right of the agent's avatar. The smaller HKBs can be created more efficiently by applying Algorithm 3.2 to a corresponding reduced version of the input matrix, where the dimensions for all other surrounding objects are omitted (resulting in four instead of seven dimensions for each matrix). In case of $\mathcal{KB}_{\text{score}}^{\text{above}}$, the corresponding reduced input matrix will look as follows:

$$Q_{\text{score}}^{\text{above}} := (q_{s_{\text{above}}, s_{\text{orient}}, a, s_{\text{score}}})$$

with $s_{\text{above}}, s_{\text{orient}}, a$ and s_{score} as in (5.6).

After having extracted each of the four smaller HKBs from the reduced matrices using Algorithm 3.2 (including the optional filter step for removing all rules without actions in their premises), the resulting HKBs are merged to create the complete HKB $\mathcal{KB}_{\text{score}}$ by iterating over the levels of the smaller HKBs and merging the single levels. (In case of multiple rules on the same level having the same premise and conclusion, the rule with the minimal weight is kept.) □

As already mentioned before, the HKBs for the knowledge about the movement and for the knowledge about winning/losing a game can be created in a similar way. By this means, the knowledge base extraction process can be accelerated extensively.

Demonstration in the Context of the GVGAI Framework

To demonstrate the approach of learning a forward model of an a priori unknown game using HKBs, in this subsection, the game *Butterflies* from the GVGAI framework [52] will be considered as an example. The rules that are most relevant for the upcoming considerations will be quickly outlined first.

In this game, the agent controls an avatar represented by a fairy, that has to collect butterflies by touching them. The butterflies emerge from hives. Trees serve as obstacles and to delimit the bounds of a level. Collecting a butterfly increases the agent's score and the game is won if all butterflies are collected. Figure 5.7 shows one of the game's levels.

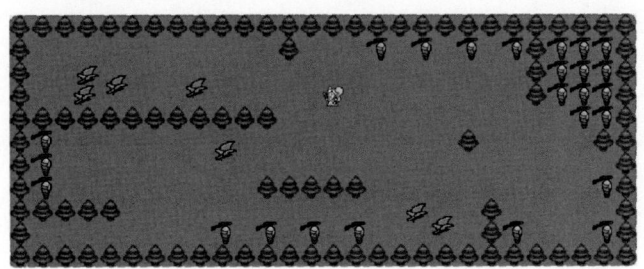

Figure 5.7 (Butterflies Game) (Source: GVGAI framework [52])
A level of the game *Butterflies* from the GVGAI framework [52], where the agent has to collect the butterflies by touching them with the fairy avatar in the upper middle of the scene. The butterflies emerge from the hives and the trees serve as obstacles and as bounds of the level. Collecting a butterfly increases the score; the game is won if all butterflies are collected.

The game shown in Figure 5.7 comprises three different types of objects that can be perceived by the agent in the surrounding area of its avatar. These are:

- butterflies (which increase the score when being collected and which lead to winning the game if all are collected)
- hives (which emit butterflies)
- trees (which prevent the avatar's movement)

The different types of objects are distinguished by numeric identifiers.

Furthermore, besides the current position of the agent's avatar, the agent is also able to perceive the game's overall state, i.e., whether or not the game has been won.

5. Enhancing Learning Agents

Since the game is a priori unknown to the agent, the agent has to learn the mentioned game mechanics on its own. For this purpose, the agent starts with random exploration by performing random actions, to learn relative frequencies for the states and the resulting subsequent states. The relative frequencies are collected in corresponding (reduced) matrices, as described in the previous subsection (see Example 5.1). After that, Algorithm 3.2 is applied to each of the matrices (including the additional filter step to remove all rules without having an action in their premises) and the resulting IIKBs are merged. This is done for every aspect of the game mechanics, as described earlier in the subsection "Meta-HKB" of this section. Figure 5.8 shows the resulting learned HKBs for all three aspects of the meta-HKB after a short training phase.

As can be seen in Figure 5.8, after a short learning phase, the agent learned HKBs for the three aspects of the game's forward model that represent the game mechanics compactly and in a way that is easy to comprehend.

Figure 5.8 (a) represents the game's forward model regarding the movement of the agent's avatar. The topmost rule $\top \to x-1, y\pm 0$ on level R_1 of the HKB $\mathcal{KB}_{\text{move}}$ was not learned correctly here, since it states that usually (when performing no action), the agent's avatar moves to the left—which is obviously incorrect. This could be the case, since the agent might have experienced more examples of moving to the left than of no movement in the short learning phase. However, this has no further impact here, since on level R_2 of $\mathcal{KB}_{\text{move}}$, there are exceptions for each of the four relevant movement actions, which reflect the game's movement mechanics correctly and completely. Level R_3 of $\mathcal{KB}_{\text{move}}$ contains the (second order) exceptions concerning the obstacles in the game (trees and hives). If one of these objects (represented by object types 0 and 3) is in the adjoining environment above, below, to the left or to the right of the agent's avatar, no movement can be performed by the corresponding actions.

Figure 5.8 (b) represents the game's scoring system, i.e., how the agent can increase the score with the avatar. The HKB $\mathcal{KB}_{\text{score}}$ was properly learned and reflects the scoring mechanics perfectly: The topmost rule $\top \to \text{score}\pm 0$ on level R_1 states that usually, there is no score change (which covers most of all cases, as indicated by the rule's weight of 0.94). This is because the agent usually only gets points when collecting butterflies by intention (i.e., by performing the corresponding action when a butterfly is around). Level R_2 is empty here, since butterflies can usually not be collected by just moving around. Only in case a butterfly is in the direct environment above, below to the left or to the right of the agent's avatar, the agent can increase the score by performing the action for the corresponding direction. This is stated on the bottommost level R_3 of $\mathcal{KB}_{\text{score}}$.

5.2 Forward Model Learning

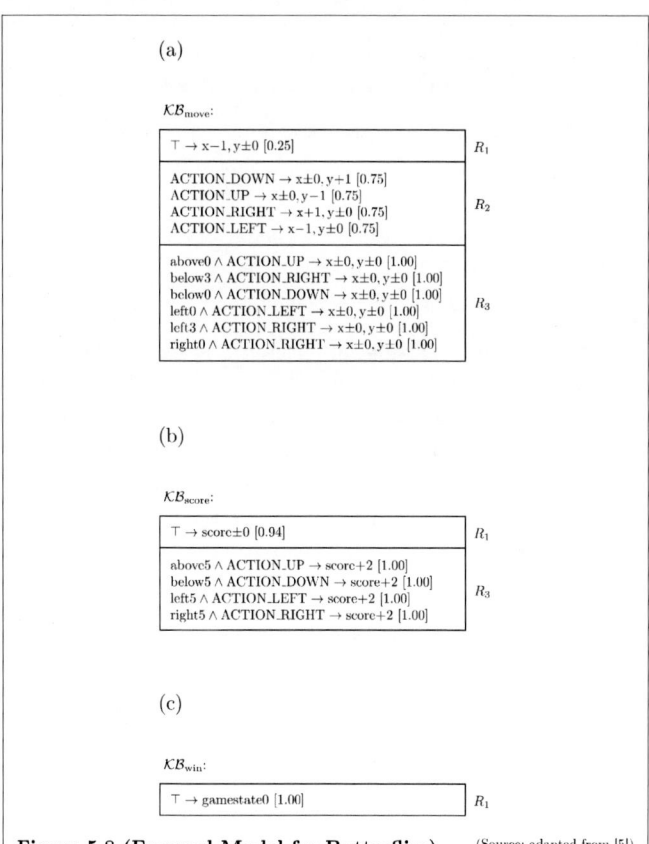

Figure 5.8 (Forward Model for Butterflies) (Source: adapted from [5])
The learned forward model for the GVGAI game *Butterflies* from Figure 5.7 is shown here after a short training phase. The three HKBs represent the three different aspects of the game mechanics: (a) how the movement works ($\mathcal{KB}_{\text{move}}$), (b) how to score ($\mathcal{KB}_{\text{score}}$) and (c) how the game can be won ($\mathcal{KB}_{\text{win}}$). In $\mathcal{KB}_{\text{move}}$, level R_2 reflects the coordinate changes depending on the agent's actions, whereas level R_3 contains the exceptions depending on different obstacles above, below, to the left or to the right of the agent's avatar (object types 0 and 3). $\mathcal{KB}_{\text{score}}$ states that usually the score does not change, except when an object of type 5 (butterfly) is around and a corresponding action is performed. $\mathcal{KB}_{\text{win}}$ does not provide useful information, since the agent never won the game in the short training phase (gamestate0).

In Figure 5.8 (c), the HKB $\mathcal{KB}_{\text{win}}$ represents the knowledge about how to win or lose the game. $\mathcal{KB}_{\text{win}}$ comprises only the topmost level R_1, which contains the only rule that the game is always lost. This is the case, since the agent never managed to win the game during the short learning phase. Thus, no further knowledge about the mechanics how to win or lose the game could be learned here.

As has been presented here, the proposed approach results in a forward model comprising different aspects of a game. Such a model can later be used to let the agent forward simulate a game, even if the game mechanics are unknown in advance to the agent. By this means, algorithms like Monte Carlo Tree Search (MCTS) [21], that are well-known from the GVGAI planning track, can be used by the agent to forward-simulate a game for determining good actions.

However, since the presented approach does not always provide perfect forward models (depending on the agent's experiences during the learning phase, cf. $\mathcal{KB}_{\text{win}}$), and since the environment may change after learning, a mechanism should be provided, that allows the agent for quickly adapting a learned forward model, when experiencing inconsistencies in its current environment (e.g., in a new level of the same game). In the context of the GVGAI competition [65], this can easily occur, since (depending on the rules of the competition's current round) the agent may be trained in other levels than those used for evaluation.

In knowledge representation, such kinds of problems can be tackled by *belief revision* approaches. This will now be considered in the context of HKB forward models in the following section.

5.2.2 Revising Forward Models of Games

Belief revision is a traditional field of knowledge representation, concerning the incorporation of new pieces of information into existing knowledge. In this sense, belief revision can be considered (with some respect) a "symbolic way of machine learning". Besides common challenges that are usually tackled by belief revision approaches, such as avoiding potential inconsistencies or the question which parts of the knowledge are affected when a piece of information has to be forgotten (see, e.g., [13] for an overview), a further interesting aspect in relation to learning agents lies in the observation that revising knowledge seems to have the potential of being much faster than "relearning" it on a sub-symbolic or statistical level: In the case of revision, the new information is usually assured to be immediately available after performing the revision. In contrast, sub-symbolic approaches often need many iterations until an agent gets "convinced" that formerly learned knowledge is no longer valid, since numeric weights (e.g., relative frequencies and the like) are usually adapted stepwise during a sub-symbolic learning process.

5.2 Forward Model Learning

In the context of the GVGAI competition [65], where a learning agent may be evaluated in other levels than those being trained in during a short evaluation phase, a faster adaption mechanism is essential for quickly adapting to the changes of a new unknown level. At the same time, larger parts of the knowledge that were learned before about the general game mechanics should be preserved. For this purpose and to further extent the capabilities of HKBs as a knowledge representation paradigm for learning agents in games, a simple yet effective revision approach for HKB forward models is presented and applied here in the context of games. (An evaluation of the approach against common quality criteria for revision approaches is provided in [5].)

Due to the origins of the idea of creating a revision approach for HKBs with respect to the requirements of the GVGAI competition (see also the bibliographic remarks in Section 5.4 for details), the revision algorithm was designed to be used in (nearly) real-time environments and therefore has to be extremely lightweight and efficient. The algorithm is based on the idea of *adding*, *removing* or *exchanging* an exception in a forward model HKB $\mathcal{KB}$, in case the reasoning algorithm $\mathfrak{R}$ (see Algorithm 3.1 in Section 3.2) provides a *wrong* result compared to what is observed by the agent.

Note that here, $\mathcal{KB}$ consists of forward model rules (see Definition 5.2) and, consequently, $\mathfrak{R}$ is provided with a state-action conjunction $st^a := s_1 \wedge ... \wedge s_n \wedge a$ (representing a state and and action performed in that state) as input, and returns an information about the resulting subsequent state st' (instead of an action). Thus, the forward model represented by $\mathcal{KB}$ has to be revised, if the returned information about the subsequent state st' does not conform to the corresponding information about the real subsequent state of the agent's environment after performing action a (i.e., if $\mathfrak{R}(\mathcal{KB}, st^a) \neq \{st'\}$).

To determine whether or not a conclusion inferred from an HKB does not conform to the corresponding information about the real subsequent state st', the revision algorithm uses at most two calls to the reasoning algorithm. (For a closer study on the efficiency of the HKB reasoning algorithm, see Krüger et al. [41].)

Whether an exception is *added*, *removed* or *exchanged* in the existing knowledge base depends on the level of an HKB $\mathcal{KB}$, on which the rule causing the wrong conclusion is located (according to [26]):

- If a rule ρ_{st^a}, that causes the wrong conclusion for a given state-action conjunction $st^a := s_1 \wedge ... \wedge s_n \wedge a$ and the subsequent state information st' is not located on level $R_{n+1} \in \mathcal{KB}$, a new exception will be *added* on level R_{n+1}.

- Otherwise, if ρ_{st^a} is located on level R_{n+1}, a new exception is only added, if *removing* the wrong exception on level R_{n+1} does not cause the reasoning algorithm to provide the correct conclusion. (In other words: The rule is *exchanged*, if removing it would not lead already to the desired conclusion.)

By this, it will be avoided that, in case of multiple revisions, the number of rules on the most specific level R_{n+1} of the HKB successively increases over time, until it degenerates to a trivial HKB (cf. Section 3.3).

Algorithm 5.1 formalizes the described approach.

Input: HKB $\mathcal{KB} := \{R_1, ..., R_{n+1}\}$, state-action conjunction $st^a := s_1 \land ... \land s_n \land a$,
  subsequent state information st'
Output: Revised HKB $\mathcal{KB}' := \{R_1, ..., R_n, R'_{n+1}\}$

```
01    % If a wrong conclusion is inferred for the given state-action conjunction
02    if {st'} ≠ ℜ(𝒦ℬ, st^a) then
03
04        % Add new exception, if firing rule not on most specific level...
05        if ρ_{st^a} ∉ R_{n+1} then    % ρ_{st^a} is the rule firing for ℜ(𝒦ℬ, st^a)
06            R_{n+1} := R_{n+1} ∪ {st^a → st' [1.0]}
07
08        % ...else remove or exchange existing exception
09        else
10            R_{n+1} := R_{n+1} \ {ρ_{st^a}}
11            if {st'} ≠ ℜ(𝒦ℬ, st^a) then
12                R_{n+1} := R_{n+1} ∪ {st^a → st' [1.0]}
13            end if
14        end if
15    end if
```

Algorithm 5.1 (Revision Algorithm for HKBs)   (Source: adapted from [26])

The algorithm calls the reasoning algorithm $\mathfrak{R}$ (Algorithm 3.1) to determine whether the HKB leads to the wrong conclusion about the subsequent state for the given state-action conjunction. A new exception is *added* on the most specific level if the wrong conclusion is produced by a rule firing on a more general level. Otherwise, an exception is *removed* if the removal causes the reasoning algorithm to infer the correct conclusion, or *exchanged* (i. e., added again after removal), if the reasoning algorithm still infers the wrong conclusion after the removal.

To assure that Algorithm 5.1 provides HKBs that adequately represent both the new information and the knowledge that has already been known before, a corresponding evaluation of the algorithm can be found in [5].

The following example will demonstrate the ideas of Algorithm 5.1 in the context of a fictive more difficult level of the game *Butterflies* from Figure 5.7):

Example 5.2 (Revising a Forward Model: Changes)   After having learned the forward model from Figure 5.8 in the context of several levels of the game Butterflies (as shown in Figure 5.7), an agent is assumed to play a (fictive) more difficult level of the game. There, collecting butterflies increases the score by just one (instead of two).

Starting from the learned forward model HKB for scoring[32]

$$\mathcal{KB}_{\text{score}} = \{\{\top \to \text{score}\pm 0 \ [0.94]\},$$
$$\emptyset,$$
$$\{\text{above5} \land \text{ACTION\_UP} \to \text{score}+2 \ [1.00],$$
$$\text{below5} \land \text{ACTION\_DOWN} \to \text{score}+2 \ [1.00],$$
$$\text{left5} \land \text{ACTION\_LEFT} \to \text{score}+2 \ [1.00],$$
$$\text{right5} \land \text{ACTION\_RIGHT} \to \text{score}+2 \ [1.00]\}\}$$

from Figure 5.8 (b), it is assumed that the agent is in a state with a butterfly (object of type 5) being above its avatar, which is represented by the sensor symbol "above5". For the avatar's orientation, the neutral sensor symbol "orientNil" is provided, since the game mechanics of the game Butterflies do not require to distinguish different orientations of the avatar (i.e., the avatar simply moves in the corresponding direction when performing an action). Furthermore, it is assumed that the agent decides to perform ACTION_UP for a score increase of two by collecting the butterfly (according to $\mathcal{KB}_{\text{score}}$). After performing the action, the agent observes the subsequent state and remarks that the score increased by only one (instead of the expected increase of two, as stated by the corresponding rule above5 ∧ ACTION_UP → score+2 of $\mathcal{KB}_{\text{score}}$).

The forward model HKB $\mathcal{KB}_{\text{score}}$ will now be revised using Algorithm 5.1 with $\mathcal{KB} := \mathcal{KB}_{\text{score}}$, the state-action conjunction $st^a :=$ above5 ∧ orientNil ∧ ACTION_UP and the observed new subsequent state information $st' :=$ score+1 as input: Since it is $\{st'\} \neq \mathfrak{R}(\mathcal{KB}, st^a)$ (see lines 1–2 of Algorithm 5.1), and since the firing rule above5 ∧ ACTION_UP → score+2 providing the wrong conclusion is not located on the bottommost level of the HKB (see lines 4–5 of Algorithm 5.1), a new rule reflecting the change will be added on the bottommost level of the HKB (see line 6 of Algorithm 5.1). After that, the revised version of $\mathcal{KB}_{\text{score}}$ returned by the algorithm will be

$$\mathcal{KB}'_{\text{score}} = \{\{\top \to \text{score}\pm 0 \ [0.94]\},$$
$$\emptyset,$$
$$\{\text{above5} \land \text{ACTION\_UP} \to \text{score}+2 \ [1.00],$$
$$\text{below5} \land \text{ACTION\_DOWN} \to \text{score}+2 \ [1.00],$$
$$\text{left5} \land \text{ACTION\_LEFT} \to \text{score}+2 \ [1.00],$$
$$\text{right5} \land \text{ACTION\_RIGHT} \to \text{score}+2 \ [1.00]\},$$
$$\{\text{above5} \land \text{orientNil} \land \text{ACTION\_UP} \to \text{score}+1 \ [1.00]\}\} \quad (5.7)$$

and $\mathfrak{R}(\mathcal{KB}'_{\text{score}}, st^a)$ will provide the correct inference now. □

---

[32] Note that the HKB is denoted here as ordered set of sets, similar to Formula (4.3) on page 109.

Note that, since the avatar's orientation is not relevant in the game of Butterflies, it might appear cumbersome that an exception is created here on the bottommost level of the HKB, instead of exchanging the rule above5 ∧ ACTION_UP → score+2. However, in *general video game playing*, it should not be assumed that such a property will remain unused in other levels of a game: As an example, a new level could introduce a *butterfly net* as a new object, which has to be used in the direction of the avatar's current orientation to be able to catch a butterfly.

The following example will consider revision in the case of a new object:

Example 5.3 (Revising a Forward Model 2: New Object) Continuing with the revised version $\mathcal{KB}'_{\text{score}}$ from Example 5.2 (see (5.7)), it is assumed here, that the agent plays an even more difficult (fictive) version of the game Butterflies, where a new type of object appears: *hornets*. Hornets decrease the score by one, when being touched by the agent's avatar. Also here (as in Example 5.2), the agent's orientation is not of relevance and thus only the neutral sensor symbol "orientNil" is provided for the corresponding sensor.

The agent is assumed now to be in a state with one of the new hornet objects (object of type 6) above its avatar and the agent performs the action ACTION_UP. Since the agent does not know anything about hornets, for the corresponding state-action conjunction above6 ∧ orientNil ∧ ACTION_UP, the reasoning algorithm $\mathfrak{R}$ (Algorithm 3.1) falls back to the most general rule ⊤ → score±0 and thus no score change will be expected. After having performed the action, the agent observes the subsequent state and remarks that the score decreased by one (instead of no score change, as expected).

Thus, the forward model HKB $\mathcal{KB}_{\text{score}}$ will be revised again using Algorithm 5.1 with $\mathcal{KB} := \mathcal{KB}'_{\text{score}}$, $st^a := $ above6 ∧ orientNil ∧ ACTION_UP and the observed new subsequent state information $st' := $ score−1 as input. This results in the HKB

$$\mathcal{KB}''_{\text{score}} = \{\{\top \to \text{score}\pm 0 \ [0.94]\},$$
$$\emptyset,$$
$$\{\text{above5} \land \text{ACTION\_UP} \to \text{score}+2 \ [1.00],$$
$$\text{below5} \land \text{ACTION\_DOWN} \to \text{score}+2 \ [1.00],$$
$$\text{left5} \land \text{ACTION\_LEFT} \to \text{score}+2 \ [1.00],$$
$$\text{right5} \land \text{ACTION\_RIGHT} \to \text{score}+2 \ [1.00]\},$$
$$\{\text{above5} \land \text{orientNil} \land \text{ACTION\_UP} \to \text{score}+1 \ [1.00],$$
$$\text{above6} \land \text{orientNil} \land \text{ACTION\_UP} \to \text{score}-1 \ [1.00]\}\} \quad (5.8)$$

for which $\Re(\mathcal{KB}''_{\text{score}}, st^a)$ provides the correct conclusion both for $st^a := \text{above}6 \wedge \text{orientNil} \wedge \text{ACTION\_UP}$ as well as for $st^a := \text{above}5 \wedge \text{orientNil} \wedge \text{ACTION\_UP}$ (from Example 5.2). □

In case the agent will now play a level again where a collected butterfly increased the score by two, instead of one (e. g., as in one of the levels from which the original forward model HKBs from Figure 5.8 were learned), and assuming the same situation as in Example 5.2 with a butterfly above the agent's avatar and the agent performing ACTION_UP, a revision of $\mathcal{KB}''_{\text{score}}$ from Example 5.3 (see (5.8)) using Algorithm 5.1 would simply remove the rule above5 ∧ orientNil ∧ ACTION_UP → score+1.

Note that by this means, the number of rules is *reduced*, which may prevent the forward model HKB from steadily growing on the bottommost level through multiple subsequent revisions. Furthermore, note that the knowledge is selectively changed by Algorithm 5.1, without affecting other parts of the knowledge that were previously learned (like the knowledge about the hornets or the original common scoring mechanics of the game that was learned before).

5.2.3 An Agent Model Combining Learning and Revision

In Section 5.1.2 a hybrid HKB/reinforcement learning agent model was described, which supports an underlying reinforcement learning approach with the extraction and exploitation of found rules in the state-action space. Similarly, here an agent model will be described that integrates the learning of a game's forward model, the exploitation of the forward model and the possibility of revising it with environment changes in the context of the GVGAI framework [52].

However, the agent model presented here differs from the one that was described in Section 5.1.2 (see Figure 5.5), as it aims not at accelerating a learning process with found rules, but at making it possible to learn to play different a priori unknown games by means of HKBs. Furthermore, by learning a forward model, the agent model contributes to bridge the gap between the GVGAI *learning track* and the GVGAI *planning track*, by offering the possibility of applying common techniques used by the GVGAI planning community (such as *monte carlo tree search*, MCTS [21]) also in the learning track (see the beginning of Section 5.2).

According to [5] and following ideas from the GVGAI competition [65], the agent model is separated into the agent's training phase and the agent's evaluation phase: The former realizes the learning of the forward model, whereas the latter concerns the exploitation and revision of the learned model. Figure 5.9 shows the agent model.

5. Enhancing Learning Agents

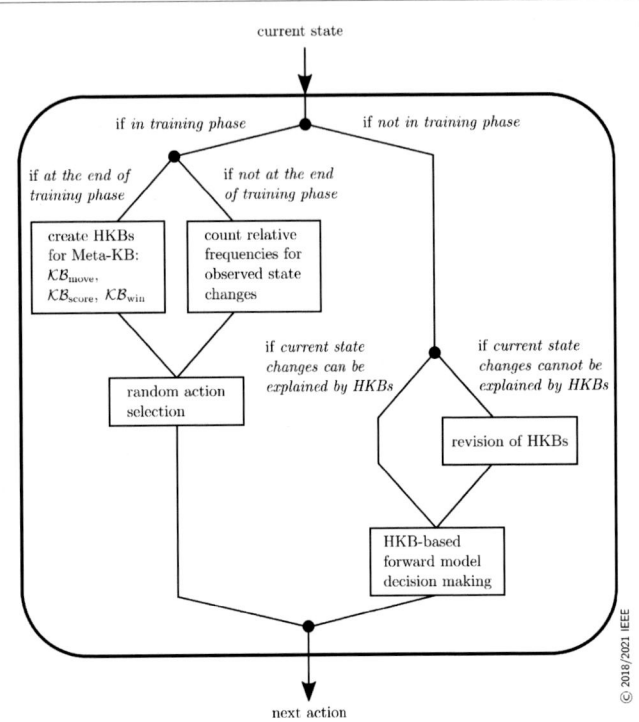

Figure 5.9 (Learning and Revision Agent Model) (Source: a. f. [26])
According to [5], in the training phase (left side of the figure), the agent performs random exploration and collects data about the environment for learning the forward model HKBs. At the end of the training phase, the agent creates the forward model HKBs from the data collected so far. When being evaluated (right side of the figure), the agent revises the forward model HKBs if they are not able to explain observations made in the evaluation environment.

The process described by the agent model from Figure 5.9 usually starts in the training phase (cf. [5]): In this phase, the agent explores the environment through random actions to collect data about the game. At the end of the training phase, the forward model HKBs are created (see Section 5.2.1).[33]

---

[33] In the GVGAI competition, the training phase could be rather short in the past (e. g., five minutes in the competition's round of 2017). However, for the presented approach, only about 50 seconds of training time were used in the context of several different games for learning eligible forward model HKBs from the collected data (see [5, 26]).

5.2 Forward Model Learning

The subsequent evaluation phase usually comprises new levels of the game that were not seen by the agent during the training phase. These new levels can involve changed circumstances, like new objects or a different anatomy of the level. In this phase, after every action, the agent observes whether the changes of the environment fit to the forward model HKBs that were learned and created at the end of the training phase: If a state change cannot be explained by the corresponding learned forward model HKB, then this HKB is revised with the observed changes using Algorithm 5.1 (as described in Example 5.2 and Example 5.3). The agent's decision-making is then based on the (revised) forward model HKBs using techniques like MCTS [21] for performing forward simulations of the game to determine the possibly best next action.

The agent model presented here integrates machine learning, knowledge representation and revision. Moreover, it allows to incorporate established techniques known from the *computational intelligence in games* community (such as MCTS [21]), which are commonly used in the GVGAI planning track. The GVGAI framework represents a challenging environment here, since agent models must be very responsive (40 milliseconds per decision, as described in [5]).

The presented agent model performed well in experiments made in the context of the GVGAI framework [52] and outperformed several previous agents, that were participating earlier in the GVGAI competition [65]: According to the results in [5], the presented agent model (with MCTS being used for decision making based on the learned HKB forward model) dominated four previously participating agents regarding the average reached game score in five out of ten diverse games from a training set of the GVGAI competition. Only three of the other competing agents were able to dominate the presented agent model (each of which in only one of the ten games). This resulted in the agent model being the best among the considered competitors. It increased the overall performance by $\approx 23\%$ according to the used scoring system in comparison to the second best agent (which was the one by İlhan and Etaner-Uyar, see the description of the learning track agents in Section 2.3.3). The evaluation details of the presented agent model can be found in [5, 26].

As a further result, the agent model also allows to inspect the learned forward model HKBs, which may help to explain what the agent learned and can contribute to better understand the learned agent behavior as well as the decision-making.

5.3 Summary

This chapter presented two HKB-based agent models that incorporate learning techniques and decision making based on symbolic knowledge. Analyses and evaluations of the benefits of this incorporation were provided in the context of grid world scenarios and different games from the GVGAI competition [65].

It was shown in Section 5.1 that incorporating the HKB extraction algorithms into an agent's learning process can speed up learning. Depending on how eligible the exploitation of heuristics is for the underlying problem, this can be beneficial already in the first 10%–15% of the learning process. Moreover, Section 5.1 showed, that these approaches can also help to master games that are in principle easy to solve but typically cause problems for common algorithms (see Table 5.3 and Appendix B).

In Section 5.2, an HKB-based agent model was described that incorporates learning, the exploitation of learned symbolic knowledge and the revision of such knowledge in the context of new levels of the same game. The agent model was developed in the context of a joint work together with Jun.-Prof. Dr.-Ing. Alexander Dockhorn (see bibliographic remarks in Section 5.4). It contributed to *general video game artificial intelligence* (GVGAI) [53] by enabling the use of state-of-the-art methods known from the GVGAI competition's planning track (such as *monte carlo tree search*, MCTS [21]) in the context of the competition's learning track as well, where no forward model of the game is provided to an agent. By this means, the performance in the learning track could be increased by about 23% compared to the best agent model of one of the GVGAI competition's previous rounds at that time (see [5, 26] for a detailed evaluation).

5.4 Bibliographic Remarks

Section 5.2 has its origins in the field of *general video game playing* [53] and resulted from joint works with Jun.-Prof. Dr.-Ing. Alexander Dockhorn (from Leibniz University Hannover). In our joint works [5, 26], HKBs were used to enable agents to quickly learn forward models of different video games from the *general video game artificial intelligence* (GVGAI) competition [65].

As described earlier, in this setting, agents were first trained on several levels of a game and were then evaluated on different levels of the same game. In the training phase, means of machine learning were used to statistically learn the forward model of the game, whereas in the evaluation phase, due to time constraints from the

GVGAI competition, it was not possible to perform a statistical "relearning" in case changes of the game where noticed by the agent. For this purpose, the revision algorithm provided in Section 5.2.2 of this chapter was implemented to let the agent react quickly to changes of the environment, while still considering the knowledge learned in the training phase.

The cooperation resulted in a conference paper [26], where HKBs were first introduced together with revision algorithm as an efficient knowledge representation paradigm for general video game playing. As an extension to this work, the journal article [5] has been published in the IEEE journal *Transactions on Games* at the end of 2020 (date of early access). Besides a formalization of the revision algorithm and further extended contents, this work also provides intuitions for the validation of the revision algorithm against an adapted version of the basic postulates by Alchourrón, Gärdenfors and Makinson [2, 35].

In the context of the cooperation, the author's work focused on the representation of the learned forward models as HKBs and their integration to an agent model, as well as on the development of the revision approach and its validation. The work by Jun.-Prof. Dr.-Ing. Alexander Dockhorn focused on the exploitation of the learned (and revised) forward models using search algorithms like *monte carlo tree search* (MCTS) [21] and the study of the resulting agent model in the context of different games from the GVGAI framework by Perez-Liebana et al.

6. Conclusion and Future Work

After having studied the concept of hierarchical knowledge bases (HKBs) in different applications in the context of games (and related scenarios), this chapter summarizes the results of this work and provides the conclusions (Section 6.1). After that, an outlook on possible future work will be outlined, which also comprises some further hints to applications outside the scope of games (Section 6.2).

6.1 Summary of the Results and Conclusions

This work investigated ideas for extracting knowledge bases from learning agents, to be able to explain their behavior in a comprehensible way. Moreover, it was investigated, how the exploitation of such extracted knowledge can contribute to increase an agent's learning capabilities.

To achieve these goals, different algorithms have been described, which allow for learning an entire knowledge base that represents the behavior learned by an agent. The need for a compact representation of the resulting knowledge led to the concept of HKBs: These knowledge bases have been designed to represent the knowledge in the form of rules with exceptions on different levels of abstraction. Thereby, HKBs are not only a compact representation paradigm but are also easy to read and intuitively comprehensible to people not having a strong background in logic (the comprehensibility of HKBs has been studied in [41]). HKBs have been developed with simplicity in mind, both regarding comprehensibility, reasoning and revision efficiency. This renders them especially useful in the context of (near) real-time environments, such as games (and related domains).

More detailed, the main results of this work can be summarized as follows:

- *HKBs as an intuitive and comprehensible knowledge representation approach*: With HKBs (Section 3.1), an approach has been developed that is able to compactly represent the behavior of agents. The resulting representations show some interesting properties regarding comprehensibility (see also [41]) and thereby are also potentially accessible to people without a strong background in logic.

- *Different extraction approaches to learn comprehensible representations in the form of HKBs from data*:
  A preliminary approach and its extension based on the APRIORI algorithm by Agrawal et al. [1], as well as a more elaborate algorithm have been developed to learn HKBs from data (Section 3.4 and Section 3.5). The latter is more transparent than its precursors and able to produce eligible (rougher) HKBs when being stopped before finishing the extraction. It has been shown that the algorithm is complete for deterministic state-action sequences of an agent. Using these algorithms, the behavior of different agents, that learned to act meaningful in the context of games (and similar scenarios) could be explained (Section 4.1).

- *Efficient reasoning and revision algorithms for the resulting HKBs*:
  Both the reasoning algorithm (Section 3.2) for HKBs and the revision algorithm for forward model HKBs (Section 5.2.2) are efficient enough to be used by agents in (near) real-time environments, such as games. The efficiency of the reasoning algorithm has also been considered in [41].

- Two hybrid agent models incorporating learning and knowledge representation:

  - *A hybrid machine learning/knowledge representation agent model that accelerates an agent's reinforcement learning process*:
    The concepts of HKBs and the corresponding extraction algorithms have been incorporated into an agent model to increase the learning speed of a reinforcement learning agent (Section 5.1). The approach conforms to common modularization criteria from software engineering, since the incorporation of the HKBs and the extraction algorithms are independent from the underlying reinforcement learning approach, that is used for the machine learning part. Thereby, the presented HKB approaches are combinable with different reinforcement learning approaches.

  - *An agent model incorporating learning, exploitation and revision of forward models in the context of a priori unknown environments (games)*:
    In the joint works [5, 26] with Jun.-Prof. Dr.-Ing. Alexander Dockhorn (from Leibniz University Hannover), the ideas of HKBs could be successfully adapted to be able to learn forward models (i.e., "how things work") of a priori unknown environments in the context of video games (Section 5.2). The representations of such forward models could be learned and exploited efficiently to be applied in the (near) real-time framework for *general video game playing* (GVGAI) by Perez-Liebana et al. By this means, it was possible to apply state-of-the-art algorithms from the GVGAI planning community (like *monte carlo tree search*, MCTS [21]) in

case no forward model of the game is provided to the agent, which increased the performance over other agents in the learning track's previous rounds of the GVGAI competition (see Section 5.3 and [5, 26]). The results contributed to the incorporation of knowledge representation techniques and other approaches from the AI in games community and were mentioned in the book on general video game artificial intelligence [53].

- *The InteKRator toolbox for using HKBs in practice*:
  Since this work is strongly geared toward practical aspects, an important result is the implementation of the most relevant approaches into the INTEKRATOR toolbox [38]. Besides the idea of making the approaches accessible to a broader community, it can also be considered a proof-of-concept for their practical usefulness. The toolbox is implemented in JAVA as an open source library/command line applications. It allows for learning HKBs from data and for efficiently performing reasoning and revision on HKBs. Furthermore, it is also possible to combine these techniques with continuous numeric sensory data. INTEKRATOR was meanwhile also used outside the scope of games, e. g., in *medical informatics* (for hospital logistics/process optimization research) [6] or for educational purposes at the *Summer School in Bioinformatics and High-Dimensional Statistics* [37] at the Institute of Medical Biostatistics, Epidemiology and Informatics (IMBEI) of the University Medical Center of the Johannes Gutenberg University Mainz in 2020. In a more recent joint work at IMBEI [10], the INTEKRATOR toolbox has also been proposed for automatically creating expert systems from data (see bibliographic remarks in Section 3.7).

- As a side product, *a model for subjectively experienced strategic depth*:
  As a further result emerging from HKBs, a model for the strategic depth that is subjectively experienced by humans when playing games was developed in a joint work [11] with Dr. Vanessa Volz (formerly at TU Dortmund University, at the time of writing at Queen Mary University of London and modl.ai, Copenhagen). This result served as a foundation for an interactive educational exhibit that was created for the company Z Quadrat GmbH in Mainz, Germany. With this exhibit, users can play different levels of a game and evaluate the strategic depth estimates of the algorithm against their personal feeling. Moreover, users can learn about knowledge representation, by inspecting HKBs representing the knowledge of their playtraces. The exhibit was accepted at the German exhibition ship *MS Wissenschaft* [50] and was shown in a large number of German and Austrian cities in 2019. It was later selected for the *ScienceStation* traveling exhibition (another project of the German scientific communication organization *Wissenschaft im Dialog*, WiD) [59] and, in this context, it was shown at several

train stations in Germany in 2019. It was furthermore selected by the *Deutsches Museum Bonn* (German Museum in Bonn) [24] for an exhibition on AI [48].

The concepts resulting from this work stimulated bachelor's and master's theses (e. g, [40, 12]), partly contributed to other's PhD work [25] and resulted in further joint works by the author [6] as well as by others [42].

Besides the opportunity of growing this work in stimulating environments and thereby getting in touch with ambitious scientists and students over time (see Section "Acknowledgments" for details), further possible reasons for that are:

- Reasoning for HKBs (as well as revision) is lightweight and very efficient, and can therefore be used in (near) real-time environments (cf. [41]). This distinguishes HKBs from several other knowledge representation approaches and renders HKBs an eligible approach for agents, especially in the context of games.

- The proposed learning/extraction algorithms create HKBs with rule weights representing conditional probabilities $P(conclusion \mid premise)$—a concept widely-used both in knowledge representation and other communities. Together with the created HKBs being *compact* (in case the intrinsic structure of the input data allows for a compact representation) and *complete* (for deterministic data in case of the advance extraction algorithm), this renders HKB extraction a sound and easily interpretable way for getting insights into data (such as state-action sequences produced by agents).

- With the INTEKRATOR toolbox, the concepts are available in a well-documented and easy to use open source software, that can be used both stand-alone and as a programming library (also outside the scope of games; first experiences have been made, e. g., in medical informatics).

- The representation of knowledge in the form of rules with exceptions appears to be "natural" and easily accessible, also to people outside the knowledge representation community (cf. [41]). This is underpinned by the educational interest in HKBs (as shown, e. g., in the context of the exhibit that was mentioned earlier).[34]

With the aforementioned points, the work contributed to the practical usage of combined machine learning/knowledge representation approaches in the context of agents, with applications especially (but not solely) in games. This may help to further establish the usage of such approaches in the *AI in games community* (see [53]),

---

[34] The author's personal experiences of explaining the basic ideas of HKBs to many people in different contexts (e. g., to AI classes at school [4], to non-computer science researchers and students [37] or to diverse communities at exhibitions) also conforms to that.

and hopefully also to other communities. Some first attempts to that will be briefly outlined in the following section.

6.2 An Outlook on Future Work

Despite the results provided in the previous section (Section 6.1), there are further ideas that might be interesting to be considered for future work. Some of these ideas will be briefly outlined here.

An important and still open question in the context of this work is when a machine learning approach should be used and when an agent should preferably rely on a revision approach for adapting to changes in the environment. In Section 5.1, it was shown that the exploitation of symbolic knowledge can vastly improve the performance of an agent (at least if the environments allows for such exploitation, which is assumed to be usually the case for meaningful environments) and that this usually helps early in the learning process. However, these sections do not state anything about when to *revise* the extracted HKBs. Moreover, in Section 5.2, it was described that meaningful forward models of unknown environments can be learned quickly using HKBs in conjunction with a corresponding learning algorithm. Even if this approach already incorporates revision, the decision when to perform revision instead of relying on the machine learning approach was implied by the switch between the training and evaluation phase of the GVGAI competition's framework [65]. The incorporation of a mechanism that lets an agent decide this on its own (e. g., from observing the environment) into an agent model as shown in Figure 5.9, could be an interesting next improvement here.

From a more theoretical point of view, it could be interesting to have a closer look on the complexity of the presented algorithms. Although the efficiency of the algorithms and the resulting performance gain in the context of learning agents has been shown already in several experiments in Section 5.1 and Section 5.2 (the latter representing a near real-time setting) as well as in the study [41]: Having a closer look on it from a complexity theoretical point of view could further underpin these results. Furthermore, HKBs in conjunction with the reasoning algorithm (Algorithm 3.1) could be investigated regarding its inference properties. Although this work already showed the functionality and usefulness in several different contexts, it might be interesting to interconnect it more tightly with logic-based approaches. In [8] and [40], it had already been outlined that it is in principle possible to translate HKBs into answer set programs, which can be considered a first step in this direction. Since it has been shown in [41] that reasoning for HKBs can outperform reasoning for answer set programs, it could also be beneficial to consider the inverse direction (i. e., translating answer set programs to HKBs).

As the introductory citation in the beginning of this work states that games might be interesting subjects to prepare for "real-world problems", one of the most interesting future works might be the transfer of the concepts and approaches mentioned here to other domains outside the scope of games. First attempts to this have already been made in *medical informatics* in the context of multi-agent simulations for optimizing hospital processes [6]. There, a hospital process involving patients, doctors and nurses has been simulated to learn behavioral rules in the form of HKBs for the different individuals participating in the process. The HKBs have been learned using an earlier version of the INTEKRATOR toolbox [38] (see also Appendix A) and have been further processed manually to simplify and adapt them. More recently, in [10], INTEKRATOR has also been proposed for the automated creation of expert systems from data in the medical context. This shows the potential of the work also for further applications outside the scope of games.

Appendix

A. Introduction to the INTEKRATOR Toolbox

This part of the appendix serves as a basic introduction to the INTEKRATOR toolbox. The INTEKRATOR toolbox implements the most important results of this work to be used in practice. It is intended as a lightweight toolbox geared toward being used in the context of agent applications, however, it can also be used in other areas outside the scope of agents. The toolbox has recently been accepted for publication in the context of automatically learning expert systems from medical data [10], showing that this work's results can also be transferred to other applications. The content presented here represents a selection of the most important features of the INTEKRATOR toolbox, mainly following [38].

After providing some general information about the interface (Section A.1), the main features of the learning module (Section A.2) will be presented. After that, the usage of the inference module (Section A.3) and the revision module (Section A.4) will be explained. Finally, the checking functionality for analyzing the knowledge quality will be described (Section A.5).

A.1 Basic Interface

The INTEKRATOR toolbox is written in the JAVA programming language. According to [38], it can be both used as a command line application (for calling it manually or as an external process) and as a JAVA library. The library is extensively documented using JAVADOC (see, e.g., [16], Chapter 7, pp. 203–208). The toolbox is lightweight, consisting only of a single .jar-file without any external dependencies. By this means, it can be easily integrated into other applications (such as web applications). The command line interface is geared toward usability and efficiency. It operates on simple text files and also allows for calling the toolbox as an external process from other (non-JAVA) applications.

Following [38], the basic command structure of the INTEKRATOR toolbox is

$$\texttt{java -jar InteKRator.jar PARAMETERS INFILE [OUTFILE] [...]} \quad (A.1)$$

where `INFILE` is the input file to be processed according to the `PARAMETERS`, `[OUTFILE]` is an optional output file to which the results are written in addition to the standard out (if provided) and [...] indicates that multiple `PARAMETERS INFILE [OUTFILE]` sequences can be used for sequential processing with a single call.

The following sections will provide information on how the `PARAMETERS` look in detail depending on the respective use case. The parameters and their respective options are similar to the interface offered by the corresponding methods when using the JAVA library instead.

A.2 Learning

Learning is implemented using the results from Section 3.5 (especially Algorithm 3.3 and the extensions from Section 3.5.3 and Section 3.5.4).

According to [38], to learn an HKB from a state-action sequence, each line of the file provided by `INFILE` from (A.1) must contain state-action pairs of the form `s1 ... sn` (separated by space characters), where `s1 ... sn` describe an agent's state in which action `a` has been performed. The `PARAMETERS` from (A.1) are of the form

$$\text{-learn [OPTIONS]}$$

where `[OPTIONS]` represent one or more optional learning parameters, that can be used in arbitrary order as well as in combination (if not otherwise stated). Some of the most important ones will be described here, following [38] (a more complete list can be found in [38]):

- `top`
  Ensures that the resulting HKB has a top level rule (even if not needed for any of the state-action pairs of the input data to infer the action from the state).

- `all`
  Ensures that the resulting HKB includes all rules learned from data (even those that are not needed for any of the state-action pairs of the input data to infer the action from the state).

- `discretize [C}N ...] [C}NAMES ...] [info C ...]`
  Discretizes columns containing numeric data by clustering (see Section 3.5.3).[35]
  - If the optional `C}N ...` is provided, each column `C` (where 1 denotes the first column) will be discretized to at most `N` sensor symbols, each repre-

---

[35] The possibly unusual appearing syntax of the curly bracket after the column number can be considered a "funnel" that concentrates the numeric values to learned sensor symbols.

senting one cluster. Multiple C}N can be provided, one for each numeric column that should be discretized.

- If the optional C}NAMES ... is provided, NAMES must be a comma-separated list of names (without space characters). Each column C (where 1 denotes the first column) will be discretized to a maximum number of clusters according to the number of names provided, and the names will be used for the resulting sensor symbols representing the clusters. Multiple C}NAMES can be provided, one for each numeric column that should be discretized.

- If the **info**-option is provided, additional information about the number of clusters and the percentage covered by a specific cluster symbol will be provided for each column C (see (3.3) in Section 3.5.3). Multiple columns C can be provided, one for each numeric column for which additional information should be provided.

In either of the three cases here, the **any**-keyword can be used for C to refer to *all columns*.

- **preselect [N]**
Only the most potentially relevant sensors are considered for learning to accelerate the learning process in case of higher-dimensional data (see Section 3.5.4). If the optional N is provided, only the N most potentially relevant sensors are considered. Otherwise N is determined automatically from data using a clustering approach (as described at the end of Section 3.5.4).

- **sample N[%]**
Only N state-action pairs from the input state-action sequence are randomly selected for learning. If % is provided, N percent of the state-action pairs are randomly selected instead. Sampling can drastically speed up the learning process, but may result in *incomplete* HKBs (i.e., it might not be possible to infer the correct action from the state of each state-action pair from the original state-action sequence, even if the original state-action sequence was *deterministic*; see Definition 3.1). However, -check might be used subsequently to evaluate the quality of the resulting HKB (see Section A.5). In case of the original state-action sequence being deterministic, completeness of the learned HKB can be ensured by revising it subsequently with every state-action pair of the original state-action sequence (see Section A.4). However, this will probably result in a less compact representation with additional exceptions on the most specific level.

A.3 Reasoning

The reasoning approach of the INTEKRATOR toolbox is based on the results from Section 3.2 (especially Algorithm 3.1).

To infer one or more action(s) from a provided state and a learned (or manually created) HKB, according to [38], the HKB must be contained in the `INFILE` from (A.1). The `PARAMETERS` from (A.1) must be of the form

`-infer [why] STATE`

where `why` is an optional parameter for providing additional explanatory information and `STATE` represents the state from which the action(s) will be inferred.

The parameter `STATE` must be of the form `s1 ... sn` (separated by space characters). If the optional parameter `why` is provided, then the rule(s), based on which the results are inferred, will also be provided.

If more than one action is provided as result, still following [38], this means that these actions are equally good according to the HKB of the `INFILE`.

A.4 Revision

Revision is based on Algorithm 5.1. However, the INTEKRATOR toolbox implements the revision approach in a more general way, which allows to revise any HKB (not only those representing forward models of games; cf. Section 5.2.2).

To revise a learned (or manually created) HKB, according to [38], the HKB must be contained in the `INFILE` from (A.1) and the `PARAMETERS` from (A.1) must be of the form

`-revise PAIR`

where `PAIR` is a state-action pair representing the new knowledge that has to be integrated in the HKB.

The parameter `PAIR` must be of the form `s1 ... sn a` (separated by space characters) and states that it should be possible to infer action `a` from state `s1 ... sn` after revision.

Note that, in principle, INTEKRATOR also allows for performing revision on levels other than the most specific one (in case the state provided in `PAIR` is not a complete state). However, even if this is technically possible in the same way, it does neither conform to Algorithm 5.1 (where revision is only done on the most specific level), nor is the validation of the revision approach done in [5] guaranteed to hold in this case. For this reason, the INTEKRATOR toolbox provides a warning, if revision is not done on the most specific level (as far as this can be determined from the HKB to be revised). Also here, `-check` might be used subsequently to evaluate the impact of the revision on the overall quality of the resulting HKB (see Section A.5).

A.5 Checking

To check the quality of a learned (or manually created) HKB, it is possible to perform a check of the HKB against a state-action sequence. In this case, it is measured for how many of the state-action pairs contained in the state-action sequence the action is correctly inferred from the corresponding state.

According to [38], the `INFILE` from (A.1) must be the HKB to be checked and the `PARAMETERS` from (A.1) must be of the form

`-check [details] FILE`

where `details` is an optional parameter resulting in more detailed results if provided and `FILE` is the state-action sequence against which the HKB is checked.

Every line in `FILE` must be a state-action pair of the form `s1 ... sn a`. If the `details` option is provided, the percentage of state-action pairs that are correctly covered by the HKB is in addition shown individually for every action.

B. Online Appendix

This part of the appendix refers to the online appendix that accompanies this work. There, especially videos will be provided to further underpin some of the presented results in a visual way.

The online appendix can be accessed through [51] or by scanning the code provided in Figure B.1.

Figure B.1 (Access to Online Appendix) (Source: created using [58])
Common software can be used to scan the code as an alternative way to access the online appendix.

List of Algorithms

Algorithm 3.1 (Reasoning on HBKs) (Source: adapted from [7])..63
Algorithm 3.2 (Preliminary Knowledge Base Extraction) (Source: based on [7])..........................70
Algorithm 3.3 (Advanced Extraction of HKBs) (Source: adapted from [6])..................................84
Algorithm 5.1 (Revision Algorithm for HKBs) (Source: adapted from [26])................................158

List of Figures

(Note that "a. f." is used in some cases to abbreviate the term "adapted from".)

Figure 2.1a (Basic Agent Model) (Source: adapted from [14])..29
Figure 2.1b (Basic Agent Model: Alternative Representation)..29
Figure 2.2 (Agent, Sensors, Actions)
(Source: a. f. FLAIRS'17 poster by Apeldoorn & Kern-Isberner)...32
Figure 2.3 (States, Actions and State Transitions)..33
Figure 2.4 (Grid World with Water) (Source: adapted from [7–9, 62])......................................39
Figure 2.5 (Q-Learning in a Grid World) (Source: adapted from [7–9, 62])..............................46
Figure 2.6 (A "Black Box" by Learned Rules)..49
Figure 3.1 (HKB for an Agent in a Grid World) (Source: adapted from [11])...........................61
Figure 3.2 (Horse Racing Game)
(Source: a. f. exhibit software by the author for Z Quadrat GmbH)..72
Figure 3.3 (Road Following Task)
(Source: a. f. teaching software by the author used for Z Quadrat GmbH)..................................94
Figure 3.4 (HKB for Fuzzy-Controlled Road Following)...96
Figure 4.1 (GVGAI Games for HKB Extraction) (Source: [52], adapted from [11])................105
Figure 4.2 (Extracted HKB for Camel Race Level 2)..109
Figure 4.3 (Extracted HKB for Run Level 2)..110
Figure 4.4 (Extracted HKB for Eighth Passenger Level 3)...112
Figure 4.5 (Evaluation of the Strategic Depth Measure) (Source: adapted from [11])............120
Figure 5.1 (Grid Worlds for Learning with Explicit Knowledge) (Source: a. f. [7])................128
Figure 5.2 (Extracted HKBs after Completed Learning Process) (Source: a. f. [7])................132
Figure 5.3 (Results for Incorporating HKBs during Learning) (Source: adapted from [7])....132
Figure 5.4 (Subjective Strategic Depth during Learning) (Source: adapted from [9])............137
Figure 5.5 (Hybrid Reinforcement Learning/HKB Agent Model) (Source: a. f. [9])...............139
Figure 5.6 (Knowledge Evolution during Learning Process)...147
Figure 5.7 (Butterflies Game) (Source: GVGAI framework [52])..153
Figure 5.8 (Forward Model for Butterflies) (Source: adapted from [5])...................................155
Figure 5.9 (Learning and Revision Agent Model) (Source: a. f. [26])......................................162
Figure B.1 (Access to Online Appendix) (Source: created using [58])....................................181

List of Tables

Table of Notations..15
Table 3.1 (Data for Potential Relevance)..98
Table 5.1 (Parameters for Learning Agent Experiments) (Source: adapted from [7])...................131
Table 5.2 (Plain Q-Learning vs HKB Approach) (Source: a. f. [9])..141
Table 5.3 (Q-Learning vs HKB Approach in a Game) (Source: a. f. [9]).......................................144

References

[1] Agrawal, R., Mannila, H., Srikant, R., Toivonen, H., Verkamo, A. I.: Fast Discovery of Association Rules. In: Fayyad, U. M., Piatetsky-Shapiro, G., Smyth, P., Uthurusamy, R. (eds.) Advances in Knowledge Discovery and Data Mining, pp. 307–328. The MIT Press, Cambridge, Massachusetts, 1996.

[2] Alchourrón, C., Gärdenfors, P., Makinson, D.: On the Logic of Theory Change: Partial Meet Contraction and Revision Functions. Journal of Symbolic Logic, 50(2):510–530, 1985.

[3] Apeldoorn, D.: AbstractSwarm – A Generic Graphical Modeling Language for Multi-Agent Systems. In: Klusch, M., Thimm, M., Paprzycki, M. (eds.) Multiagent System Technologies – 11th German Conference, MATES 2013, Koblenz, Germany, September 16-20, 2013 Proceedings, pp. 180–192. Springer, Berlin, Heidelberg, 2013.

[4] Apeldoorn, D.: KI in der Schule – Teil 1: Einführung in die künstliche Intelligenz. LOG IN – Informatische Bildung und Computer in der Schule, 195/196:126–131, 2021.

[5] Apeldoorn, D., Dockhorn, A.: Exception-Tolerant Hierarchical Knowledge Bases for Forward Model Learning. IEEE Transactions on Games, 13(3):249–262, 2021.

[6] Apeldoorn, D., Hadidi, L., Panholzer, T.: Learning Behavioral Rules from Multi-Agent Simulations for Optimizing Hospital Processes. In: Chomphuwiset, P., Kim, J., Pawara, P. (eds.) Multi-disciplinary Trends in Artificial Intelligence – 14th International Conference, MIWAI 2021, Virtual Event, July 2–3, 2021, Proceedings, pp. 14–26. Springer, Cham, 2021.

[7] Apeldoorn, D., Kern-Isberner, G.: When Should Learning Agents Switch to Explicit Knowledge? In: GCAI 2016. 2nd Global Conference on Artificial Intelligence. EPiC Series in Computing, vol. 41, pp. 174–186. EasyChair Publications, 2016.

[8] Apeldoorn, D., Kern-Isberner, G.: Towards an Understanding of What is Learned: Extracting Multi-Abstraction-Level Knowledge from Learning Agents. In: Rus, V., Markov, Z. (eds.) Proceedings of the Thirtieth International Florida Artificial Intelligence Research Society Conference, pp. 764–767. AAAI Press, Palo Alto, 2017.

[9] Apeldoorn, D., Kern-Isberner, G.: An Agent-Based Learning Approach for Finding and Exploiting Heuristics in Unknown Environments. In: Gordon, A. S., Miller, R., Turán, G. (eds.) Proceedings of the Thirteenth International Symposium on Commonsense Reasoning, London, UK, November 6-8, 2017. CEUR Workshop Proceedings (Vol-2052), Aachen, 2018.

[10] Apeldoorn, D., Panholzer, T.: Automated Creation of Expert Systems with the InteKRator Toolbox. Studies in Health Technology and Informatics, 283:46–55, 2021.

[11] Apeldoorn, D., Volz, V.: Measuring Strategic Depth in Games Using Hierarchical Knowledge Bases. In: 2017 IEEE Conference on Computational Intelligence and Games (CIG), pp. 9–16. IEEE, Piscataway, 2017.

[12] Barbi, M.: Erlernen von Wissensbasen mittels Reinforcement Learning und Neuronalen Netzen. Master's thesis, Technische Universität Dortmund, Dortmund, 2017.

References

[13] Beierle, C., Bock, T., Kern-Isberner, G., Ragni, M., Sauerwald, K.: Kinds and Aspects of Forgetting in Common-Sense Knowledge and Belief Management. In: Trollmann, F., Turhan, A.-Y. (eds.) KI 2018: Advances in Artificial Intelligence, pp. 366–373. Springer International Publishing, Cham, 2018.

[14] Beierle, C., Kern-Isberner, G.: Methoden wissensbasierter Systeme – Grundlagen, Algorithmen, Anwendungen (4. Auflage). Vieweg+Teubner, Wiesbaden, 2008.

[15] Beierle, C., Kutsch, S., Sauerwald, K.: Compilation of Conditional Knowledge Bases for Computing C-Inference Relations. In: Ferrarotti, F., Woltran, S. (eds.) Foundations of Information and Knowledge Systems, pp. 34–54. Springer International Publishing, Cham, 2018.

[16] Bloch, J.: Effective Java (Second Edition). Addison-Wesley, Upper Saddle River, Boston, Indianapolis, San Francisco, New York, Toronto, Montreal, London, Munich, Paris, Madrid, Capetown, Sydney, Tokyo, Singapore, Mexico City, 2008.

[17] Borgelt, C., Braune, C., Kruse, R.: Unsicheres, impräzises und unscharfes Wissen. In: Görz, G., Schmid, U., Braun, T. (eds.) Handbuch der Künstlichen Intelligenz (6. Auflage), pp. 279–341. De Gruyter Oldenbourg, Berlin, Boston, 2020.

[18] Borgida, A., Etherington, D. W.: Hierarchical Knowledge Bases and Efficient Disjunctive Reasoning. In: Brachman, R. J., Levesque, H. J., Reiter, R. (eds.) Proceedings of the First International Conference on Principles of Knowledge Representation and Reasoning, pp. 33–43. Morgan Kaufmann Publishers, San Francisco, 1989.

[19] Brewka, G., Eiter, T., Truszczyński, M.: Answer Set Programming at a Glance. Commun. ACM, 54(12):92–103, 2011.

[20] Browne, C.: Elegance in Game Design. IEEE Transactions on Computational Intelligence and AI in Games, 4(3):229–240, 2012.

[21] Browne, C. B., Powley, E., Whitehouse, D., Lucas, S. M., Cowling, P. I., Rohlfshagen, P., Tavener, S., Perez, D., Samothrakis, S., Colton, S.: A Survey of Monte Carlo Tree Search Methods. IEEE Transactions on Computational Intelligence and AI in Games, 4(1):1–43, 2012.

[22] Clingo – A Grounder and Solver for Logic Programs: https://github.com/potassco/clingo. Visited on Oct 24th, 2020.

[23] de Finetti, B.: La prévision : ses lois logiques, ses sources subjectives. Ann. Inst. Henri Poincaré, 7(1):1–68, 1937.

[24] Deutsches Museum Bonn: https://www.deutsches-museum.de/bonn. Visited on Feb 8th, 2021.

[25] Dockhorn, A.: Prediction-based Search for Autonomous Game-Playing. PhD thesis, Otto-von-Guericke-Universität Magdeburg, Magdeburg, 2020.

[26] Dockhorn, A., Apeldoorn, D.: Forward Model Approximation for General Video Game Learning. In: Browne, C., Winands, M. H. M., Liu, J., Preuss, M. (eds.) Proceedings of the 2018 IEEE Conference on Computational Intelligence and Games (CIG'18), pp. 425–432. IEEE, Piscataway, 2018.

[27] Dörner, D.: Die Logik des Mißlingens – Strategisches Denken in komplexen Situationen. Rowohlt Taschenbuch, Reinbek bei Hamburg, 1992.

[28] Duarte, F. F.: Review of Recent Work on Computational Intelligence in Games. In: Rua, R., Silva, V., Muhammad, S., Duarte, F. (eds.) MAPiS 2019 – First MAP-i Seminar Proceedings, pp. 6–14. UA Editora, Aveiro, 2019.

[29] Eichhorn, C., Volz, V., Niland, R., Schendekehl, T.: A Vision on Analysing Approaches for Knowledge Representation and Reasoning Using Computer Games. In: Beierle, C., Kern-Isberner, G., Ragni, M., Stolzenburg, F. (eds.) Proceedings of the 6th Workshop on Dynamics of Knowledge and Belief (DKB-2017) and the 5th Workshop KI & Kognition (KIK-2017) co-located with 40th German Conference on Artificial Intelligence (KI 2017), Dortmund, Germany, September 26, 2017, pp. 31–42. CEUR Workshop Proceedings (Vol-1928), Aachen, 2017.

[30] Fierens, D.: Learning Directed Probabilistic Logical Models from Relational Data (Het leren van gerichte probabilistisch-logische modellen uit relationele gegevens). PhD thesis, Lirias, Katholieke Universiteit Leuven, Leuven, 2008.

[31] Garnelo, M., Arulkumaran, K., Shanahan, M.: Towards Deep Symbolic Reinforcement Learning. arXiv:1609.05518 [cs.AI], 2016.

[32] Ghallab, M., Nau, D., Traverso, P.: Automated Planning – Theory and Practice. Morgan Kaufmann Publishers, Amsterdam, Boston, Heidelberg, London, New York, Oxford, Paris, San Diego, San Francisco, Singapore, Sydney, Tokyo, 2004.

[33] Glunk, F. R., Illustrated by Rosenzweig, F., Piel, A.: Computer und Roboter. Loewe, Bindlach, 1993.

[34] Greulich, C., Edelkamp, S., Gath, M.: Agent-Based Multimodal Transport Planning in Dynamic Environments. In: Timm, I. J., Thimm, M. (eds.) KI 2013: Advances in Artificial Intelligence – 36th Annual German Conference on AI, Koblenz, Germany, September 16-20, 2013 Proceedings, pp. 74–85. Springer, Berlin, Heidelberg, 2013.

[35] Hansson, S. O.: Logic of Belief Revision. In: Zalta, E. N. (ed.) The Stanford Encyclopedia of Philosophy. 2017.

[36] Hertzberg, J., Lingemann, K., Nüchter, A.: Mobile Roboter – Eine Einführung aus Sicht der Informatik. Springer Vieweg, Berlin, Heidelberg, 2012.

[37] IMBEI Summer School in Bioinformatics and High-Dimensional Statistics: https://www.unimedizin-mainz.de/transmed/training-program/training-in-scientific-skills/summer-school-in-bioinformatics-and-high-dimensional-statistics.html. Visited on May 29th, 2021.

[38] InteKRator Toolbox: https://gitlab.com/dapel1/intekrator_toolbox. Visited on Oct 15th, 2020.

[39] Junges, R., Klügl, F.: Learning Tools for Agent-Based Modeling and Simulation. Künstliche Intelligenz, 27:273–280, 2013.

[40] Krüger, C.: Statistische Evaluation unterschiedlicher Repräsentationsformen für die Wissensextraktion aus Reinforcement Learning. Bachelor's thesis, Technische Universität Dortmund, Dortmund, 2016.

References

[41] Krüger, C., Apeldoorn, D., Kern-Isberner, G.: Comparing Answer Set Programming and Hierarchical Knowledge Bases Regarding Comprehensibility and Reasoning Efficiency in the Context of Agents. In: Proceedings of the 30th International Workshop on Qualitative Reasoning (QR 2017) at International Joint Conference on Artificial Intelligence (IJCAI 2017) in Melbourne, Australia. Northwestern University, Evanston, Illinois, 2017.

[42] Kuhn, I.: Heuristische Optimierung durch menschliche Intuition – Das Beste aus zwei Welten. In: Becker, M. (ed.) SKILL 2019 – Studierendenkonferenz Informatik, pp. 97–108. Gesellschaft für Informatik e. V., 2019.

[43] Kurniawati, H.: Partially Observable Markov Decision Processes (POMDPs) and Robotics. arXiv:2107.07599 [cs.RO], 2021.

[44] Kutschinski, E., Polani, D., Uthmann, T.: A Decentralized Agent-Based Platform For Automated Trade and Its Simulation. Computing in Economics and Finance 2000, No 276, Society for Computational Economics, 2000.

[45] Lang, J.: Twenty-Five Years of Preferred Subtheories. In: Eiter, T., Strass, H., Truszczyński, M., Woltran, S. (eds.) Advances in Knowledge Representation, Logic Programming, and Abstract Argumentation – Essays Dedicated to Gerhard Brewka on the Occasion of His 60th Birthday, pp. 157–172. Springer, Cham, 2015.

[46] Lantz, F., Isaksen, A., Jaffe, A., Nealen, A., Togelius, J.: Depth in Strategic Games. In: Kiekintveld, C., Wingate, D. (eds.) The Workshops of the Thirty-First AAAI Conference on Artificial Intelligence: Technical Reports WS-17-01 – WS-17-15, pp. 967–974. AAAI Press, Palo Alto, 2017.

[47] Lucas, S. M., Dockhorn, A., Volz, V., Bamford, C., Gaina, R. D., Bravi, I., Perez-Liebana, D., Mostaghim, S., Kruse, R.: A Local Approach to Forward Model Learning: Results on the Game of Life Game. arXiv:1903.12508 [cs.AI], 2019.

[48] Mission KI – erleben . verstehen . mitgestalten: https://www.deutsches-museum.de/bonn/information/aktuell/veranstaltungen-2021/mission-ki. Visited on May 29th, 2021.

[49] Mnih, V., Kavukcuoglu, K., Silver, D., Graves, A., Antonoglou, I., Wierstra, D., Riedmiller, M.: Playing Atari with Deep Reinforcement Learning. arXiv:1312.5602 [cs.LG], 2013.

[50] MS Wissenschaft – The Floating Science Centre: https://ms-wissenschaft.de. Visited on Feb 8th, 2021.

[51] Online Appendix to Knowledge Base Extraction for Learning Agents: https://gitlab.com/kb-extraction-for-learning-agents/online-appendix. Visited on Sep 10th, 2021.

[52] Perez-Liebana, D., Liu, J., Khalifa, A., Gaina, R. D., Togelius, J., Lucas, S. M.: General Video Game AI: A Multitrack Framework for Evaluating Agents, Games, and Content Generation Algorithms. IEEE Transactions on Games, 11(3):195–214, 2019.

[53] Perez-Liebana, D., Lucas, S. M., Gaina, R. D., Togelius, J., Khalifa, A., Liu, J.: General Video Game Artificial Intelligence. Morgan & Claypool Publishers, San Rafael, 2019.

[54] Poole, D.: A Logical Framework for Default Reasoning. Artificial Intelligence, 36(1):27–47, 1988.

[55] Reiter, R.: A Logic for Default Reasoning. Artificial Intelligence, 13(1–2):81–132, 1980.

[56] RoboCup Soccer Simulation League: https://ssim.robocup.org. Visited on Mar 21st, 2020.

References

[57] Russel, S. J., Norvig, P.: Artificial Intelligence: A Modern Approach (Third Edition). Pearson Education, Harlow, 2016.

[58] Scannable Code Generator: https://goqr.me. Visited on Sep 10th, 2021.

[59] ScienceStation – Wissenschaft im Bahnhof: https://www.wissenschaft-im-dialog.de/projekte/sciencestation. Visited on May 29th, 2021.

[60] Silver, D., Huang, A., Maddison, C. J., Guez, A., Sifre, L., van den Driessche, G., Schrittwieser, J., Antonoglou, I., Panneershelvam, V., Lanctot, M., Dieleman, S., Grewe, D., Nham, J., Kalchbrenner, N., Sutskever, I., Lillicrap, T., Leach, M., Kavukcuoglu, K., Graepel, T., Hassabis, D.: Mastering the Game of Go with Deep Neural Networks and Tree Search. Nature, 529:484–489, 2016.

[61] Steinley, D.: K-means clustering: A half-century synthesis. British Journal of Mathematical and Statistical Psychology, 59(1):1–34, 2006.

[62] Sutton, R. S., Barto, A. G.: Reinforcement Learning: An Introduction (Second Edition). The MIT Press, Cambridge, Massachusetts, 2018.

[63] Sutton, R. S., Precup, D., Singh, S.: Between MDPs and semi-MDPs: A framework for temporal abstraction in reinforcement learning. Artificial Intelligence, 112(1):181–211, 1999.

[64] Tesauro, G.: Temporal Difference Learning and TD-Gammon. Communications of the ACM, 38(3):58–68, 1995.

[65] The General Video Game AI Competition: http://www.gvgai.net. Visited on Apr 17th, 2021.

[66] TweetyProject: https://tweetyproject.org. Visited on Dec 7th, 2021.

[67] Volz, V., Rudolph, G., Naujoks, B.: Demonstrating the Feasibility of Automatic Game Balancing. In: Friedrich, T. (ed.) GECCO'16: Proceedings of the 2016 Genetic and Evolutionary Computation Conference, pp. 269–276. Association for Computing Machinery, New York, 2016.

[68] Watkins, C. J. C. H.: Learning from Delayed Rewards. King's College, Cambridge, 1989.

[69] Wooldridge, M.: An Introduction to MultiAgent Systems (Second Edition). John Wiley & Sons, Chichester, 2009.

[70] Wooldridge, M.: Intelligent Agents (Second Edition). In: Weiss, G. (ed.) Multiagent Systems (Intelligent Robotics and Autonomous Agents), pp. 3–50. The MIT Press, Cambridge, 2013.

Index

A
Action 31-33, 60
   Sequence 38
   Space 36
   Symbol Set **31,** 33, 36, 106
Agent 27, 35, 36
   Behavior **37,** 45, 47, 64, **103**
   Knowledge-based 41
   Learning 42, 45, **125**
   Model 28, 54, 58, **134, 161**
Answer Set Programming 22, 42, 48, 52
Apriori Algorithm 51, 75
   Confidence 76
   Support 76
Artificial Intelligence 19
   Sub-symbolic 19
   Symbolic 19
ASP 22, 42, 48, 52
   Solver 22

B
Bayesian Network 50
Black Box **42, 46,** 47, 103

C
Clustering 51, 91
   Centroid 92
   K-means 51, **92,** 99
Completeness **88**

D
Decision Tree 50
Decision-making Component **36,** 37, 41
   Non-deterministic 40
Default 52
   Logic 42, 48, 52
   Negation 48, 52

E
Environment 28, 32, 34, 36
   Non-deterministic 34, 59
Exception 59, 60
   Needed 60
Exhibit 23, **122**
Exploration-exploitation Dilemma 43, 45

F
Forward Model 55, 148
   Learning **149**
   Revision 157
Fuzzy Controller 95

G
Game 27
General Video Game Artificial Intelligence 55
   Framework **104**
Generalization 52, 53, 59, 66
Grid World **33,** 45, 61, 63
GVGAI 27, 55
   Competition 27, 55
   Framework **104**
   Game 104

H
Higher-dimensional Data **97**
HKB 57, 58, 60
   Extraction 68, **80**
   Knowledge Engineering 64
   Reasoning Algorithm 62, **63**
   Trivial 64

I
InteKRator 24, **175**

K
Knowledge Base 57
   Exception-Tolerant Hierarchical **57, 60**

Index

Extraction 57, **66**
Knowledge Representation 19, 48

M
Machine Learning 19, 50, 52
    Unsupervised 51
MCTS 23, 55, 148
Monte Carlo Tree Search 23, 55, 148

N
Neural Network 19, 21, 46, 50, 127
    Convolutional 19
    Deep Learning 50
    Function Approximator 21, 46, 50
Numeric Action Data 94
Numeric Sensor Data **91**

P
Percept **30**
Playtrace 106
    Human 104, 108
POMDP 32, 34

Q
Q-learning 44, 46, 126
    Discount Factor 44, 129
    Exploration Probability **45**
    Exploration Rate 129
    Learning Rate 44, 129
    Update Rule 44

R
Reasoning **62**
Reinforcement Learning 21, **43,** 55, 125
    Hierarchical 51
Reward 42
    Global 43
    Local 42
Robot 27
    Fuzzy-Controlled 95
Rule 47, 52, 59
    Association 51
    Complete **60**
    Generalized **60**
    Premise Set **60**

S
Sensor 30
    Numeric Data **91**
    Potential Relevance 97
    Preselection **97**
    Symbol Name 30, 93
    Symbol Set **30,** 33, 36, 107
    Unreliable 34
    Value **30,** 36, 50
Simulation 27
State 30, 32, 33, 36
    Complete **31,** 60
    Partial **31,** 60
    Sequence 39
    Space 36, 107
    Transition 32, 33
State-Action Pair **39**
State-action Sequence 39
    Deterministic 40, 58, **59,** 80
    Non-deterministic **40,** 59
State-action Set 40
State-Action Space 36
Subjective Strategic Depth 22, 113
    Measure 22, **113, 114**

W
Weight Matrix 43, 44